Complete EnglishSmart®

GRADE 2

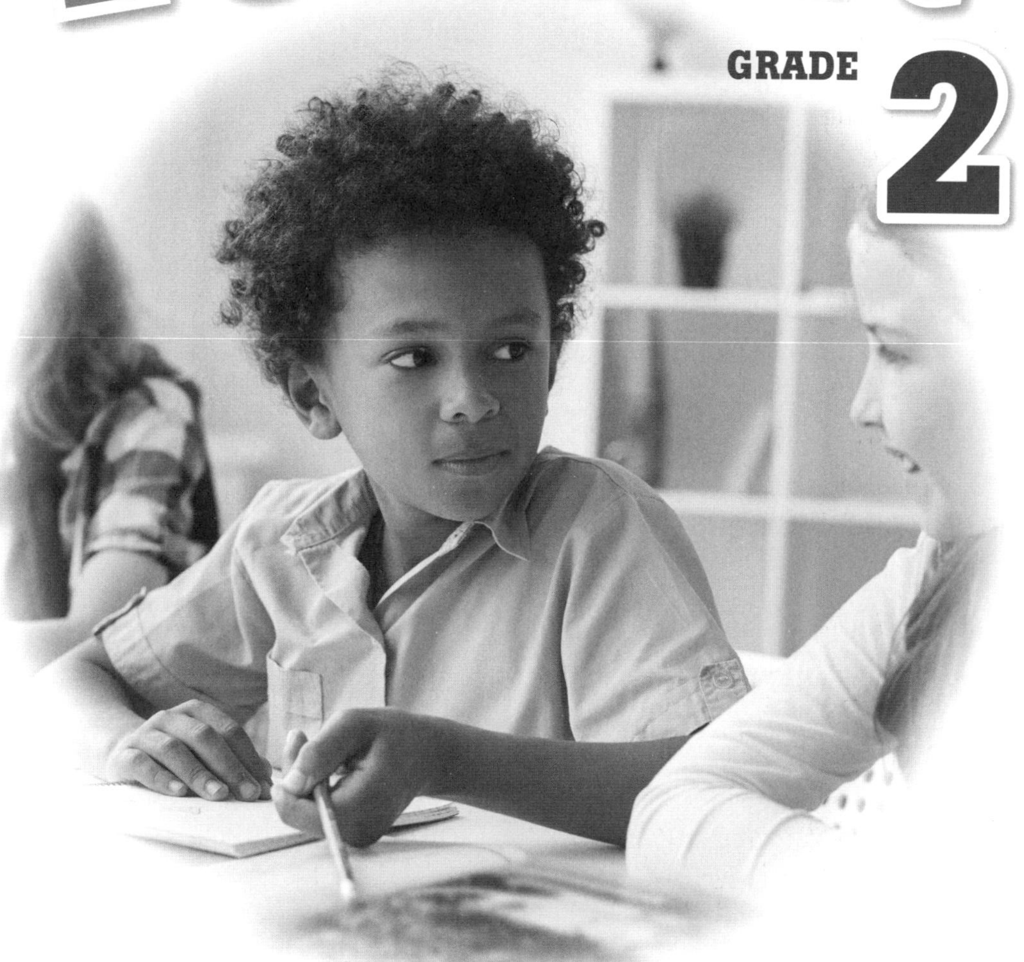

Contents

Grade 2

Dear Parent,

Thank you for choosing our *Complete EnglishSmart* as your child's learning companion.

We are confident that *Complete EnglishSmart* is the ultimate supplementary workbook your child needs to build his or her English language skills.

Complete EnglishSmart explores the fundamental aspects of language development – phonics, grammar, vocabulary, reading, and writing – by introducing each concept with an easy-to-understand definition and clear examples. This is followed by a variety of interesting activities to provide plenty of practice for your child. There is also a note box at the end of each unit for your child to note down what he or she has learned.

To further ensure that your child retains the language concepts and enjoys the material, there is a review at the end of each section and a Language Games section at the end of the book to help your child consolidate the language concepts in a fun and meaningful way. The accompanying online audio clips provide an interactive way for your child to learn phonics.

If your child would like to show his or her understanding of the language concepts in a creative way, we are happy to invite your child on a bonus Language Game Design Challenge. Please find the detailed information on page 271 of this book.

We hope that your child will have fun learning and developing his or her English language skills with our *Complete EnglishSmart*.

Your Partner in Education,
Popular Book Company (Canada) Limited

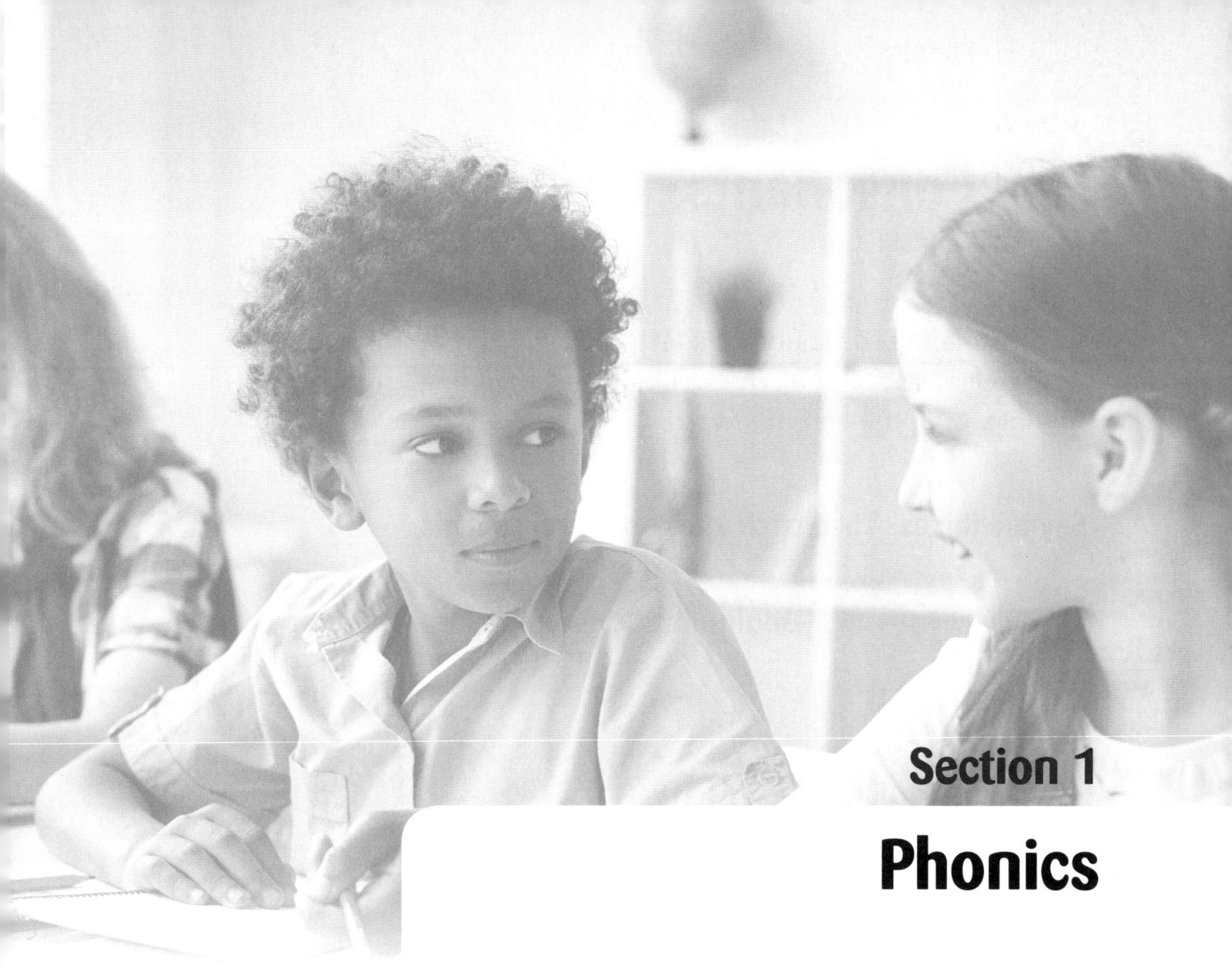

Phonics

UNIT

1 Consonants

 A consonant is the sound of a letter in a word that is not a vowel (a, e, i, o, or u). It can be at the beginning, in the middle, or at the end of a word.

A. Say the things. Then circle the correct consonants.

1.1 Beginning Consonant

sun 

leaf

pan

Beginning Consonant

bat   fish   duck

1.2 Middle Consonant

wa**t**er 

shi**v**er

co**r**al

Middle Consonant

   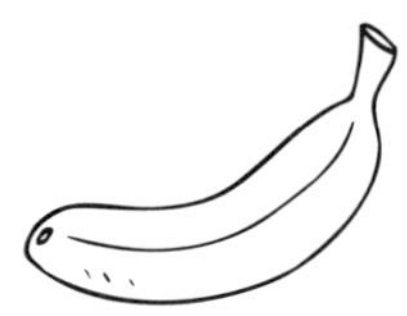

koala   petal   banana

1.3 Ending Consonant

po**t** 

bo**x**

dro**p**

Ending Consonant

bus   pen   jar

B. **Say the things and write the words. Then check to show the beginning, middle, and ending consonants.**

	Beginning Consonant		Middle Consonant		Ending Consonant	
	h	j	p	s	r	b
__ __ __ __						
__ __ __						
__ __ __ __						
__ __ __						
__ __ __ __ __						
__ __ __ __ __ __						

C. **Say the things. Then write the correct beginning, middle, and ending consonants.**

D. **Read the passage and circle the letter "n" in the words with the specified colours.**

Nunavut

Nunavut is a large territory in the north of Canada. It is near the North Pole. It is very cold there. Not many plants grow there because it is so cold.

In Nunavut, there are six months of darkness and six months of daylight. You might see the sun shining at 9 o'clock at night in June, just like it does at noon!

Words that I Have Learned

Beginning Consonant	Middle Consonant	Ending Consonant
_______	_______	_______
_______	_______	_______
_______	_______	_______
_______	_______	_______

UNIT 2

Hard and Soft "c" and "g"

The letters "c" and "g" have both hard and soft sounds.

A. Say the things. Write "c" or "g". Then match.

2.1

c

| **hard** |
| comb  |
| magi**c** |

| **soft** |
| **c**ent 1¢ |
| fa**c**e |

1.

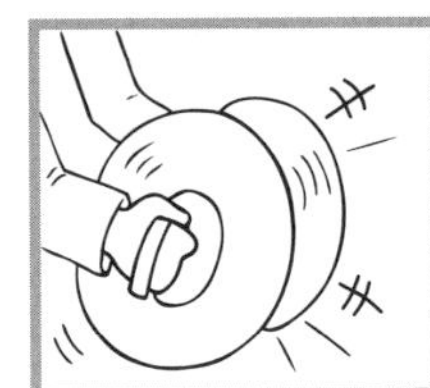

atti__   __ymbals   __andy

hard "c"   soft "c"

2.2

g

| **hard** |
| **g**ate  |
| ta**g** |

| **soft** |
| **g**in**g**er  |
| oran**g**e |

2.

an__el   __irl   fla__

hard "g"   soft "g"

B. Say the words under the pictures and write "c" or "g" to show what sounds the words contain. Then name the things that contain the same sounds.

> gift   castle   giraffe   dancer

1. **Hard** [ ]

   music   caterpillar

2. **Hard** [ ]

   guitar   dragon

3. **Soft** [ ]

   ice   city

4. **Soft** [ ]

   bridge   giant

C.   Say the things. Then write the words in the correct boxes.

D. **Read the passage and circle the letters in the words with the specified colours.**

Penguins

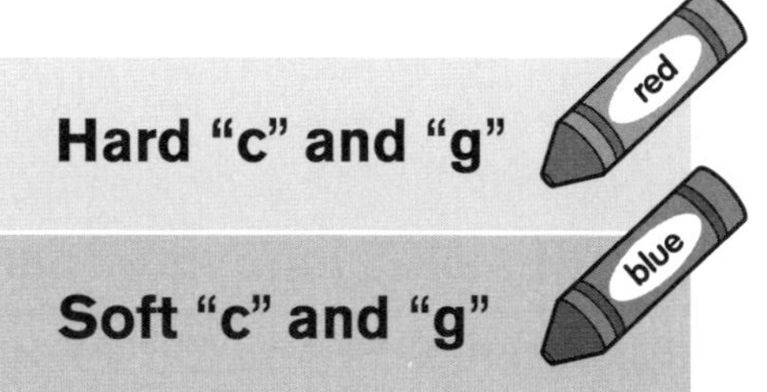

Penguins are birds that cannot fly but are good swimmers. They live in icy Antarctica and off the coast of Africa and Australia. The smallest penguin is 40 centimetres tall. It is called the Blue Fairy. The tallest penguin, the Emperor, seems huge in comparison!

The female penguin lays an egg or two and goes off in search of food. While she is gone, the male protects the eggs from danger.

Words that I Have Learned

Hard "c"	Soft "c"		Hard "g"	Soft "g"
_________			_________	
_________			_________	
_________			_________	
_________			_________	

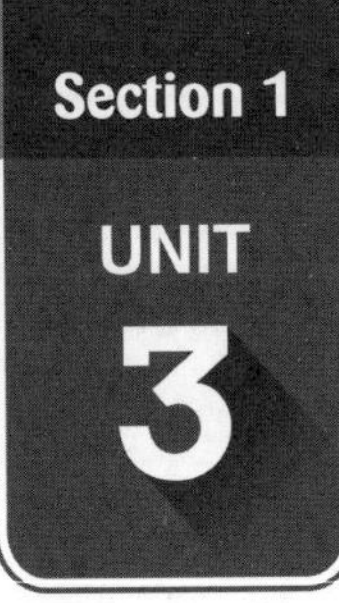

UNIT 3

Silent Consonants

Some words have silent consonants. We do not hear the sound of these consonants when we say the words.

A. Say the words. Then circle the silent consonants.

3.1 Silent Consonants

b
thum**b**
dou**b**t

h
g**h**ost
hour

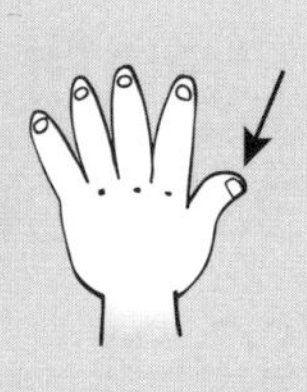

k
knife
knee

l
sa**l**mon
pa**l**m

1.

talk

2.

stalk

3.
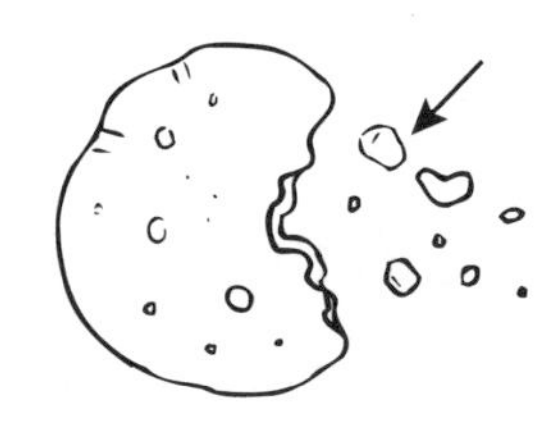
crumb

4.

knight

5.

spaghetti

6.

climb

7.
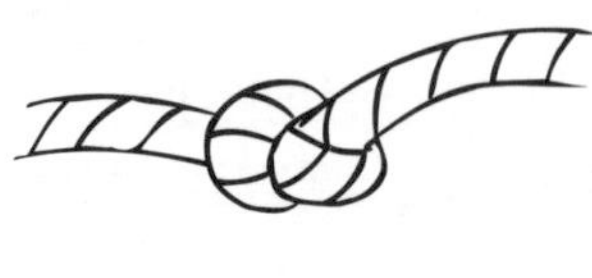
knot

8.

anchor

B. **Trace the letters. Then colour the pictures that contain the given silent consonants.**

Silent

Silent

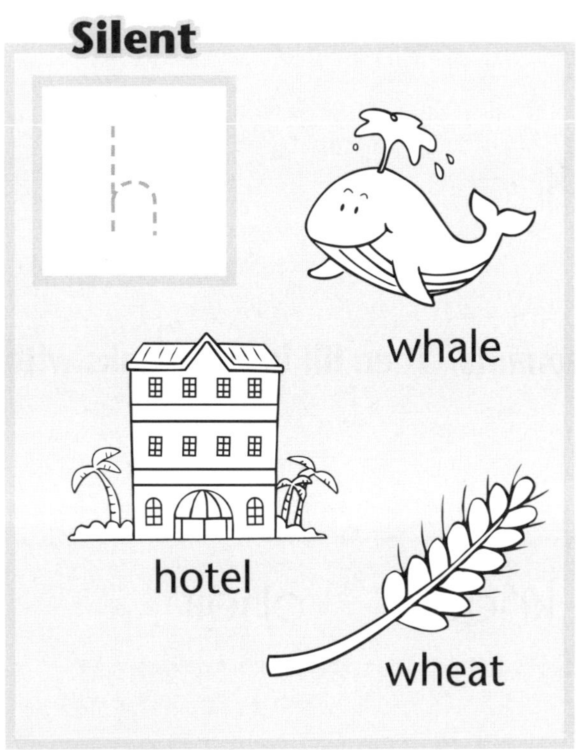

Silent

Silent

C. Say the things. Then write the silent b, h, k, and l consonants.

D. Say the words and circle the silent consonants. Then fill in the blanks with the correct words.

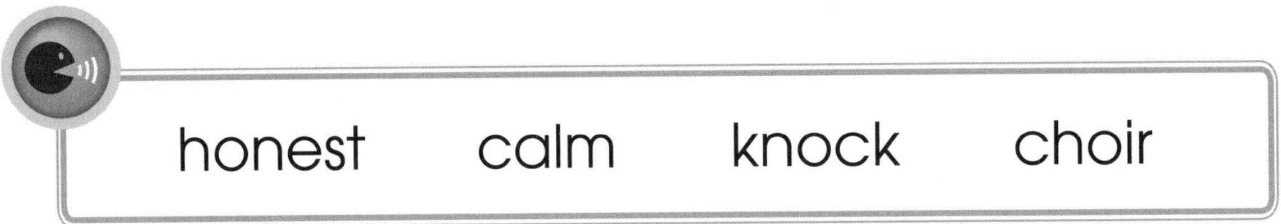

1. The words "______________" and "truthful" have similar meanings.

2. ______________ before you enter a room.

3. You should remain ______________ in an emergency.

4. Ava is a member of the school ______________.

E. **Read the story and circle the words with the silent b, h, k, and l consonants.**

Kelvin the Knight

Kelvin was an honourable knight. He was charged with capturing the thieving ghosts called Creepie and Spook. At first, Kelvin thought he would lure them with crumbs or salmon but he knew they were not that dumb. Then he came up with another scheme. He knitted a web and calmly waited for the ghosts to arrive. They got caught in his trap and Kelvin was declared the heir to the throne.

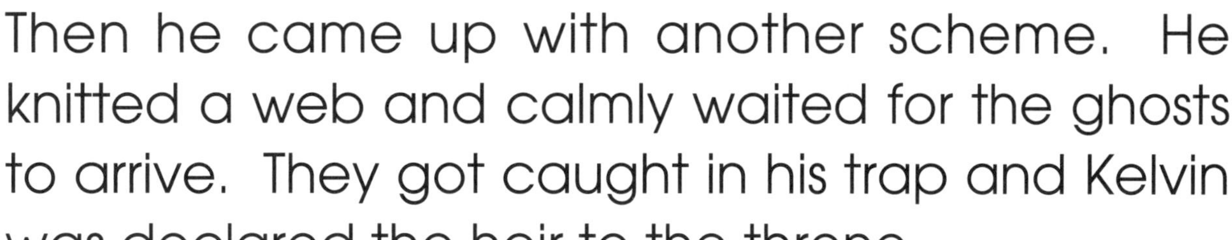

Words that I Have Learned

Words with Silent b, h, k, and l Consonants

____

____

____

____

____

UNIT

4 Consonant Blends: L Blends

A consonant blend is a blended sound usually formed by two consonants that are placed together. The L blends are blends that contain the consonant "l".

A. Say the things. Then write the correct L blends.

L Blends
4.1

black 

clown 

flag 

glad 

plane 

sleep 

1. 

__ __ock

2. 

__ __ock

3. 

__ __ouse

4. 

__ __ower

5. 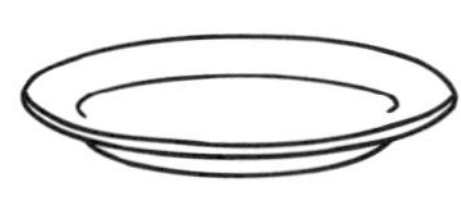

__ __ate

6. 

__ __ake

7. 

__ __ippers

8. 

__ __oves

B.   Say the things. Then match them with the correct L blends.

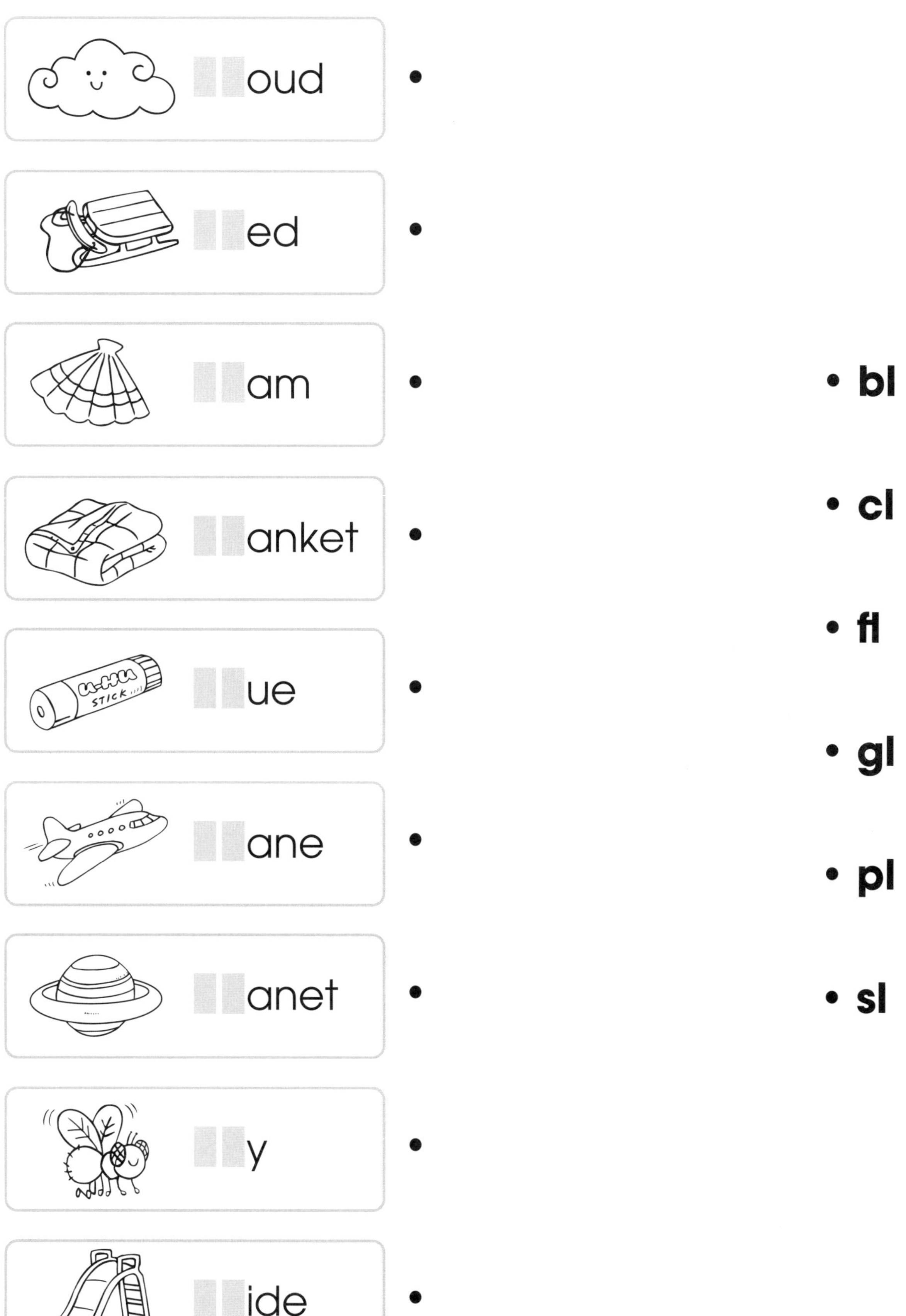

C.   Write the missing L blends to complete the words.

1. The _____ass broke into many pieces.

2. There is a Canadian _____ag outside our school.

3. At recess, we _____ay outside.

4. The heavy rain caused many _____oods.

5. "May I have some more, _____ease?" Ani asked.

6. _____oss and brush your teeth regularly.

7. I put jam on a _____ice of bread for breakfast.

8. Although the turtle was _____ow, he won the race because he did his best!

9.

D. Read the passage and circle the L-blend words.

Ladybugs

Ladybugs are insects. They are often red with black spots. Some are black with red spots. In the summer, they live on flowers, shrubs, and other plants. In the winter, they live in trees and houses.

Ladybugs are capable of flying. Although they cannot reach the clouds, they can reach great heights. On land, they are small enough to crawl on flowers and even on tiny blades of grass!

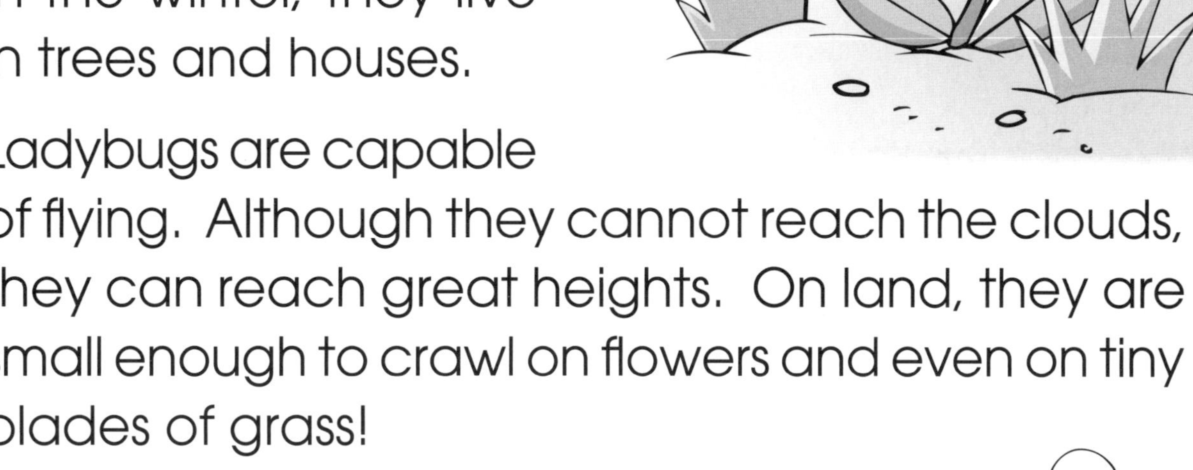

Words that I Have Learned

L-blend Words

____

____

____

____

UNIT 5

Consonant Blends: R Blends

 The R blends are consonant blends that contain the consonant "r".

A. Say the things. Then write the correct R blends.

R Blends

5.1

 **br**ick

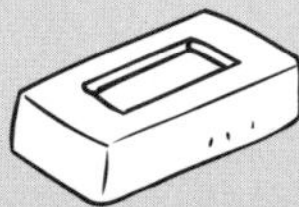 **cr**ab

 **dr**um

 **fr**uit

 **gr**ass

 **pr**ize

 **tr**ee

1. 
__ __ayon

2. 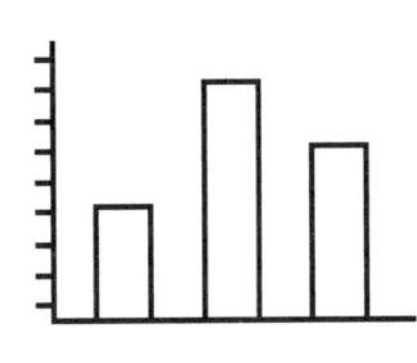
__ __aph

3. 
__ __op

4. 
__ __og

5. 
__ __oom

6. 
__ __ash

7. 
__ __ince

__ __ain

__ __ack

B. Say the things and colour the pictures with R blends. Then write the
R blends in the boxes.

R Blends

| br | cr | dr | fr | gr | pr | tr |

C. Say the things. Check the circles if the words begin with the correct R blends. If not, put a cross and write the correct spellings.

D. Say the words and circle the R blends. Then fill in the blanks with the correct words.

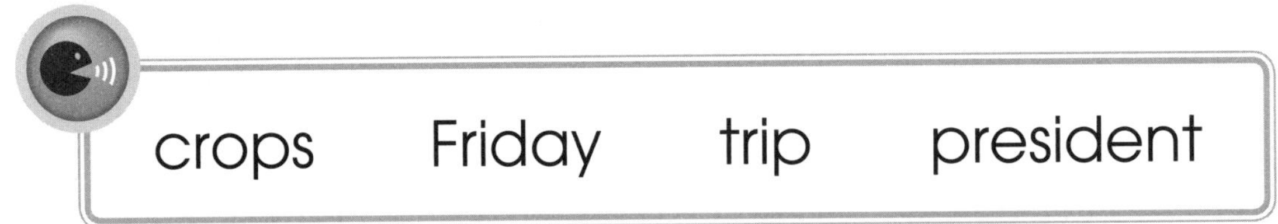

1. We are excited to go on our ____________ !

2. The farmer takes care of his ____________ .

3. I have an appointment on ____________ .

4. The ____________ made a long speech.

E.   Read the story and circle the R-blend words.

Trisha's Dream

A few days ago, Trisha had a dreadful dream. She was standing under tall trees in a scary forest. She suddenly felt huge drops of rain on her dress!

Trisha ran in the wet grass to hide inside a small brick house. It was then that she woke up to realize that in reality there was rain coming in from her window!

Words that I Have Learned

R-blend Words

____

____

____

____

____

UNIT

6 Consonant Blends: S Blends

The S blends are consonant blends that contain the consonant "s".

A. Trace the S blends. Then say the words.

6.1

S Blends

 **sc**oop

 **sk**ates

 **sl**ide

 **sm**iley

 **sn**ake

 **sp**ider

 **st**ain

 **sw**ings

1. 
scale

2. 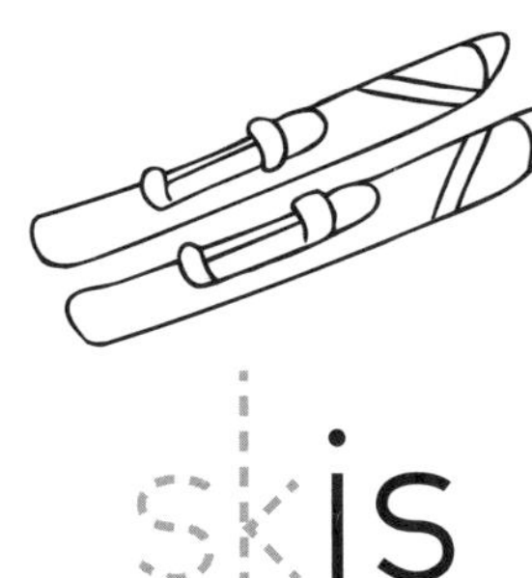
skis

3. 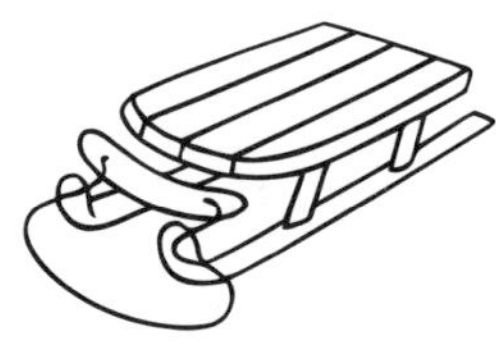
sled

4. 
smell

5. 
snow

6. 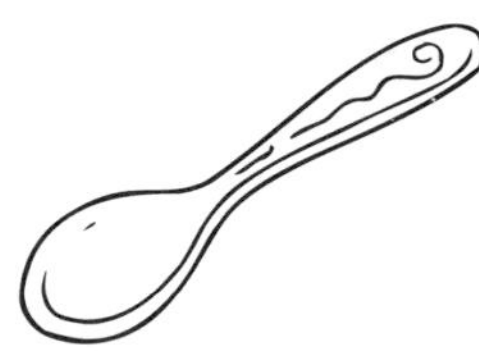
spoon

7. 
star

8. 
sweep

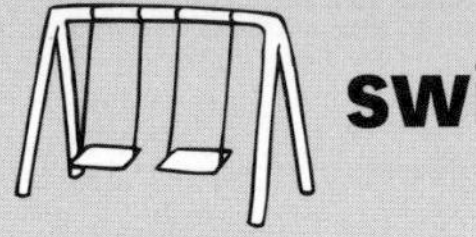

B. **Say the words and circle the S blends. Then match the words with the pictures.**

S-blend Words

sponge
snail
steam
switch
skirt
scarf

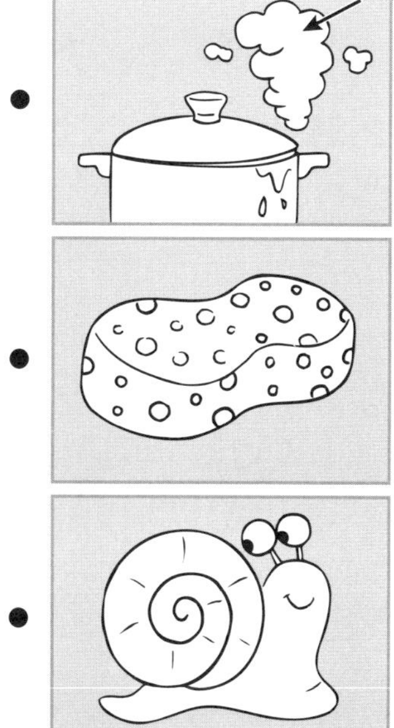

C. **Colour the correct S blends.**

1. Martha ☐ sl ☐ sn ipped on the floor.

2. The turtle was ☐ sl ☐ st ower than the hare.

3. Ana loved the ☐ sn ☐ sm all newborn kittens.

4. Cinderella used to ☐ sw ☐ st eep the castle floors.

5. The firefighter saw the ☐ sm ☐ sw oke from the window.

6. Oh, no! There's a ☐ st ☐ sk unk by the tree.

D. Say the S-blend words. Then label the pictures with the words.

S-blend Words

stairs	spot	smoothie	spade	smell
scooter	snowman	skip	swan	scarf

1.

2.

3.

4.

5.
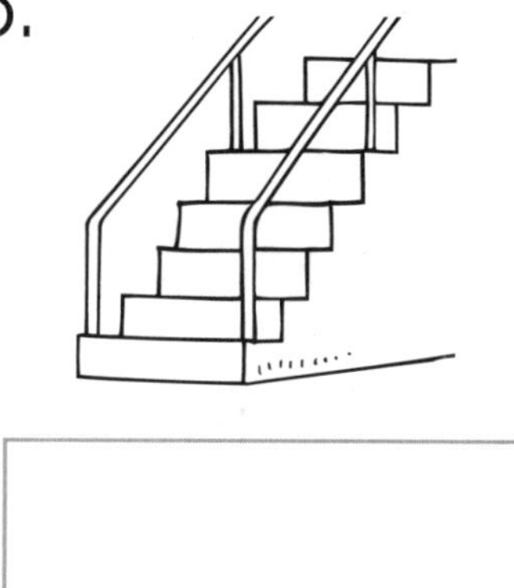

6.

7.
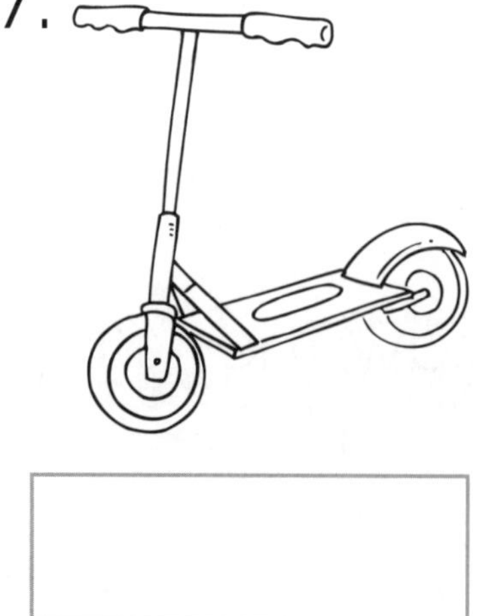

8.

E.   Read the story and circle the S-blend words.

Dance Lessons

When Stella was three years old, she started taking dance lessons. She wore a pink skirt with small ballet slippers. She practised the steps every day.

By the time she was sixteen, she was very good at ballet. Stella was offered the leading role in a play called "Swan". She quickly learned many new steps and routines. Because of her hard work, Stella spun in circles and slowly bowed as she became the star of the stage!

Words that I Have Learned

S-blend Words

____

____

____

____

____

UNIT 7

Consonant Digraphs

A consonant digraph is a group of consonants that makes only one sound. "Ch", "sh", "th", and "wh" are consonant digraphs.

A. Write the consonant digraphs ch, sh, th, and wh. Then say the words.

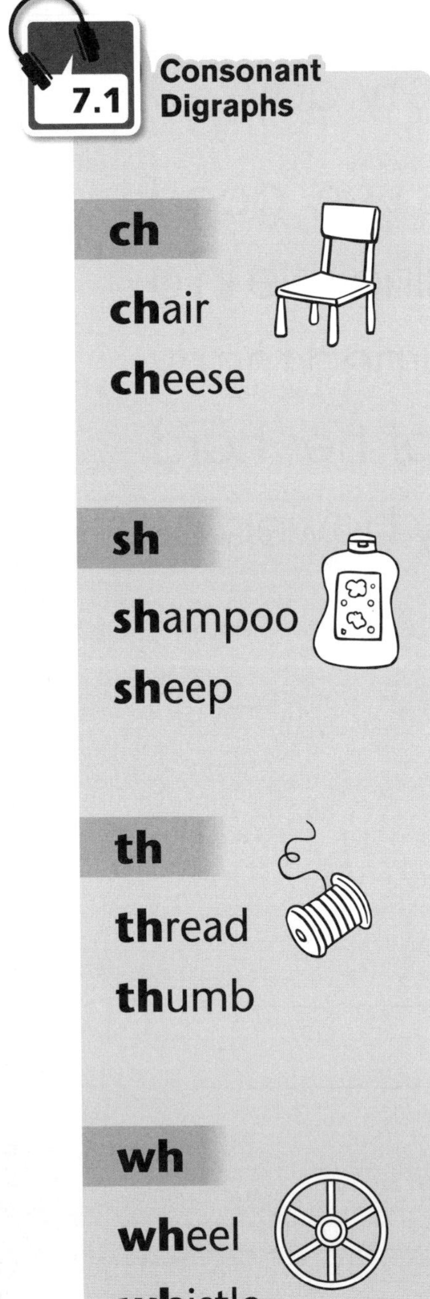

7.1 Consonant Digraphs

ch

chair
cheese

sh

shampoo
sheep

th

thread
thumb

wh

wheel
whistle

B. Say the things. Then write the correct consonant digraphs in the circles with the help of the words below.

Consonant Digraphs

ch	**sh**	**th**	**wh**
chicks	**sh**ark	**th**ief	**wh**iskers
child	**sh**ower	**th**orn	**wh**ite

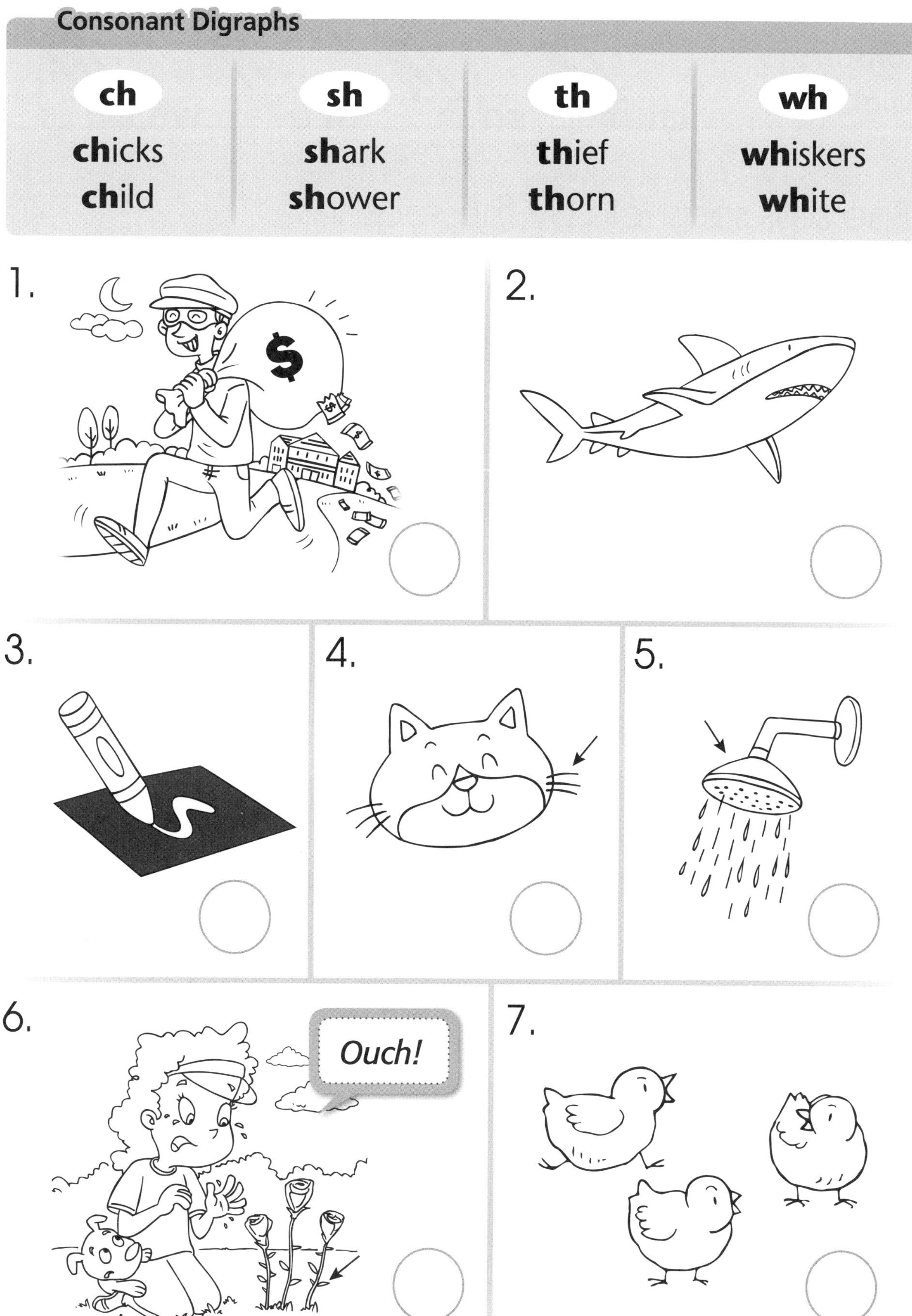

1.

2.

3.

4.

5.

6.

7.

C. Read the tongue twisters and circle the consonant digraphs with the specified colours.

| Consonant Digraphs | **ch** blue | **sh** orange | **th** yellow | **wh** green |

1. She sells seashells by the seashore.

2. Chester chewed the chewing gum cheerily.

3. The shiny shoes in Susie's Shoe Shop shimmer in the shining sun.

4. Theodore thought the thimble was thick.

5. The thin thief threw the thread to the other three thieves.

6. Willy the Whale whirled while the wheel of the white whaler whistled.

D. Say the things and write the correct consonant digraphs in the circles. Then give one more example for each.

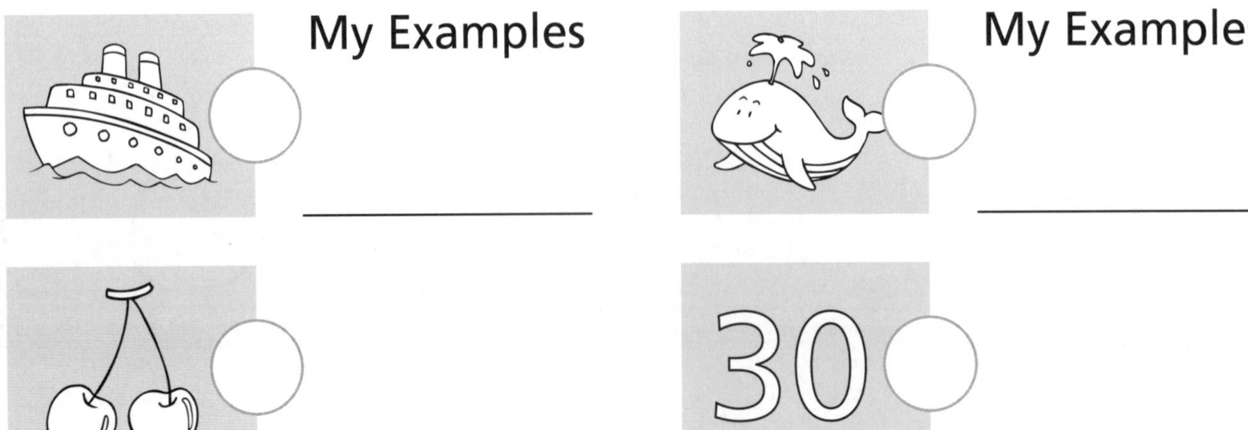

E.   Read and underline the consonant digraphs ch, sh, th, and wh.

Sheila's Shopping Adventure

Sheila was excited to go shopping with her elder brother, Chandler. She woke up early on Thursday and showered quickly. Then she threw on her favourite pink  dress with white shoes. She was going to buy things for everyone: shampoo for her dog, red thread with a shiny thistle for her grandma, delicious cherries for her mom, and a whistle to surprise Chandler.

However, once they started the car, they noticed that its steering wheel was not working. So they took the bus instead, and Sheila saw a big cheese factory, a giant chair, and a whale museum on her way to the mall!

Words that I Have Learned

Consonant Digraphs

____

____

____

UNIT

8 Short Vowels

Some words with the letter a, e, i, o, or u have the short vowel sounds.

A. Say the words. Then circle the short vowels.

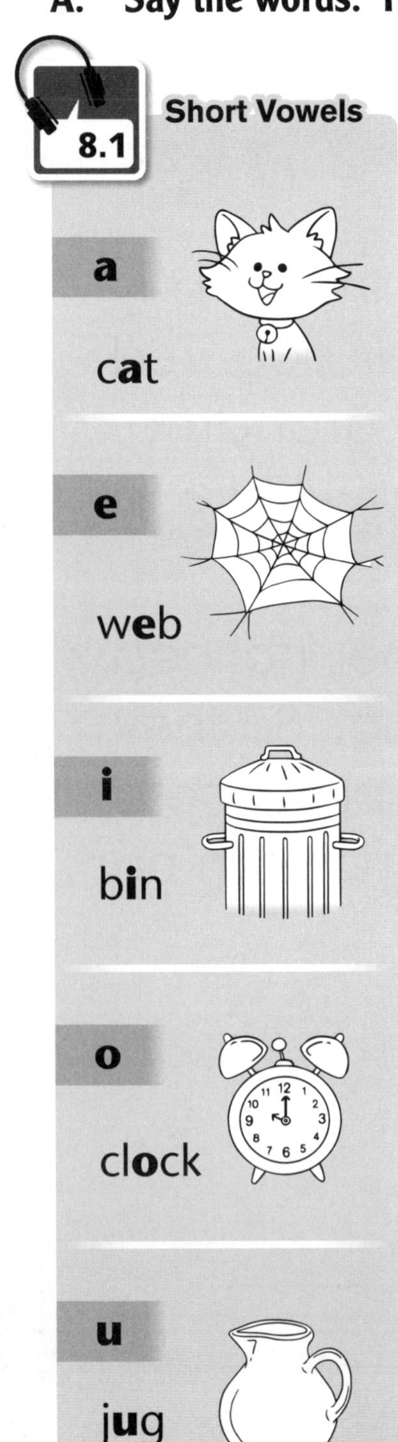

Short Vowels

8.1

a

cat

e

web

i

bin

o

clock

u

jug

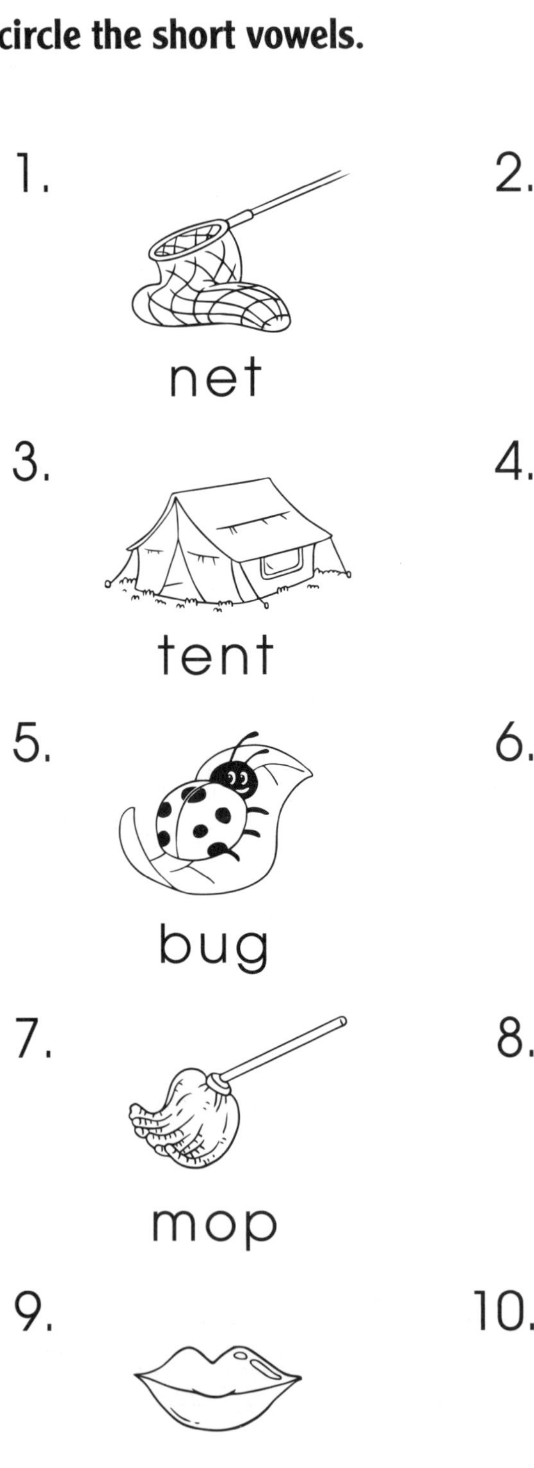

1.

net

3.

tent

5.

bug

7.

mop

9.

lips

2.

lamp

4.

six

6.

map

8.

sun

10.

rock

B. **Say the things. Then colour the ones with the short vowel sound for each group.**

Short Vowels

1. a

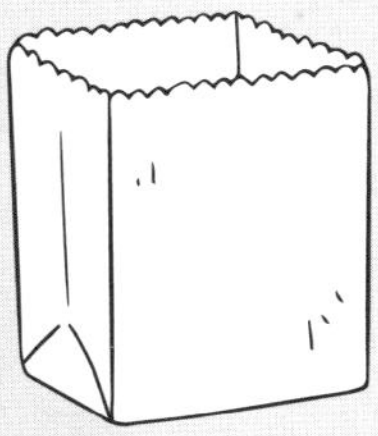

2. e

3. i

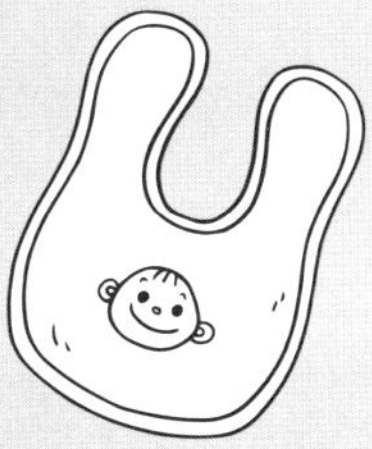

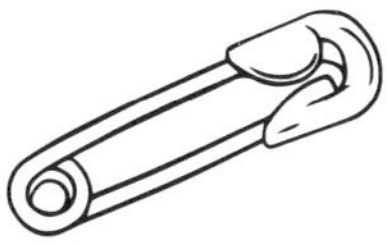

4. o

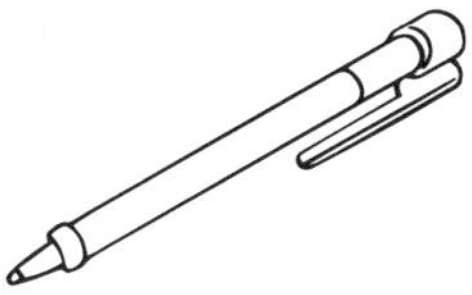

5. u

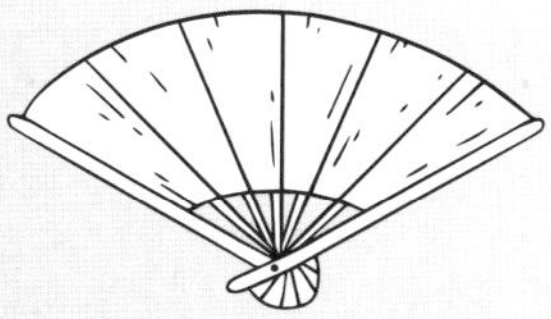

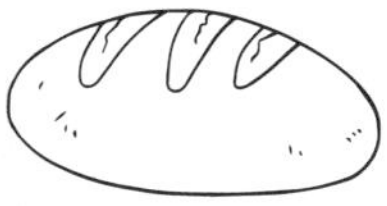

C. Say the things. Then write the short vowel sound for each.

1.

2.

3.

4.

5.

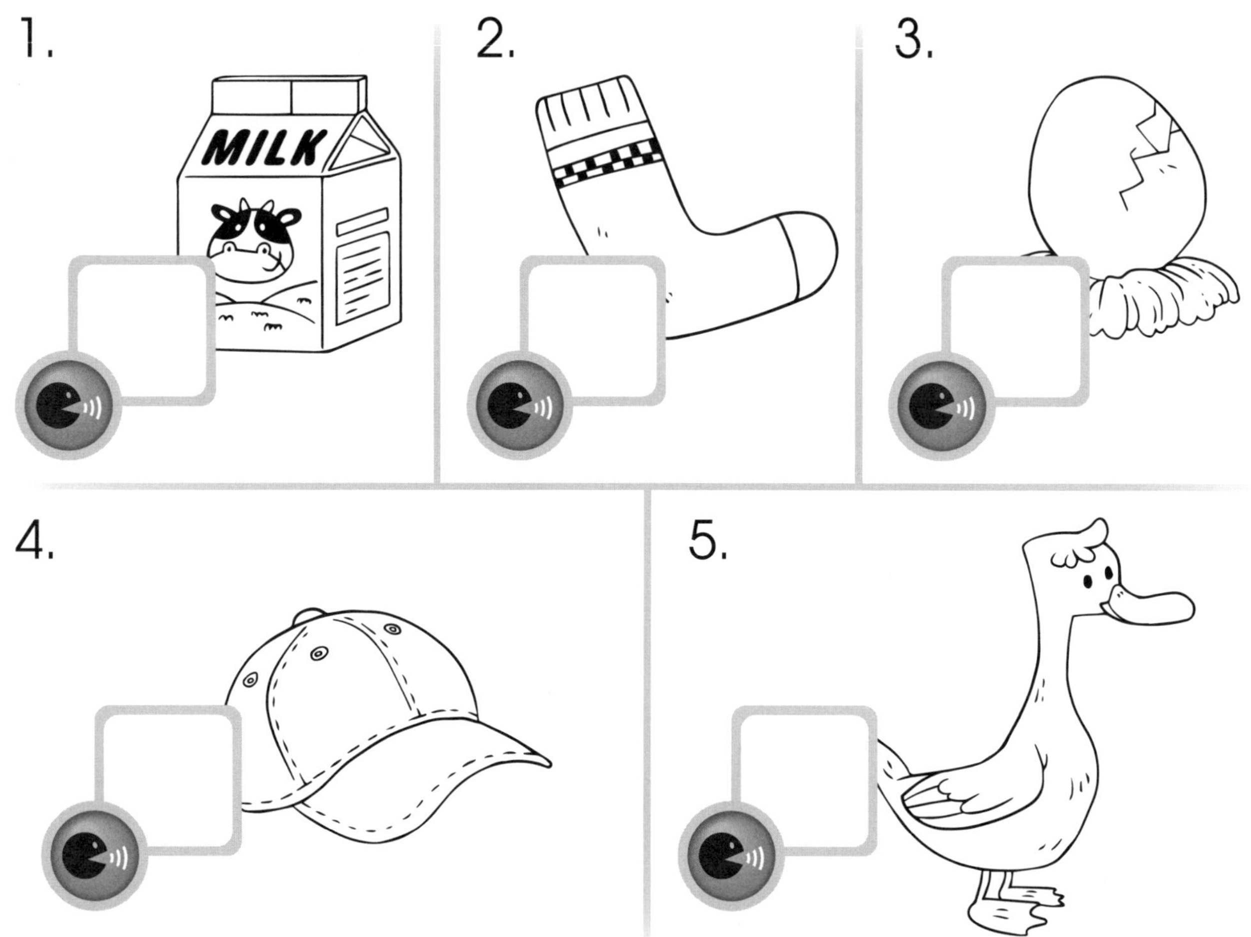

D. Fill in the blanks with the correct short vowels.

1. A fox lives in a d_____n.

2. My d_____d took me for a swim.

3. I gave Mom a big h_____g for baking me a cake.

4. The ducks were playing in the p_____nd.

5. Amy and her tw_____n sister look alike.

E. **Read the story and circle the underlined short-vowel words with the specified colours.**

Jill's Umbrella Hat

Jill has an umbrella hat. It is an umbrella but it is also a hat. It was a gift from her mom. She can use it in the rain and also in the sun. She wears it on her head. Ron likes her umbrella hat. He thinks it is fun to wear it.

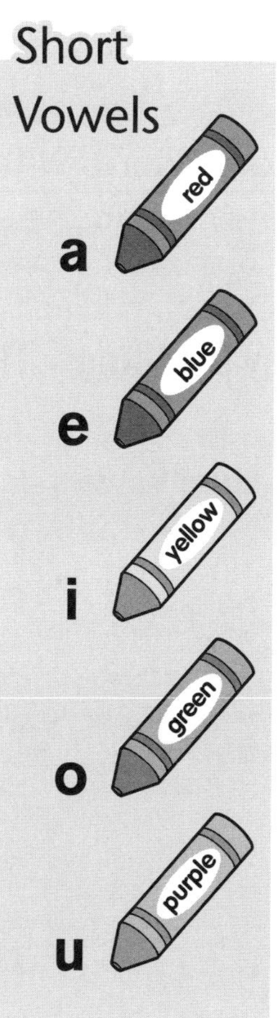

Words that I Have Learned

Short-vowel Words

a ____

e ____

i ____

o ____

u ____

UNIT 9

Long Vowels

Some words with the letter a, e, i, o, or u have long vowel sounds. They sound the same as the way you say the letters.

A. Say the things. Then write the correct long vowels.

9.1 **Long Vowels**

a cake

e evening

i kite

o bone

u flute

1. 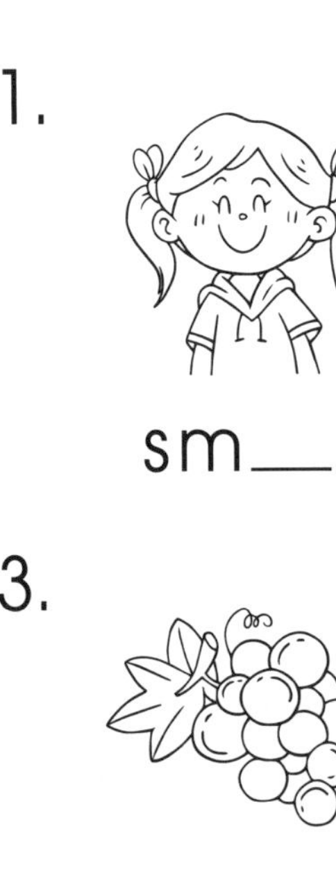
sm__le

2. 
c__ne

3. 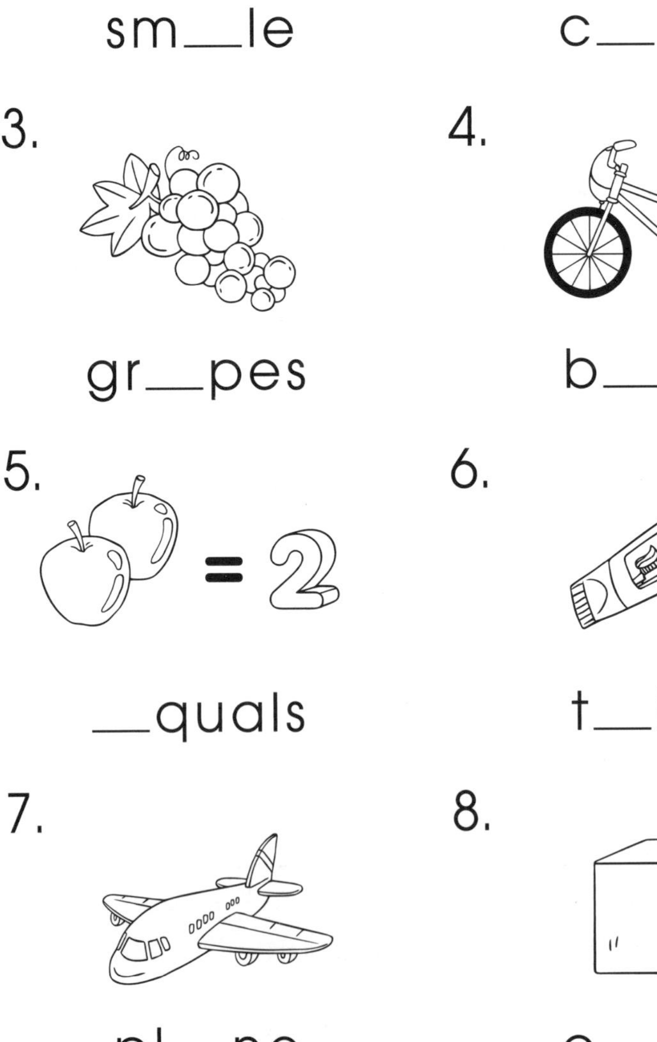
gr__pes

4. b__ke

5. __quals

6. t__be

7. pl__ne

8. c__be

B. **Say the things. Then colour the ones that contain the long vowel sound for each group.**

Long Vowels

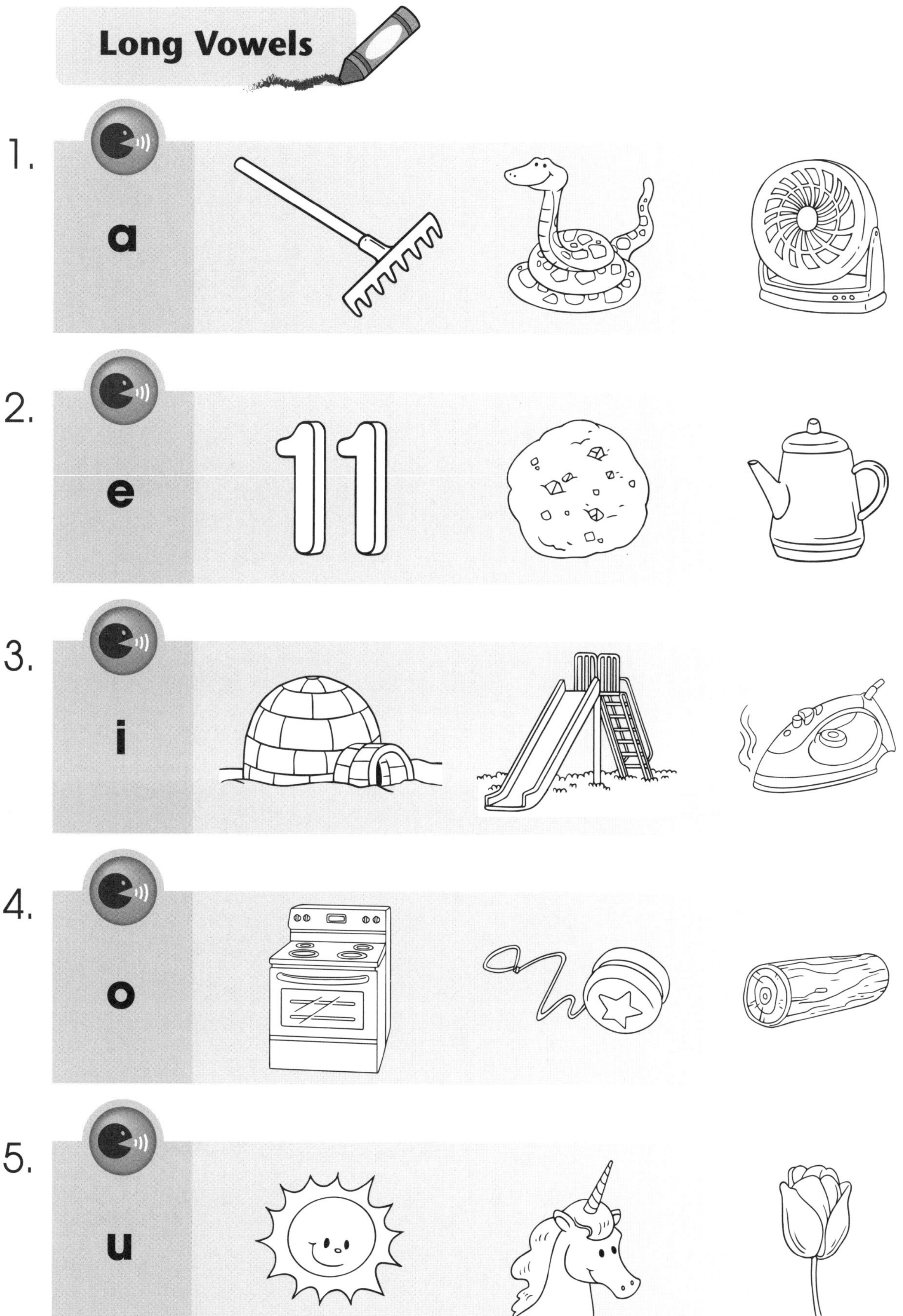

1. a

2. e

3. i

4. o

5. u

C. **Say the words and circle the long vowels. Then match the words with the pictures.**

Long-vowel Words

spider •

ruler •

whale •

globe •

acorn •

fire •

zebra •

music •

event •

ocean •

D. **Read the passage and circle the long-vowel words with the specified colours.**

All about Plants

Most plants start as a seed. Usually, you plant the seed in the garden or the yard, in the shade or the sun.

If you use a small spade, you can dig a hole to poke the seed down and cover it with soil. You plant the seed and let the sun shine down on it. When it sprouts and the stem gets stronger, leaves begin to come out.

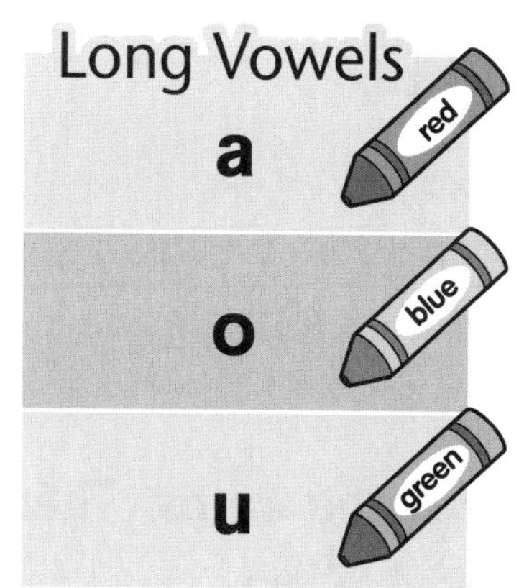

Words that I Have Learned

Long-vowel Words

a ______________________________

e ______________________________

i ______________________________

o ______________________________

u ______________________________

UNIT 10

Y as a Vowel

In some words, y sounds like a long "i". In some other words, y sounds like a long "e".

A. Say the words. Then write "i" or "e" in the boxes to show the sounds of "y" as a vowel.

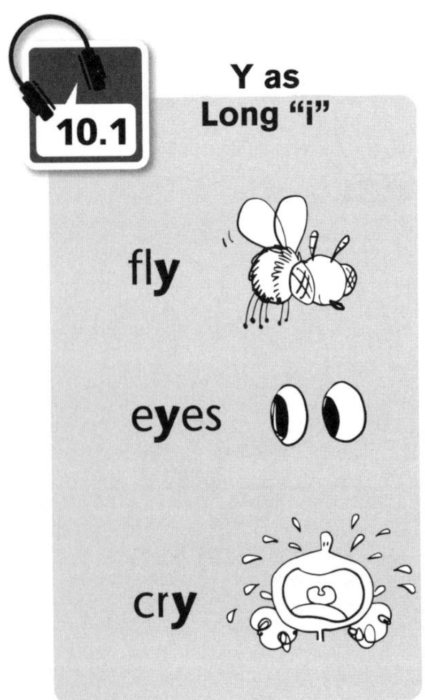

10.1

Y as Long "i"

fly

eyes

cry

1. spy ⬜

2. cherry ⬜

3. baby ⬜

4. candy ⬜

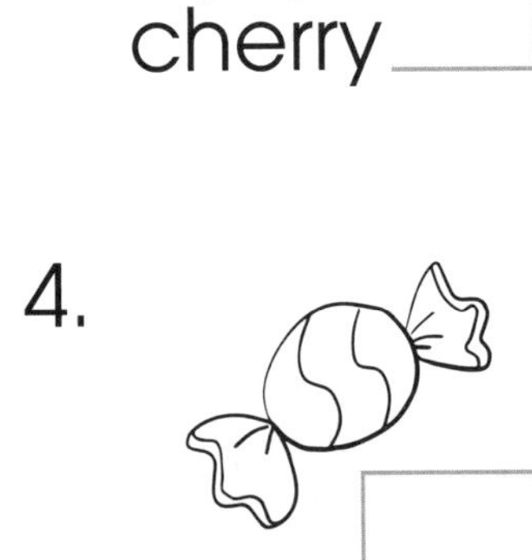

10.2

Y as Long "e"

bunny

empty

rainy

5. jelly ⬜

6. why ⬜

7. bye ⬜

8. shy ⬜

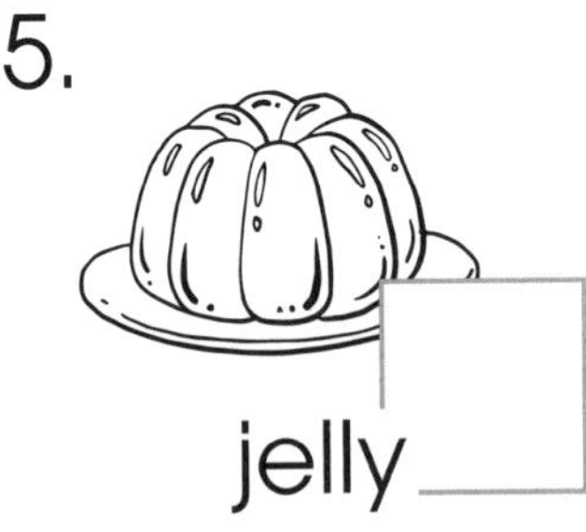

B. **Write the words in the correct boxes. Then say the words and match.**

Words with Y as a Vowel

puppy	**family**	**fairy**
July	**sky**	**butterfly**

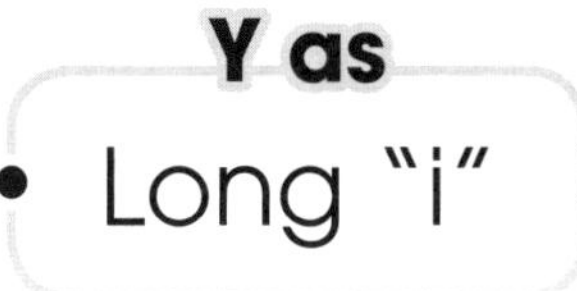

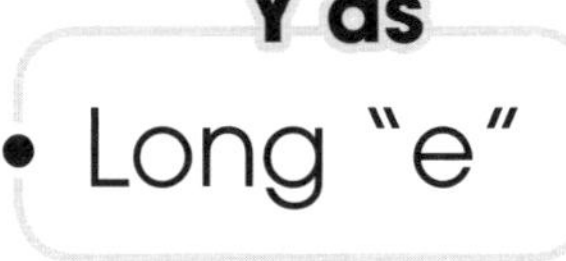

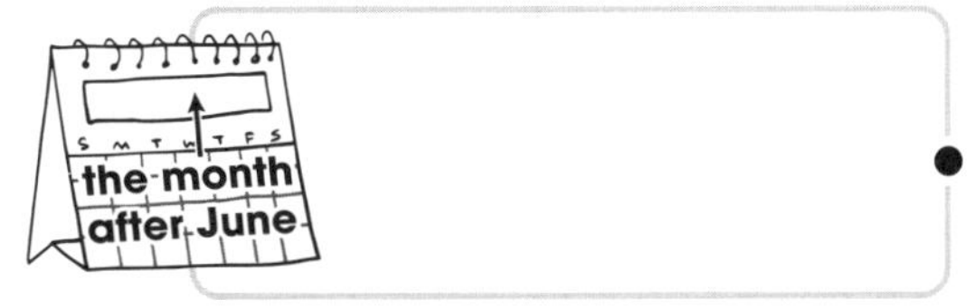

C.   Say the words and colour the boxes with the specified colours. Then fill in the blanks with the correct words.

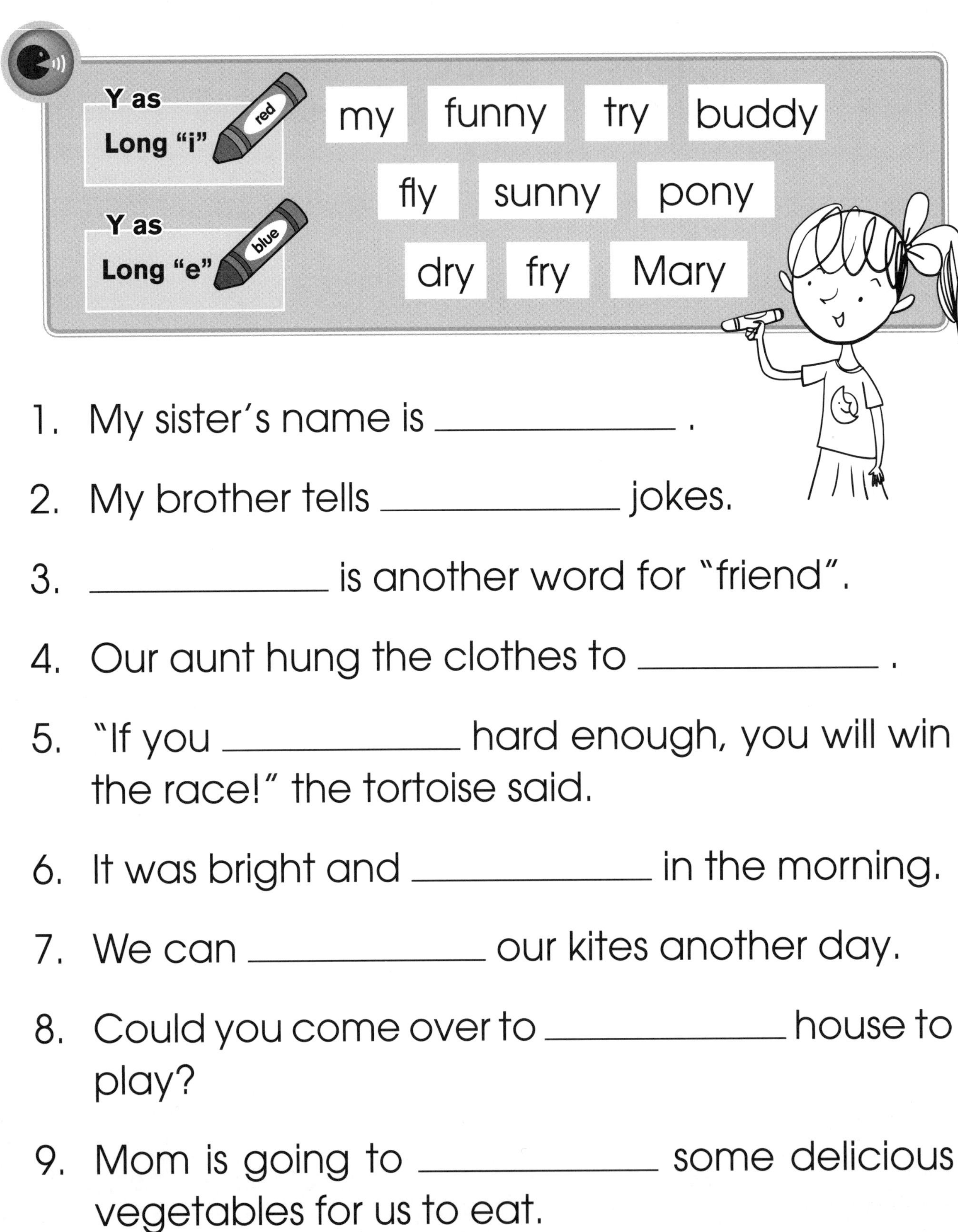

1. My sister's name is _____________ .

2. My brother tells _____________ jokes.

3. _____________ is another word for "friend".

4. Our aunt hung the clothes to _____________ .

5. "If you _____________ hard enough, you will win the race!" the tortoise said.

6. It was bright and _____________ in the morning.

7. We can _____________ our kites another day.

8. Could you come over to _____________ house to play?

9. Mom is going to _____________ some delicious vegetables for us to eat.

10. I have always wanted a small _____________ .

D. **Read the story. Then circle the words that have y with the long "i" sound and underline the words that have y with the long "e" sound.**

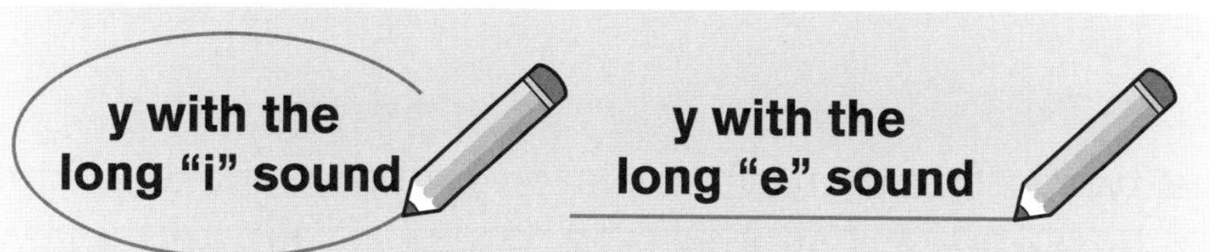

The Coin Collection

Brittany has a coin collection. She started it when she was six years old. She put the coins in a jar labelled "My Coins".

The first coins she got were from Italy, which her mom gave her after a trip there. Since then, many of her family members have given her coins for gifts. Her dad will fly to China in July and he will try to find some special coins for her.

Brittany's favourite coin is one from Sri Lanka. It is large and heavy.

Words that I Have Learned

Y as Long "i"	Y as Long "e"
_____________	_____________
_____________	_____________
_____________	_____________

UNIT

11 Vowel Digraphs

A vowel digraph is two letters that, when placed together, make a single vowel sound. The letters **ai** and **ay** make the long a sound, and **ea** and **ee** make the long e sound.

A. Say the words. Then write the correct vowel digraphs.

11.1 Vowel Digraphs

Long a

ai/ay

ch**ai**n
w**ai**st

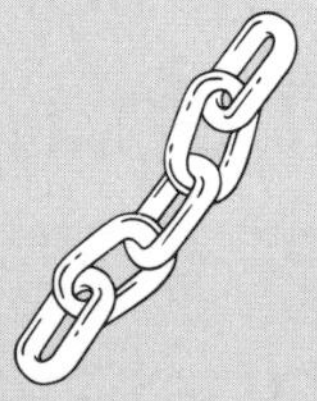

h**ay**
cl**ay**

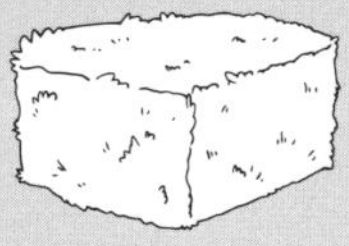

Long e

ea/ee

l**ea**f
t**ea**ch

qu**ee**n
wh**ee**l

B. Write the words with the "ai" and "ay" digraphs to solve the riddles.

Vowel Digraphs ai/ay

tray	**snail**	**jay**	**jail**	**nail**
say	**paint**	**play**	**pay**	

1. You can use me to hold things together.

____

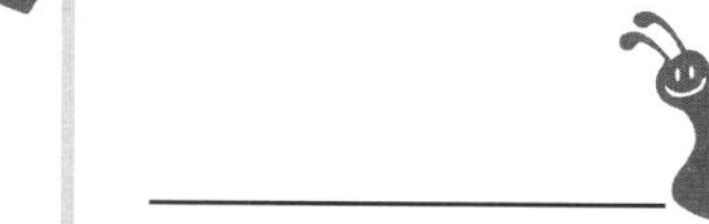

2. I carry my house on my back.

____

3. You can use me to carry things.

____

4. I am a blue bird.

____

5. You must do this if you want to buy something.

____

7. You can use me to make colourful pictures.

____

6. This is what you do when you speak.

____

8. You like to do this with your friends.

____

9. This is where people go when they commit a crime.

____

C. **Colour the correct words with vowel digraphs to complete the sentences.**

1. The | bee | | beat | makes its home in a hive.

2. The blue | jeans | | beans | are hanging on the line.

3. It is nice to have a cup of | tea | | tee | .

4. The baseball | team | | teem | plays in the summer.

5. The | bean | | been | plant grew very high.

6. We will have some | meat | | meet | for dinner.

7. Mom is going to | weed | | feed | the garden.

8. There are seven days in a | weak | | week | .

9. We will | see | | sea | the paintings at the art gallery.

10. This | seed | | seek | will grow into a plant.

D. **Write three words for each vowel digraph.**

Vowel Digraph: ea

____

____

____

Vowel Digraph: ee

____

____

____

E. **Read the letter and circle the words with the vowel digraphs ai, ay, ea, and ee.**

Adventure at the Sea

Dear Jayden,

We went to Sharaz on Thursday. On our way, we heard about a sunken ship in the deep sea. The story goes like this – a pirate ship got caught in the rain there a long time ago. It sank and a chest with precious gems and gold beads went down with it.

At first, we were afraid of the water, but then we decided to look for the ship. We boarded a small ship. Then we dived under the water. When we reached the ship, we swam inside and guess what? We found the chest!

I'll show you some photos when we're home.

Your friend,
Dean

Words that I Have Learned

Words with Vowel Digraphs

ai and **ay**	**ea** and **ee**
___________________	___________________
___________________	___________________
___________________	___________________
___________________	___________________

UNIT 12

Vowel Digraph: oo

A vowel digraph is two letters that, when placed together, make a single sound. The letters **oo** can have the long oo sound, like in "room", or the short oo sound, like in "cook".

A. Say the words. Then colour the pictures with the specified colours.

12.1 Vowel Digraphs

Long oo (blue)	Short oo (green)

Long oo

sp**oo**n

t**oo**thbrush

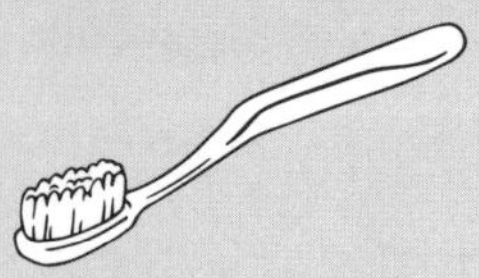

Short oo

w**oo**d

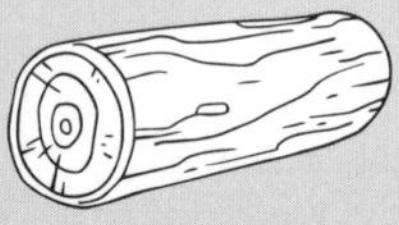

b**oo**k

1. h**oo**k

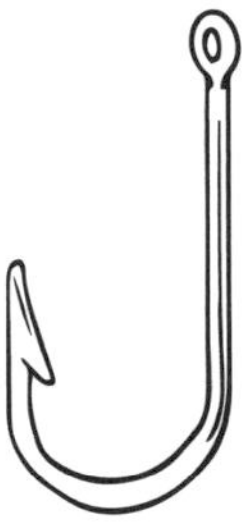

2. ball**oo**n

3. w**oo**l

4. l**oo**p

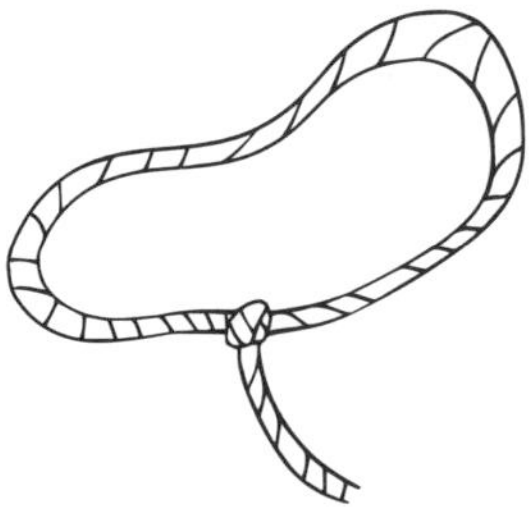

5. m**oo**n

6. m**oo**se

7. c**oo**k

B. **Write the words in the correct boxes. Then give two more examples for each.**

Long **oo**

My Examples

____

____

Short **oo**

My Examples

____

____

C. Write "long" or "short" to identify the vowel digraph of each group of words. Then fill in the blanks with the words.

1.

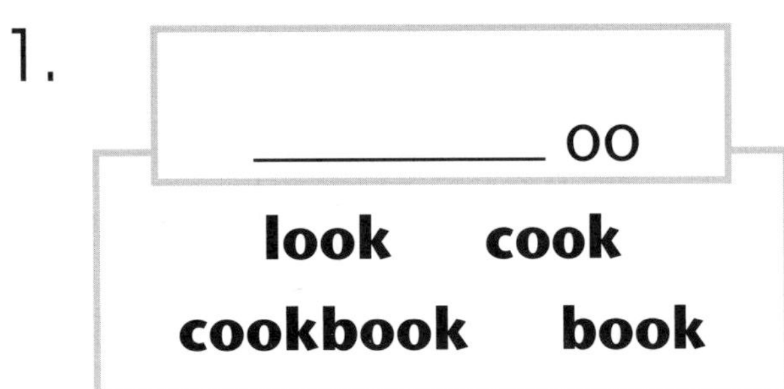

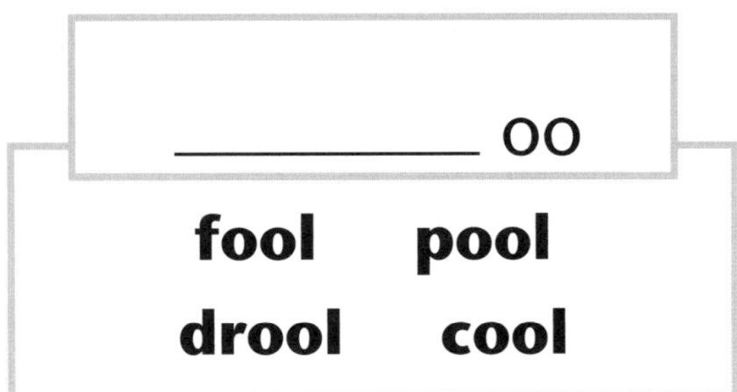

2.

My mom taught me to ____________

By reading a ____________ .

She said, "Take a ____________ .

This is called a ____________ ."

3.

The clown played the ____________ ,

Jumping in the ____________ .

He thought it was ____________

When he started to ____________ .

D.   Read the story. Then underline and circle the words.

Noor's Smoothie Recipe

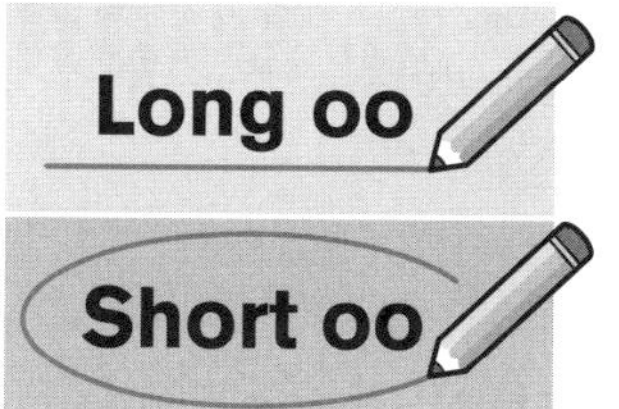

Noor was a very good cook. But she did not want to make the same food every day. So she stood in the kitchen and looked around. Finally, she decided to put some apples, strawberries, bananas, and three scoops of chocolate ice cream into the blender. She pushed the red button and "whoosh" it went as it shook the small wooden table. She excitedly poured the mixture into her glass. Noor hummed in a good mood as she drank the delicious smoothie.

Words that I Have Learned

Vowel Digraphs

Long oo	Short oo
__________	__________
__________	__________
__________	__________

UNIT 13

Diphthongs

A diphthong is a vowel sound in a single syllable that begins with the sound of one vowel and ends with the sound of another vowel.

A. Say the things. Then write the correct diphthongs.

Diphthongs

13.1

ou
couch

ow
owl

oi
oil

oy
boy

1. 

bl______se

2.

c______l

3.

m______se

4. 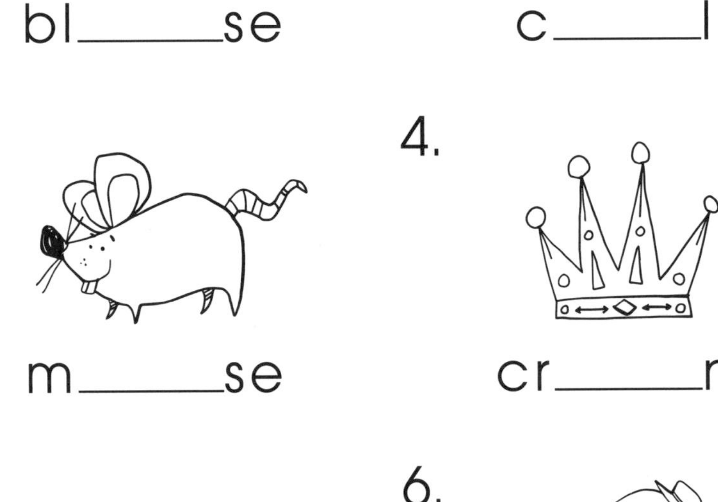

cr______n

5. 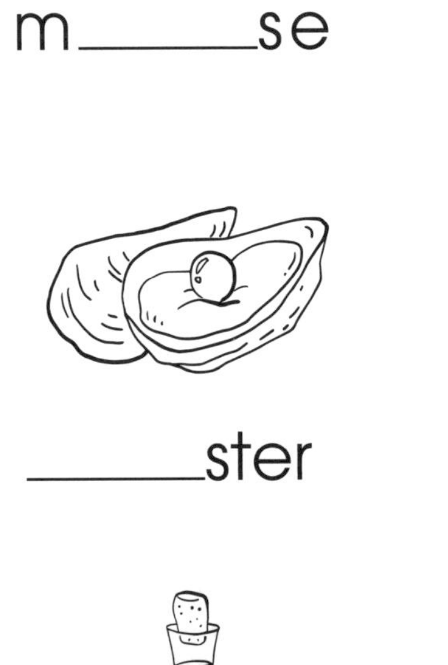

______ster

6. 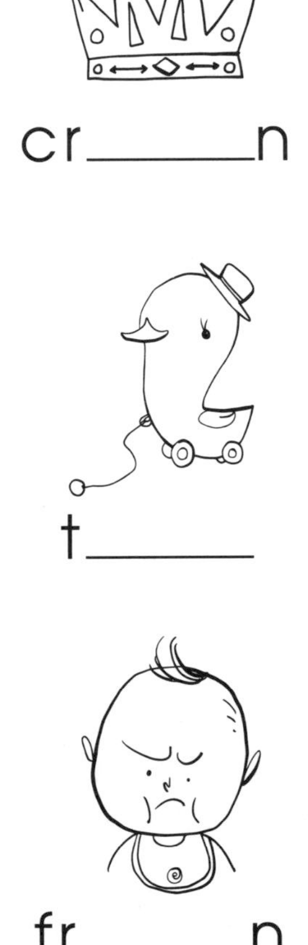

t______

7.

p______son

8.

fr______n

B. **Say the words in each group and label the box with the correct diphthong. Then fill in the blank with the correct word.**

Diphthongs

| ou | ow | oi | oy |

1. 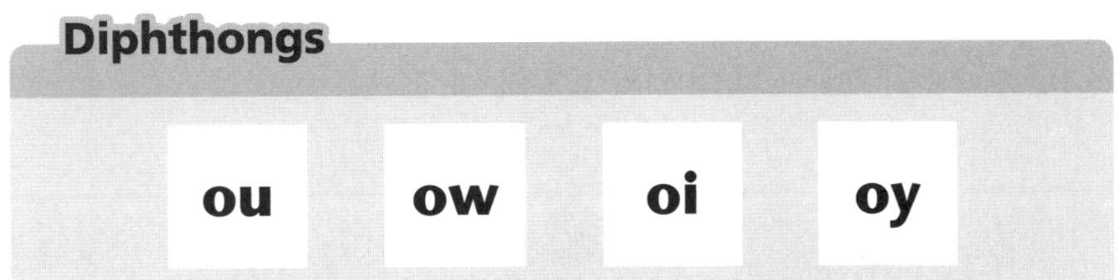

The ____________ castle was very beautiful.

2. 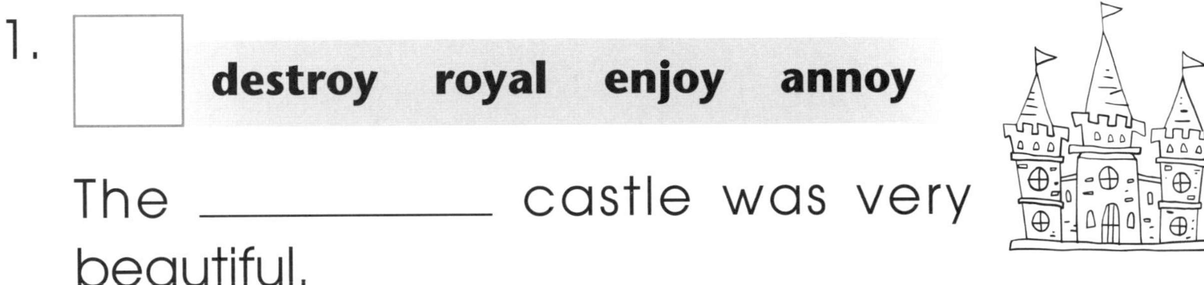

Stephanie heard a loud ____________ when the balloon popped.

3. 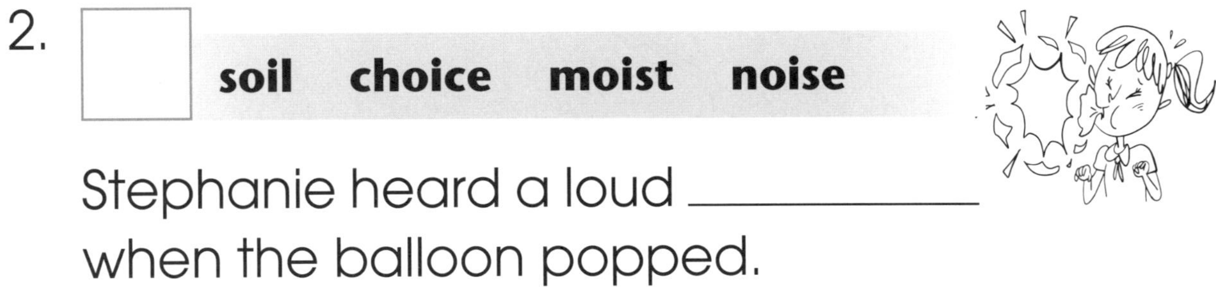

The people of the small ____________ celebrated the mayor's birthday.

4. 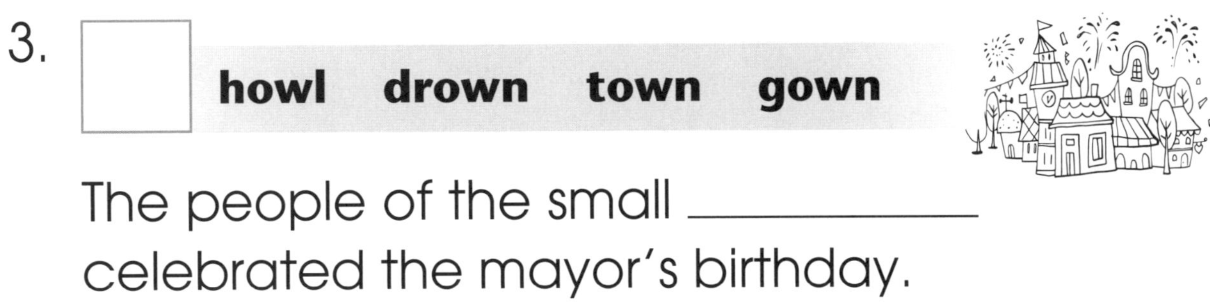

Johnny opened his ____________ to show his cavity to the dentist.

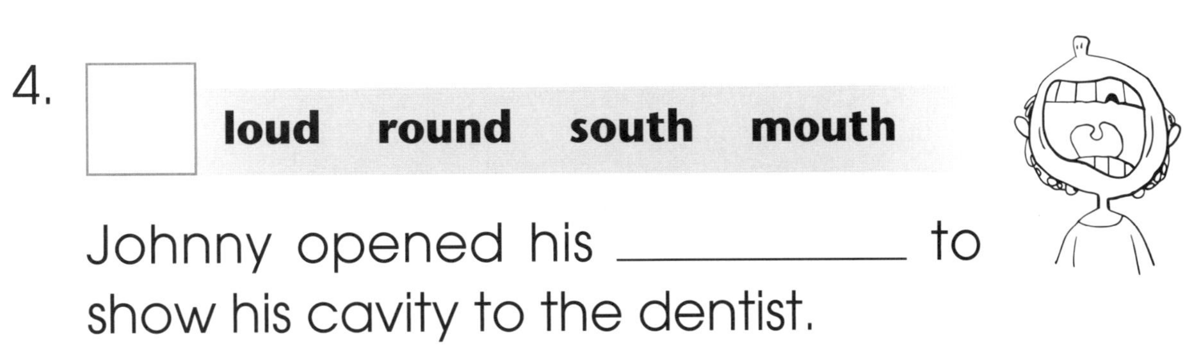

C.   Say the words. Then write them in the correct boxes.

Diphthongs

Roy the Toy Robot

Roy was very annoyed with his sister, Joy. She was around two years old and enjoyed destroying his things. She even spoiled his favourite drawing of blue clouds over a sea of trout and the one with a crowd of silly clowns. At first, Roy yelled at her in a loud voice. Then he heard her cry on the couch. So he decided to surprise her. He took a piece of foil, some brown paper, and a metal coil. After a lot of hard work, "Roy the Toy Robot" went to his sister and they both played till their mother was back home.

Words that I Have Learned

Words with Diphthongs

ou ____

ow ____

oi ____

oy ____

UNIT 14

Rhyming Words

Rhyming words are words that have the same ending sound.

A. Say the things. Then colour each rhyming pair with the same colour.

14.1 Rhyming Words

bone

cone

kite

light

pin

bin

cat

mat

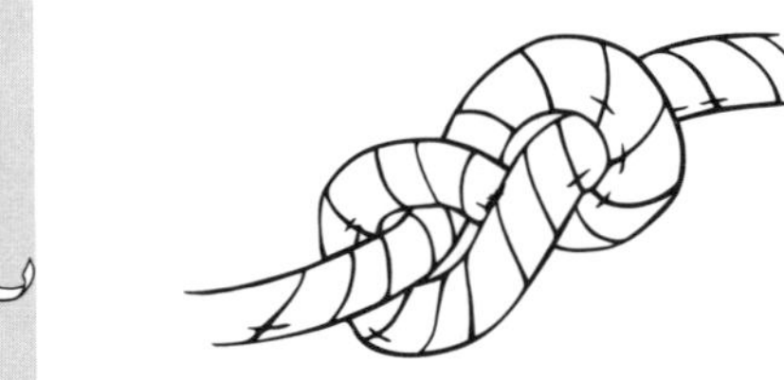
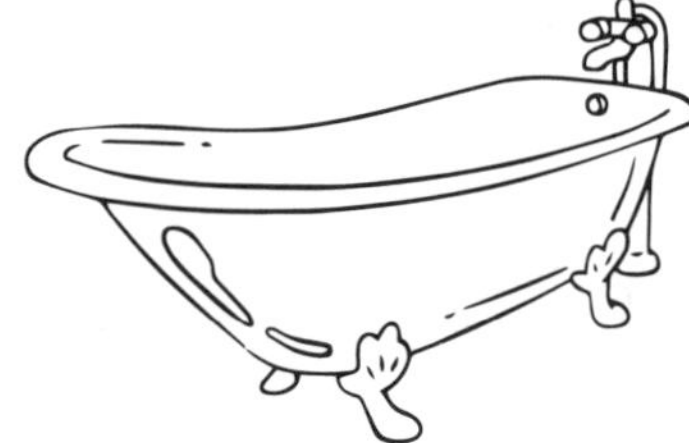

B. **Name each item. Then cross out the word that does not rhyme in each group.**

1. 

door

hook

look

2. 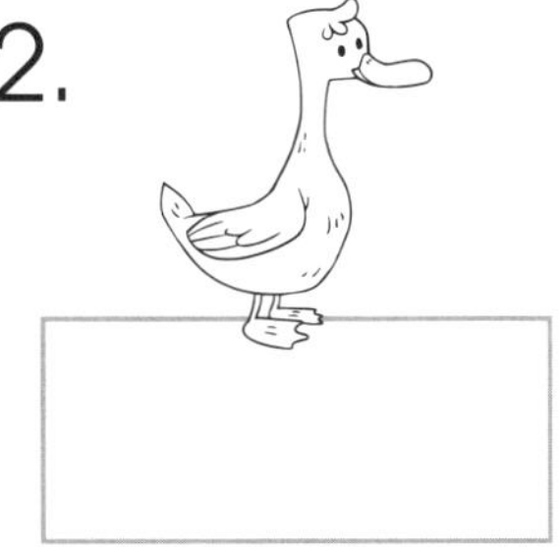

luck

truck

quack

3. 

lake

cage

bake

4. 

wok

dog

log

5. 

one

bun

mom

6. 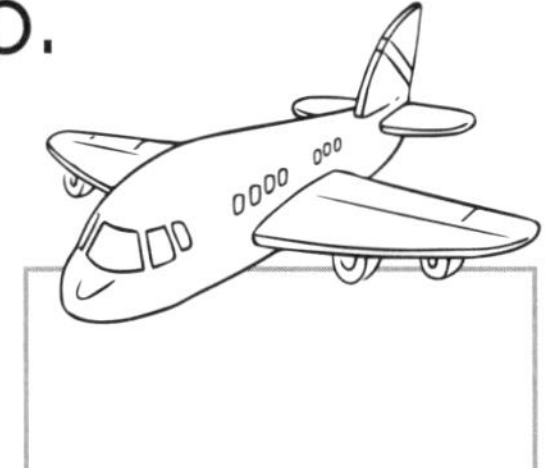

man

train

cane

C. Complete the crossword puzzle with words that rhyme with the clues.

Rhyming words do not have to end with the same spelling.

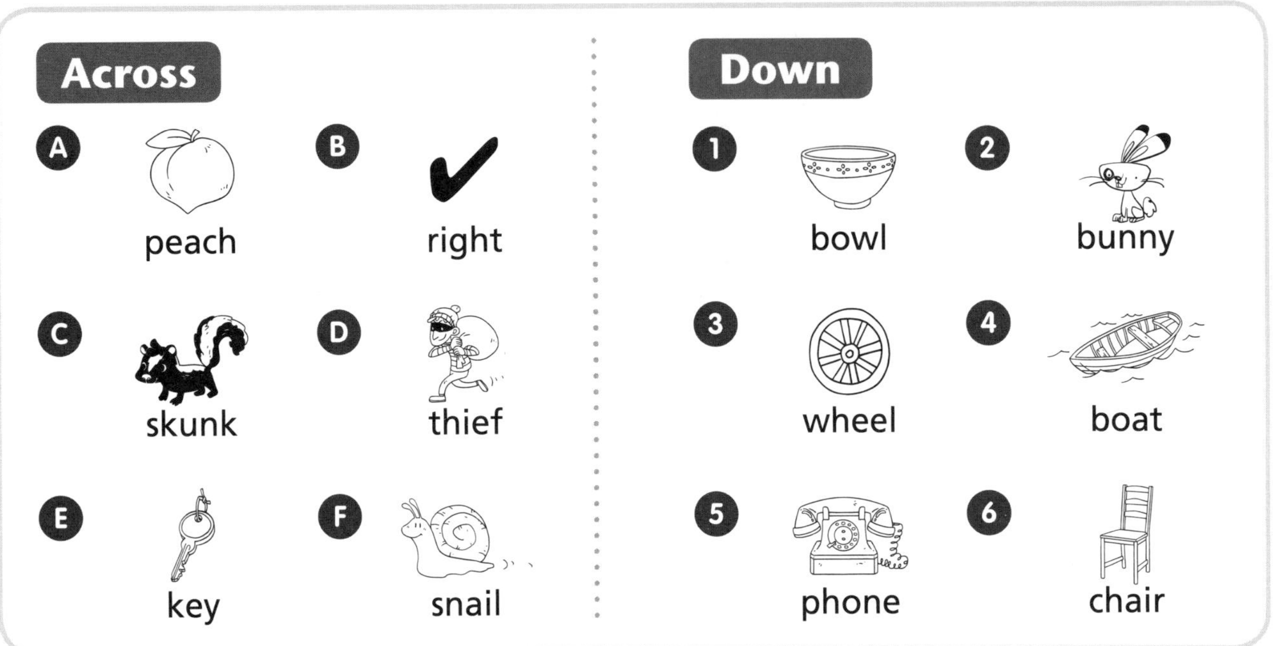

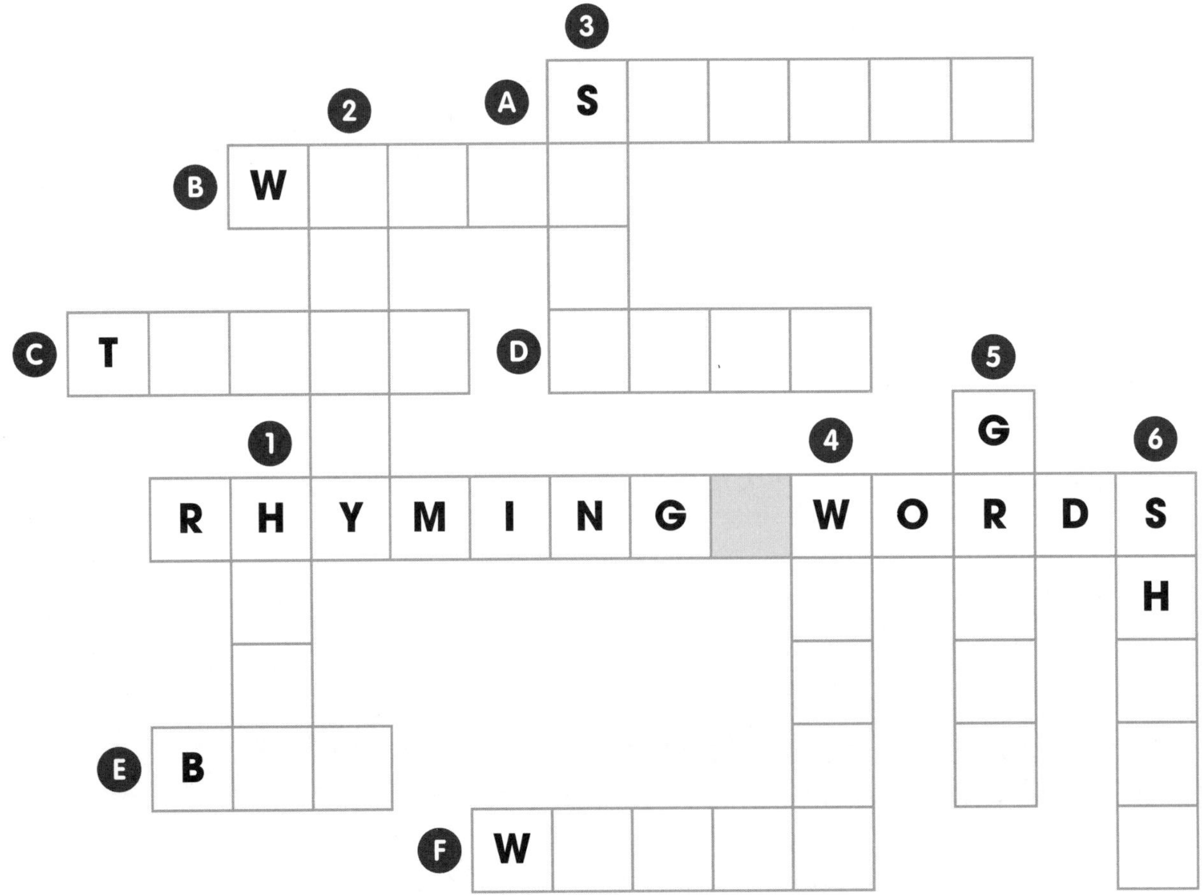

D. Circle each pair or group of rhyming words with the same colour.

Deep in the Woods

In the woods so deep,

I see a little white sheep,

A cat chasing a rat,

And a bear and a hare,

Sharing a big juicy pear!

At the pond I can hear,

A dog barking at a frog,

And a moose grunting at a goose!

In the woods so deep,

I drift off to sleep.

Words that I Have Learned

Rhyming Words

____

____

____

____

A. Circle the answers.

1. The ____ consonant of the picture is "L".

   beginning

   middle

   ending

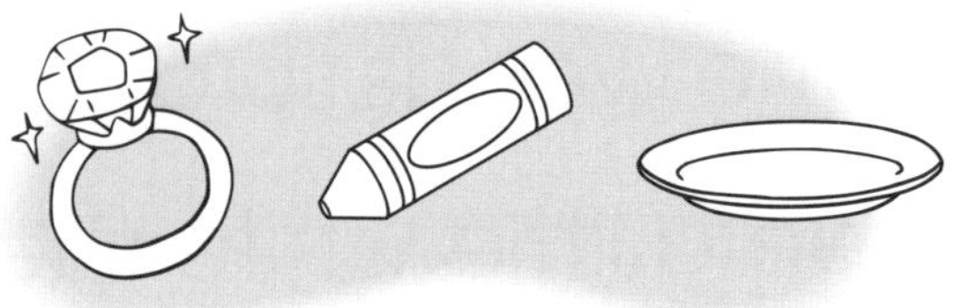

2. Which one has the hard "c" sound?

3. Which word contains the silent "k"?

   kite

   knife

   kitten

4. Which blend does this picture have?

   bl

   cl

   pl

5. Which one has an R blend?

6. This picture has the ____ blend.

   L

   R

   S

7. Which group contains all words that have consonant digraphs?

   wheel, thumb, chair

   thumb, crown, chair

   shampoo, frog, knee

8. This picture has a ____ sound.

   short vowel

   long vowel

   diphthong

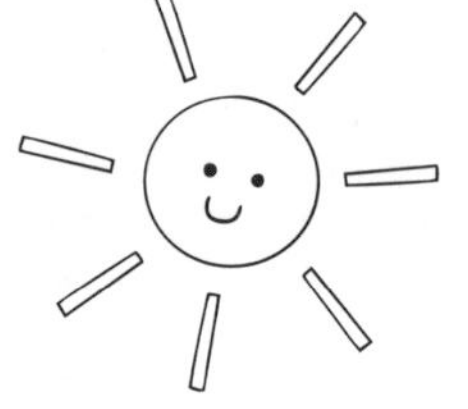

9. This picture has the _____ sound.

   short "a"

   long "a" 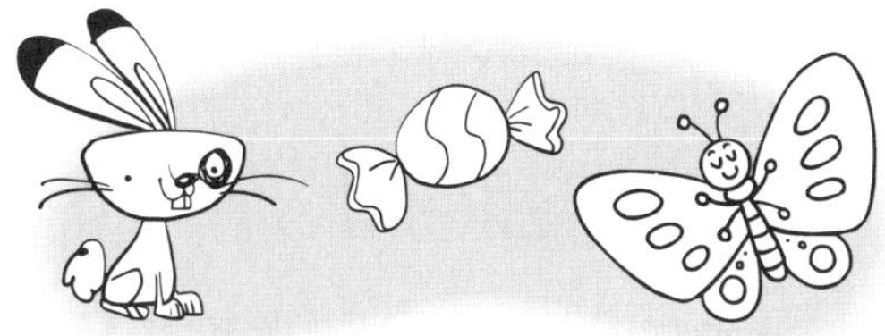

   vowel digraph "ay"

10. Which picture has y with the long "i" sound?

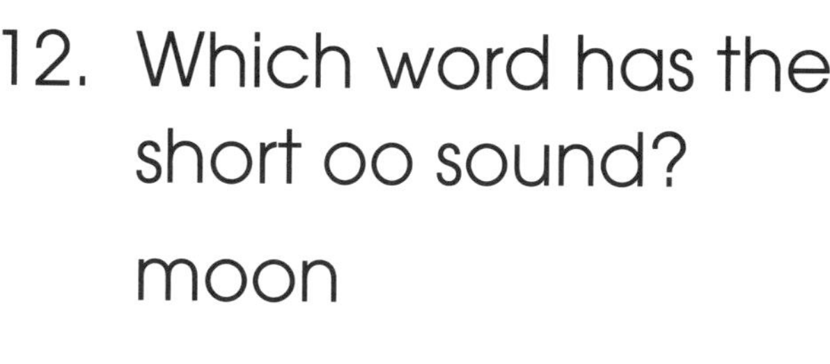

11. This picture has the vowel digraph _____ .

    ai

    ay

    ee

12. Which word has the short oo sound?

    moon

    spoon

    hook

13. Which one does not have a diphthong?

14. The word "avoid" has a _____ .

    digraph

    long vowel

    diphthong

15. Which pair of words rhyme?

    pin, been

    bite, sight

    cone, come

16. Which one does not rhyme with the others?

Consonants

B. Say the things. Then draw lines to match.

- middle consonant "m"

- ending consonant "l"

- silent consonant "b"

- silent consonant "h"

C. Read the sentences. Then circle the letters with the specified colours.

1. The gigantic giant, Gary, used magic to decorate the castle.

2. There were cakes and candies in the garden on Carl's birthday.

3. The dancers celebrated as Andy played the guitar.

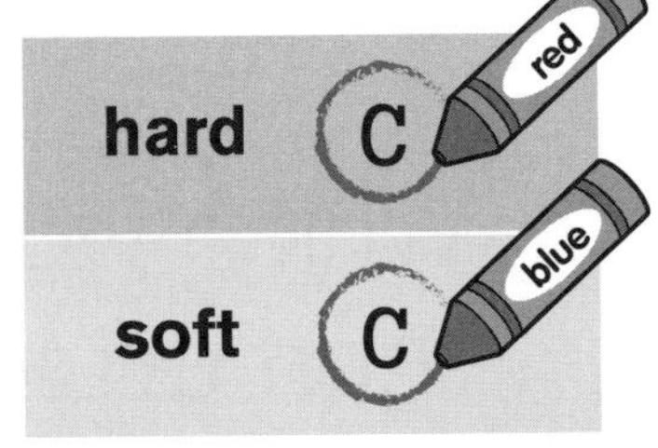

Consonant Blends and Digraphs

D.   Say the things. Then write the correct consonant blends.

1. 

__ __ock

2. 

__ __um

3. 

__ __ar

4. 

__ __ies

5. 

__ __irt

6. 

__ __ag

E.   Cross out the picture that does not belong in each group.

Consonant Digraphs

1. *ch*

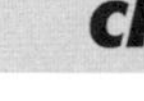

2. *sh*

3. *th*

4. *wh*

Short and Long Vowels

F. **Say the things. Write the correct short and long vowels in the circles. Then give three more examples for each.**

Short Vowel		Long Vowel	
◯	◯	◯	◯

_______________   _______________   _______________   _______________

_______________   _______________   _______________   _______________

_______________   _______________   _______________   _______________

G. **Read the sentences. Then write the underlined words in the correct columns.**

	Short-vowel Word	Long-vowel Word
1. <u>Bill</u> likes <u>grapes</u>.	__________	__________
2. They bought a <u>pink</u> <u>slide</u>.	__________	__________
3. He left a beautiful <u>rose</u> on the front <u>mat</u>.	__________	__________
4. Beatrice's <u>pet</u> dog ran away with the <u>bone</u>.	__________	__________
5. Jameson spent the <u>night</u> collecting <u>rocks</u>.	__________	__________

H. **Fill in the blanks with the correct vowel digraphs using the picture clues.**

1. The qu___n took a rest under the tr___ .

2. I saw a little sn___l on a l___f.

3. Dad hammered a n___l into the tr___ .

4. The red ball___n flew up to the m___n.

I. **Read the sentences. Then write the underlined words in the correct boxes.**

1. The sun shone through the <u>clouds</u> as the children played <u>outside</u>.

2. Alia coloured the <u>crown</u> with a yellow crayon and used a <u>brown</u> one for the <u>soil</u>.

3. The little <u>boy</u> heard an <u>annoying</u> <u>noise</u> so he went to investigate.

Words with the Diphthongs:

ou	ow	oi	oy
__________	__________	__________	__________
__________	__________	__________	__________

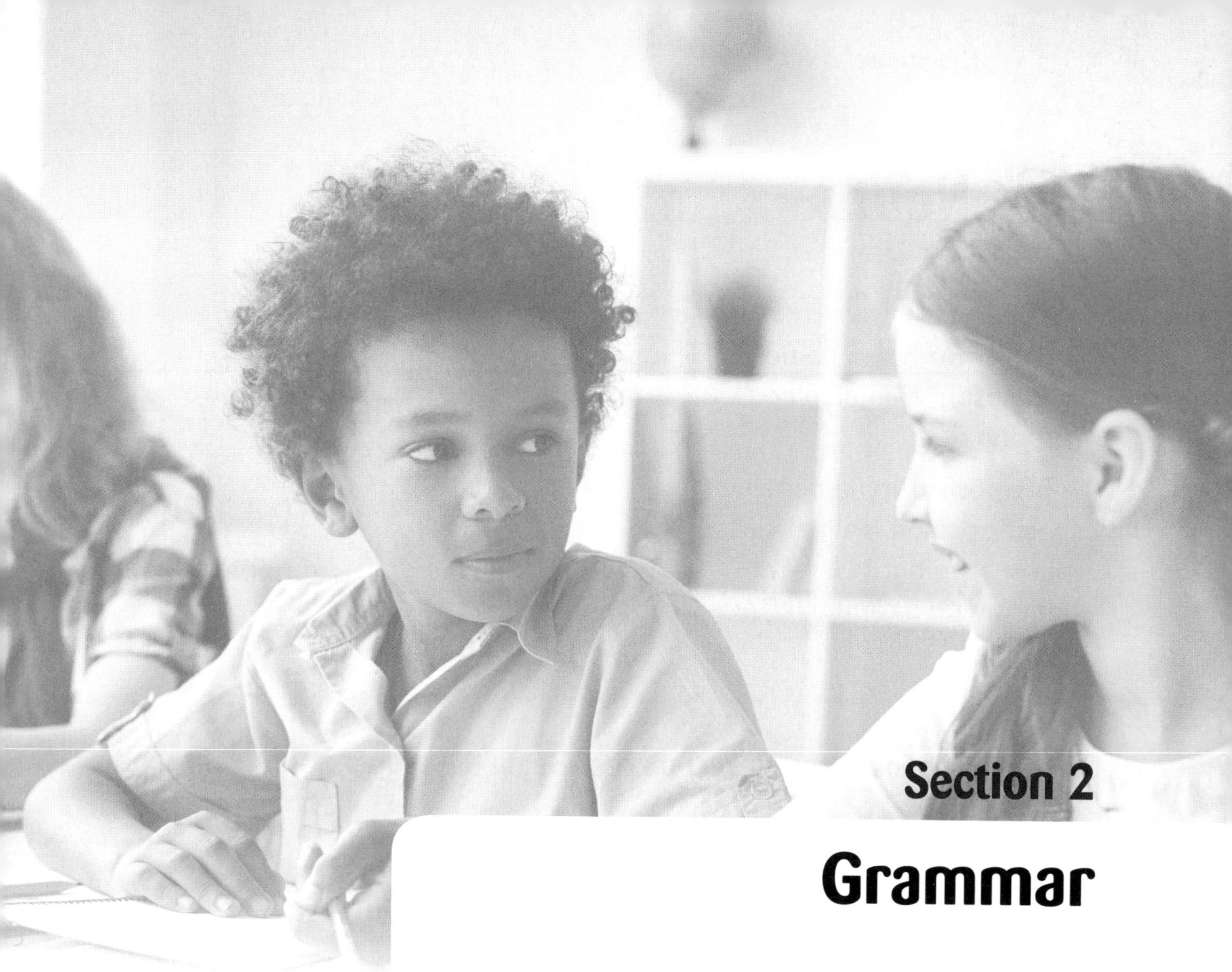

Section 2

Grammar

UNIT 1

Nouns

A **common noun** names any person, animal, place, or thing.

A **proper noun** names a specific person, animal, place, or thing. It always begins with a capital letter.

Examples

Common Noun		Proper Noun
girl		Ana
dog		Poodle
city		Halifax
movie		Bambi

A. Write the nouns in the correct places. Begin the proper nouns with capital letters.

> frisbee   city   toronto   game
> dalmatian   boy   dog   timmy

	Common Noun	Proper Noun
Person	_____________	_____________
Animal	_____________	_____________
Place	_____________	_____________
Thing	_____________	_____________

A **singular noun** names one person, animal, place, or thing. A **plural noun** names more than one person, animal, place, or thing.

Many plural nouns are formed by adding "s" to the singular nouns.

For nouns ending in "s", "x", "ch", or "sh", add "es" to form the plural.

For nouns ending in "y", change "y" to "i" and add "es".

Singular Noun	Plural Noun
girl	girls
bus	buses
box	boxes
beach	beaches
dish	dishes
berry	berries

Section 2

Grammar

B. Circle the correct words.

1. 

parrot / parrots

2. 

fairy / fairies

3. 

foxs / foxes

4. 

dress / dresses

5. 

brush / brushes

6. 

chicks / chickes

7. 

bench / benches

8. 

rat / rats

9. 

kids / kides

	Examples
Some nouns are **countable**. You can use number words before their plural forms.	• There are five <u>apples</u> in the basket. └countable
Some nouns are **uncountable**. You cannot use number words before them and they do not have any plural forms.	• <u>Milk</u> is good for us. └uncountable

C. Look at each picture. If it is countable, draw to show more than one and add "s/es" to make the noun plural.

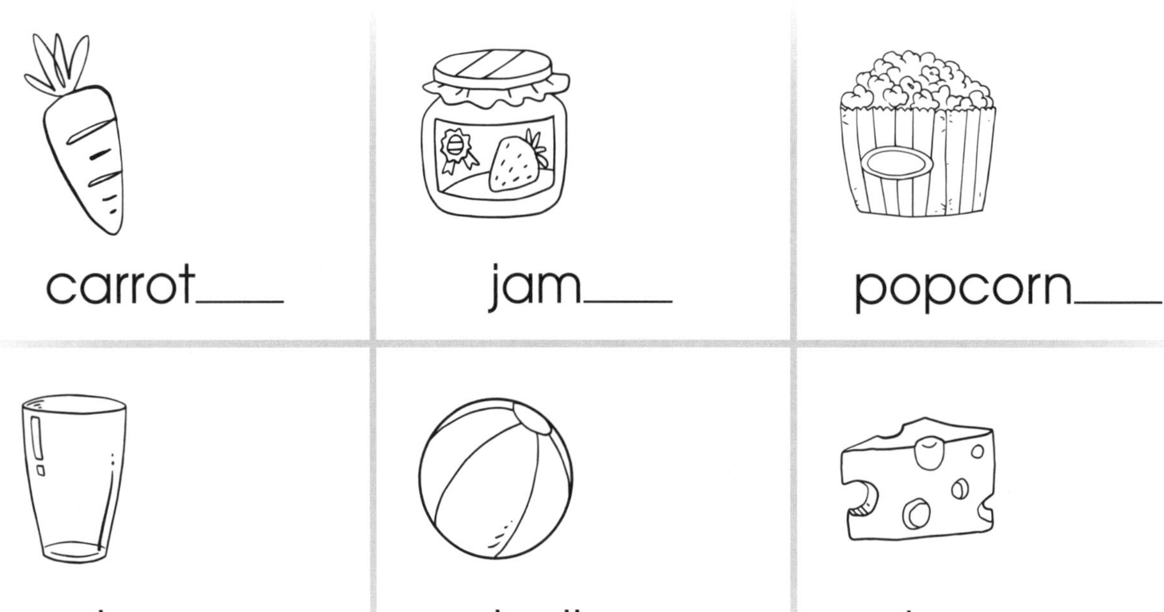

D. Colour the correct nouns for the sentences.

1. Pour some | water | waters | into the two | cup | cups |.

2. The | bottle | bottles | are made of | plastic | plastics |.

3. Add some | sand | sands | to these | pot | pots |.

4. I have | faith | faiths | in both | hero | heroes |.

E.   Read the story and write the underlined words in the correct boxes.

Arnie's Farm

Arnie's <u>farm</u> is far from the <u>market</u>. Every day, Arnie works very hard. He turns the <u>soil</u>, which is sometimes called <u>dirt</u>, to make it easier to retain <u>air</u> and drain <u>water</u>. He milks the <u>cows</u> and takes care of other <u>animals</u>. There are <u>hens</u> that lay <u>eggs</u> and <u>sheep</u> that provide <u>wool</u>. Every Saturday, Arnie drives to the market to sell the eggs, <u>milk</u>, and wool.

<table>
<tr><td>Countable Noun</td><td>Uncountable Noun</td></tr>
<tr><td></td><td></td></tr>
</table>

Words that I Have Learned

Nouns

____

____

____

UNIT 2

Articles

"A", "an", and "the" are **articles**. They come before nouns. "A" is used before a noun that begins with a consonant sound. "An" is used before a noun that begins with a vowel sound. "The" is used before a noun that names a particular person, place, or thing. It is also used with something unique.

Examples

- <u>a</u> girl
- <u>an</u> honour
- <u>the</u> GO Train
- <u>the</u> moon

A. Put the words in the correct boxes. Then give one more example for each.

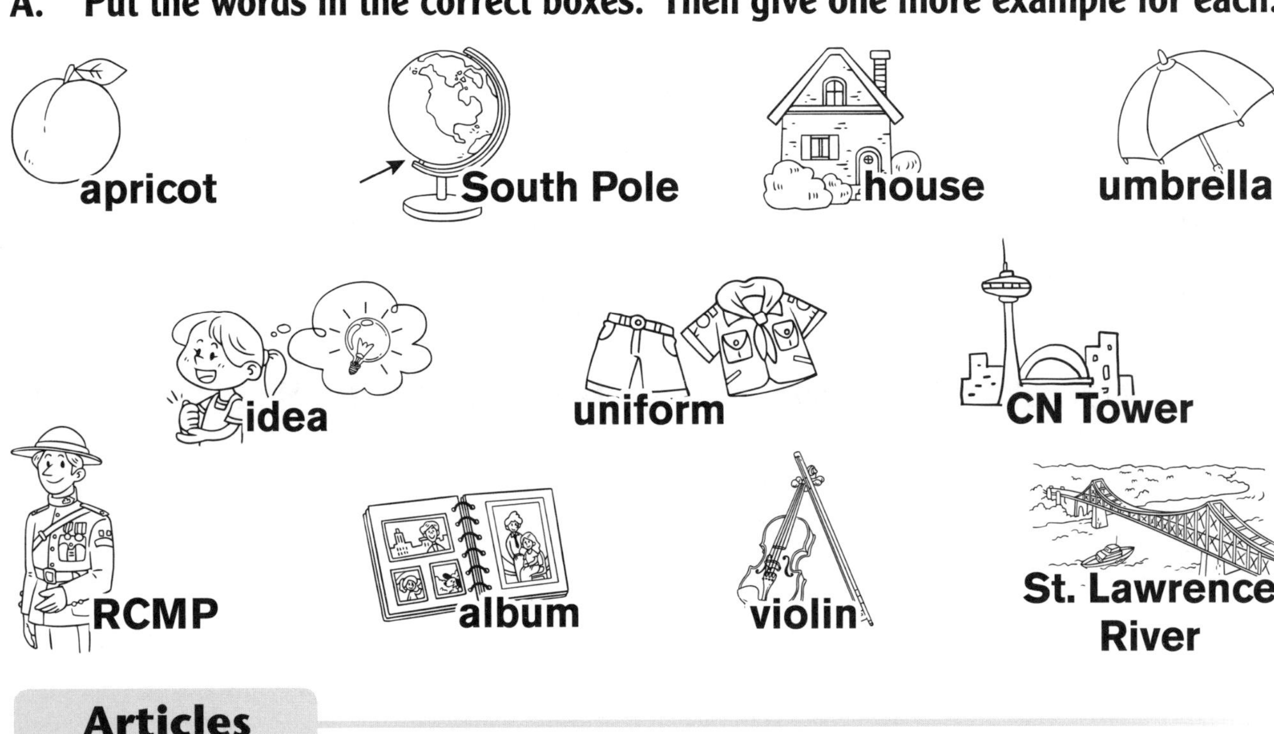

Articles

a	an	the

my example   my example   my example

B. **Write what each picture is with the correct article.**

> a/an/the
>
> **unicorn**   **Earth**   **owl**   **sun**   **airplane**
> **Olympic Games**   **elephant**   **rainbow**   **lamp**

1. 

____

2. 

____

3. 

____

4. 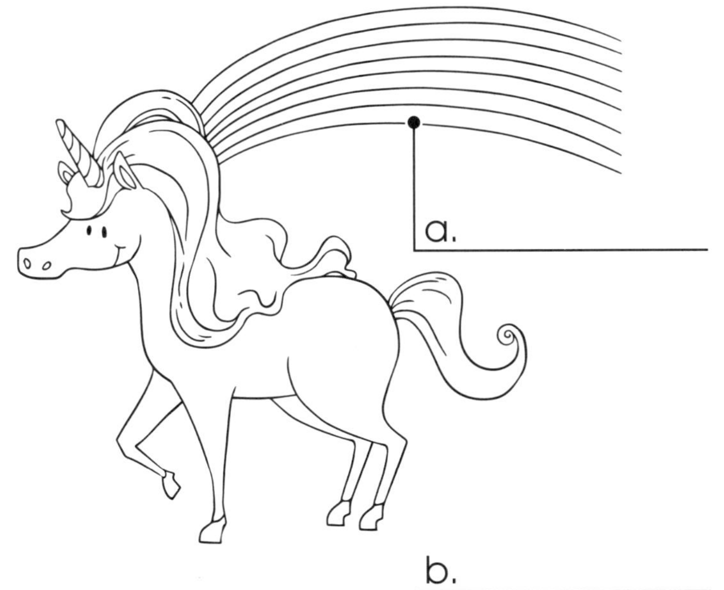

a. ____________

b. ____________

5. 

____

6. 

____

7. 

____

8. 

____

C.   **Circle the correct articles to complete the sentences.**

1. Do you know **an / the** girl over there?

2. Is this **a / an** orange or **a / the** grapefruit?

3. There are no penguins at **a / the** North Pole. You can only find them at **a / the** South Pole.

4. **An / The** Rockies lie between British Columbia and Alberta.

5. Look at **a / the** ape in **a / the** cage. Is it **a / an** chimpanzee?

6. We have forgotten to buy one of **an / the** ingredients. We need **an / the** avocado.

7. **A / The** friend should be one that cares about your feelings.

8. The train left **a / an** hour ago.

9. There is **a / the** library on **an / the** eighth floor.

10. I wish I could fly in **a / the** sky.

An article can be used before a noun with an adjective. Use "a" if the adjective begins with a consonant sound. Use "an" if it begins with a vowel sound. Use "the" if the noun after the adjective refers to a particular person, place, or thing.

Examples

- a beautiful flower
- an honest girl
- the national anthem

D. Write a sentence with the adjective and the noun. Use the correct article before them.

1. oval table

____

2. Great Lakes

____

3. Canadian flag

____

4. kind person

____

Words that I Have Learned

Articles

a _______________________________________

an _______________________________________

the _______________________________________

UNIT 3

Pronouns

A **pronoun** replaces a noun. A **subject pronoun** acts as the subject in a sentence.

"I", "you", "we", "he", "she", "it", and "they" are subject pronouns.

Example

Kim is my classmate.
He is my neighbour too.

A. Match the words and the picture with the correct subject pronouns.

The squirrel •

Ray and I •

Cindy •

The acorn •

Mr. Hopkins •

You and Liam •

Alexa and Ezra •

The flowers •

Subject Pronouns

• I

• You

• We

• He

• She

• It

• They

B. **Circle the correct subject pronouns to complete the sentences.**

1. **We / It** went to the movies last night.

2. **They / She** both like skiing.

3. Melissa likes collecting coins. **You / She** keeps them in a big jar.

4. My family and I are visiting Calgary this summer. **He / It** is in Alberta.

5. **I / You** don't know where the restaurant is. Could you show me the way?

C. **Replace the underlined words with subject pronouns. Write above the words.**

<u>Mom and Dad</u> take my brother and me to the zoo. <u>My family and I</u> go to see the zebras first.

<u>My brother Cecil</u> takes pictures of the zebras.

<u>One of the zebras</u> looks at us.

An **object pronoun** receives the action of the verb in a sentence.

"Me", "you", "us", "him", "her", "it", and "them" are object pronouns.

Example

Mrs. Lin drives Leo to school.

Mrs. Lin drives <u>him</u> to school.

D. Circle the object pronouns in the sentences.

1. I will meet you at the mall entrance.

2. Your ice cream is melting. Finish it quickly.

3. There were two mice in the corner but no one noticed them except me!

4. Janice gave him a call when she arrived at the airport.

5. Miss Hall has given us two choices for the outing. We have to let her know our pick tomorrow.

E. Write the correct object pronouns for the words.

1. my sister   __________

2. Mr. and Mrs. Hall __________

3. our class   __________

4. you and Ella   __________

5. the actor   __________

6. Lily and me   __________

7. his tall hat   __________

8.

____

____

F. **Fill in the blanks with the correct object pronouns to complete the sentences.**

1. Mom took this photo of ___________ on the farm.

2. Ginny has a dog. She walks ___________ in the park every day.

3. Hilda and Jon are my best friends. I will surely invite ___________ to my party.

4. Dennis is very upset. Do you know what happened to ___________ ?

5. Mr. Soto promised to tell ___________ the story ending tomorrow. We cannot wait to know how the story goes.

6. Ana is sick. Mom is giving ___________ some medicine.

Words that I Have Learned

Subject Pronoun	Object Pronoun
___________	___________
___________	___________
___________	___________
___________	___________

UNIT 4

Present Tense Verbs

A **present tense verb** tells what happens now. Add "s" to the base form of the verb to tell about one person or thing, except "I" and "you".

Use the "ing" form of the verb with "am/is/are" to tell what someone or something is doing.

Examples

- I <u>live</u> in Toronto.
- My aunt <u>lives</u> in Milton.
- The children <u>are reading</u>.

A. Complete the chart.

	Base Form	"s" Form	"ing" Form
1.		sings	
2.	laugh		
3.		breaks	
4.			leaping
5.	snow		
6.		finds	

B. **Write the correct forms of the underlined verbs above them.**

1. The sun <u>shine</u> brightly.

2. The children are <u>walks</u> along the pond.

3. They <u>chats</u> happily.

4. Some ducks <u>lives</u> in the pond.

5. Derek is <u>waves</u> at the ducks.

6. The ducks are <u>look</u> at Derek.

C. **Fill in the blanks with the verbs in the correct forms.**

stay	get	play	eat	collect	blow

1. I _____________ toast for breakfast every day.

2. It _____________ dark after the sun sets.

3. We _____________ in the tent at night.

4. The wind is _____________ fiercely.

5. Jerry _____________ hockey on the weekends.

6. The bees are _____________ nectar.

Examples

"**Am**", "**is**", and "**are**" are the present forms of the verb "be".

Use "am" with "I"; use "is" to tell about one person, animal, place, or thing. Use "are" to tell about more than one person, animal, place, or thing.

- I <u>am</u> a student.
- Mom's cake <u>is</u> yummy.
- Pandas <u>are</u> black and white.

D. **Circle the correct forms of "be" to complete the sentences.**

1. Bees **am / is / are** busy insects.

2. The flowers **am / is / are** in full bloom.

3. That **am / is / are** a big flower!

4. Nectar **am / is / are** my favourite treat.

5. The nectar of the flowers **am / is / are** sweet.

6. Where **am / is / are** the other bees?

7. There **am / is / are** more flowers over there!

8.

Remember that "am", "is", and "are" can be used with the "ing" form of verbs to tell what someone or something is doing.

Examples

- I <u>am watching</u> TV.
- He <u>is having</u> a good time.
- They <u>are making</u> a kite.

E. **Look at each picture and put the words in order to write about what is happening.**

A 

reading   am   I
letter.   a

B 

happily.   the   are
calves   playing

C 

is   in   tree.   the
swinging   Gavin

A ____

B ____

C ____

Words that I Have Learned

Present Tense Verbs

____

____

____

UNIT 5

Past Tense Verbs

A **past tense verb** tells about something that happened in the past. For most verbs, add "d" or "ed" to the base form to change them to the past form.

Examples

Base Form	Past Form
use	used
fold	folded

A. Circle the past forms of the verbs in the word search.

close	score	lift
brush	erase	reach
dislike	buzz	collect

c	e	p	d	r	h	l	c	o	l	r	f	a
o		l	i	t	e	b	u	z	z	e	d	
b	a	d	s	g	e	r	a	s	l	a	e	t
r	s	h	l	r	t	u	r	o	i	c	b	e
c	l	o	s	e	d	s	e	r	f	h	u	r
o	j	u	c	a	m	h	a	i	t	e	z	a
l		c	o	l	l	e	c	t	e	d	s	s
e	p	b	r	u	s	d	d	b	d		c	e
c	o	r	e	a	d		k	m	c	e	o	d
d	q	t	d	i	s	l	i	k	e	d	s	g

 Some past tense verbs are formed by repeating the last letter before adding "ed".

For verbs ending in "y", change "y" to "i" before adding "ed".

Base Form	Past Form
slip	slipped
study	studied

B. Circle the correct past forms of the verbs to complete the story.

Dodo **carryed** / **carried** a backpack to school yesterday. He **learnd** / **learned** some funny tricks at the dog school. He **balanced** / **balanceed** himself with one hand on a plank on a ball. After that, he **skiped** / **skipped** for an hour. Then he **hurryed** / **hurried** home for lunch. On his way home, he **remembered** / **rememberred** that there was no more dog food at home, so he **stoped** / **stopped** by a grocery store and **grabed** / **grabbed** some dog food. He also **tryed** / **tried** to look for a bone as a treat but he could not find one that he **liked** / **likeed** .

Irregular past tense verbs do not end in "ed". They may be spelled the same as the base form or they may be completely different.

Examples	
Base Form	**Past Form**
put	put
go	went

C. Write the past forms of the verbs.

1.

stand

____

2.

catch

____

3.

burst

____

4.

buy

____

5.

weep

____

6.

throw

____

7.

teach

____

8.
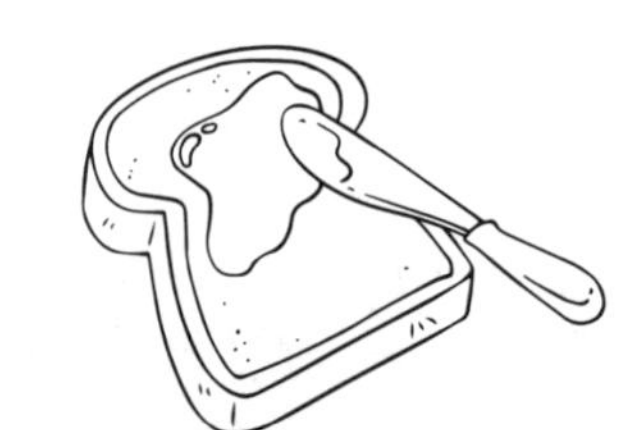

spread

____

"**Was**" and "**were**" are the past forms of the verb "be".

Use "was" to tell about one person, animal, place, or thing. Use "were" to tell about more than one person, animal, place, or thing.

"Was" and "were" can also be used with the "ing" form of a verb to tell what someone or something was doing at a past time.

Examples

- There <u>was</u> a storm last night.
- The kittens <u>were</u> frightened.
- They <u>were</u> <u>shaking</u> with fear.

D. **Check if the underlined words are correct. Correct the wrong ones by writing above the words.**

1. It <u>were</u> raining when he walked his dog.

2. There <u>was</u> a bird in the tree this morning.

3. The kids <u>were</u> singing when the teacher came in.

4. Hilary and I <u>was</u> at the show last night.

Words that I Have Learned

Past Tense Verbs

____

____

____

UNIT 6

Adjectives

An **adjective** tells about a noun. It describes a person, an animal, a place, or a thing. Colour words, number words, and shape words are all adjectives.

Examples

- The <u>little</u> girl is <u>skinny</u>.
- Bananas are <u>yellow</u>.
- There are <u>three</u> apples on a <u>square</u> plate.

A. Look at the pictures. Then match the adjectives with the correct nouns.

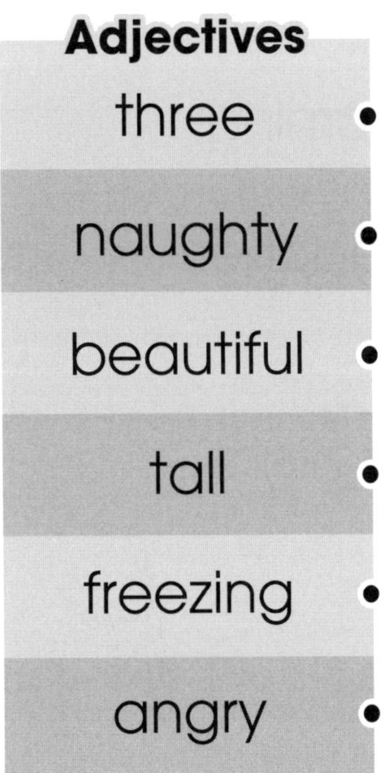

Adjectives

three •

naughty •

beautiful •

tall •

freezing •

angry •

B. Read each group of adjectives and write the noun they describe to solve the riddle.

C. Unscramble the words and fill in the blanks with the correct adjectives.

1. ______________ apples are usually sour.
   ereGn

2. I want a ______________ peach after dinner.
   yicju

3. A rainbow has ______________ colours.
   eesnv

4. Mom wants to buy a ______________ table.
   norud

5. My brother likes eating ______________ curry.
   pcsyi

6. Do you see my ______________ yo-yo? I just bought it
   enw

   yesterday. It has a ______________ star in the middle.
   oelwyl

7. Pandas are ______________ and ______________ in colour.
   lakcb   hewit

   They only eat ______________ bamboo shoots.
   sherf

8. Sam looks ______________ . He does not understand
   zuzpeld

   what Jake is doing.

9. It is such a ______________ pig.
   yazl

   It is always sleeping.

D. Circle the adjectives in the sentences. Then rewrite the sentences by replacing the adjectives with other adjectives.

1. Uncle Rowan caught a big fish yesterday.

   ____

   ____

2. She looks pretty in that costume.

   ____

3. The dog has just given birth to six puppies.

   ____

4. I dreamed of a scary monster last night.

   ____

5. The red roses in the yard were a gift from Nova.

   ____

Words that I Have Learned

Adjectives

____

____

____

UNIT 7

Prepositions

Prepositions of place are location words. They tell where people, animals, or things are.

Examples

Pete is <u>in</u> his pet shop. He is putting the paper <u>on</u> the board.

A. Circle the correct prepositions of place to complete the sentences.

1. There are lots of stars **in / on** the night sky.

2. The shy girl hides **between / behind** her mom.

3. Did you see that dog jump **under / over** the fence?

4. Please leave the books **on / over** the table **in / by** the window.

5. There is a bakery **in / between** the grocery store and the Italian restaurant.

6.

B. **Look at the picture and read the story. Check the circles if the underlined prepositions of place are correct. If not, write the correct prepositions above the words.**

Samuel is <u>under</u> ◯ a cruise ship. He is sitting <u>at</u> ◯ a table <u>in</u> ◯ the deck enjoying the cool breeze.

There are some clouds <u>over</u> ◯ the sky but the weather is still fine. There is a drink <u>under</u> ◯ the table. Samuel does not know what is <u>in</u> ◯ the glass but he thinks it tastes amazing. A little bird is <u>in front of</u> ◯ Samuel. It seems to want to share the tranquil moment with him. The cruise ship is not too far <u>on</u> ◯ the shore. Samuel can see people as tiny as ants <u>between</u> ◯ the beach.

Prepositions of time tell when someone does something or when something happens.

Examples

- We go to the park every day <u>in</u> the summer.
- The sun is high up in the sky <u>at</u> noon.

C.   Fill in the blanks with the correct prepositions of time.

Prepositions of Time

in   on   at

1. Let's go to the movies _______ Friday night.

2. The flowers bloom _______ the spring.

3. The baseball game starts _______ eight o'clock tonight.

4. We are planning a trip to Germany _______ November.

5. What are you going to dress up as _______ Halloween?

6. Dad and his friends meet _______ the first day of every month.

7. Why don't we talk about this _______ lunchtime?

8. We like going to the beach _______ weekends.

D. **Read the passage and circle the underlined prepositions with the specified colours.**

Prepositions of

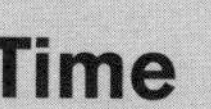

Place   **Time**

Marineland

Marineland is an adventure park <u>near</u> Niagara Falls, Ontario. There are many whales and dolphins <u>in</u> the park. If you put food <u>on</u> your hands, they will eat it right from your hands!

Marineland is such a great place to visit. You can go there early <u>in</u> the morning and spend a whole day there. Besides visiting the animals, you can go on the many rides <u>around</u> the park. You can also try different kinds of food <u>in</u> the restaurant and <u>at</u> the food kiosks.

Why not go to Marineland <u>on</u> a weekend <u>in</u> the summer and enjoy all the fun?

Words that I Have Learned

Preposition of Place	Preposition of Time
_______________	_______________
_______________	_______________
_______________	_______________

UNIT

8 Joining Words

Joining words connect ideas in sentences.

"And" adds information or lists ideas.

"Or" lists options.

"But" joins contrasting ideas.

Examples

- Let's sing <u>and</u> dance.
- Do you want hot <u>or</u> cold tea?
- That rabbit is small <u>but</u> fast.

A.   Circle the joining words in the sentences.

1. Emi, Zoe, and Jon had great fun at Brad's birthday party.

2. This machine is old but it still works well.

3. Green and purple are my favourite colours.

4. Is Rome or Venice the capital of Italy?

5. Pick one flavour combination: strawberry and banana or mango and coconut.

6. Nobody but Julian could solve the puzzle.

7. Will it be sunny or rainy tomorrow?

8. The pink candies are sweet but the yellow and green ones are sour.

9. Adalyn wanted to try the berry pie but she was already too full.

B. **Fill in the blanks with the correct joining words.**

Joining Words

and   or   but

1. A hat _________ a cap will protect you from the sun.

2. Jam _________ butter taste so good together.

3. The teacher gave us two days to study _________ it was not enough.

4. I like soccer _________ it is very hard to play.

5. Susie _________ her sister wanted to visit either the museum _________ the aquarium. They did not have time for both. _________ on the day they decided to go, they had guests over _________ they played cards with them instead.

C.   Check if the joining word in each sentence is correct. If not, cross it out and write the correct joining word above it.

1. I want to be a doctor, a lawyer, or an actor.

2. Do you want to be a chef or work in a restaurant?

3. Mom works very hard but she likes her job.

4. I have to practise hard but be better at dancing.

5. My brother only has one day off in a week. It is Saturday and Sunday.

D.   Join the two sentences with "and", "or", or "but".

1. My sister brushed her hair. She put on her favourite dress.

____

____

2. I wanted to show my picture to you. It got ruined in the rain.

____

____

3. Rehearse more. You will not remember the lines.

____

____

E.   Read the story and add joining words wherever needed.

Playing Soccer

Today I started soccer. My twin brother, Michael, *and* ∧ I went to a big field. There were lots of children none were beginners like us. Some of them were practising their skills others were playing a game.

The coach told us to pick an orange uniform a green one. I liked the green uniform Michael liked the orange one.

Our coach was very nice friendly. She told us that we would practise once a week, either on Saturday Sunday. She said that the most important thing was to have fun.

Words *that I Have Learned*	
Joining Words	**Other Words**
_________________	_________________
_________________	_________________
_________________	_________________

UNIT 9

The Sentence: Subject and Predicate

A **sentence** tells a complete thought about someone or something. It begins with a capital letter and ends with a period (.).

Example

The children are having fun.

A. Check the correct boxes to show what is missing from the sentences.

Missing

	Capital Letter	Period
1. The monkeys are playing in the tree	☐	☐
2. there is a bridge over there	☐	☐
3. I want a cup of tea	☐	☐
4. the dog is hungry.	☐	☐
5. the baby is crying loudly	☐	☐
6. she never likes wearing a cap.	☐	☐
7. my grandma makes yummy muffins.	☐	☐
8. we play badminton after school	☐	☐
9. The music fountain is in the centre of the mall	☐	☐

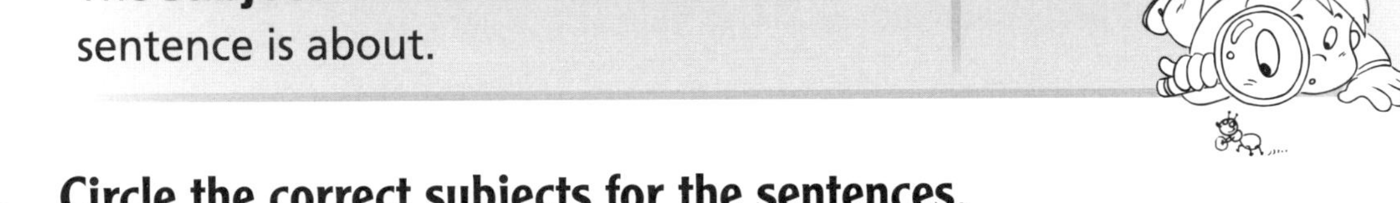

A sentence has two main parts – a subject and a predicate.

The **subject** tells whom or what the sentence is about.

Example

<u>Jerry</u> is looking at the ant.

B. **Circle the correct subjects for the sentences.**

1. **The baby / Mrs. Maddison** holds a party for Brad's birthday.

2. **Brad's father / Brad's cat** puts six candles on the cake.

3. **The birthday cake / The candles** is big.

4. **Andy / Nina** has a flower on her T-shirt.

5. **The children / The cups** are wearing party hats.

6. **Brad's parents / Brad** give him a bike for a present.

7. **The party hats / The children** play games.

8. **They / It** have great fun at the party.

9. **Mrs. Maddison / Brad** is making a wish.

10. **Andy / The bike** is telling Zoe to be quiet.

11. **The birthday / The party** ends around five.

The **predicate** is the part of a sentence that tells what the subject is or what the subject does.

Example

The dog <u>likes playing with a ball</u>.

C. Complete the sentences with the correct predicates. Write the letters.

Predicates

1. My brother _____ .

2. You _____ .

3. The shops _____ .

4. My cat _____ .

5. The bus stop _____ .

6. The book _____ .

7. The Parliament Buildings _____ .

8. The mother bird _____ .

A is in front of the park

B are closed on New Year's Day

C looks like a tiger

D are located in Ottawa

E is working on his Science project

F need a stick to play hockey

G is about animals of the jungle

H is feeding her babies in the nest

D. Look at the picture. Then complete the sentences with subjects or predicates.

1. ________________________________ are at a campsite.

2. ________________________________ sees a raccoon.

3. ________________________________ are floating in the sky.

4. The children ________________________________ .

5. The raccoon ________________________________ .

6. A bear ________________________________ .

Words that I Have Learned

____

____

____

UNIT 10   Subjects and Objects

The **subject** of a verb is the person or thing that performs the action. It can be a noun with its modifiers, or a pronoun.

Examples

- The little boy played the piano.
- He also played the violin.

A. Underline the subject of the verb in each sentence.

1. The girl is pointing at the bird.

2. The hungry lion is chasing the antelope.

3. The hamburger on the plate looks yummy.

4. My mom and dad went to the same high school.

5. The book on the shelf belongs to Heidi.

6. She has left her lunch bag in the kitchen.

7. Ted and his sister like playing board games together.

8. The cute kitten is trying to catch the butterfly.

9. That boy over there won the race last year.

10. Kayla, Miles, and I will work on the project tonight.

11. The busy beaver is building a dam.

The **object** of a verb is the person or thing that receives the action. Like a subject, it can be a noun with its modifiers, or a pronoun.

Examples

- Noah is feeding <u>his pet turtles</u>.
- He feeds <u>them</u> every morning.

B. Underline the object of the verb if there is one in the sentence. If not, put a cross in the circle.

1. Lillian likes ice cream of any flavours.

2. The naughty cat broke the vase by the window.

3. We have to leave early tomorrow morning.

4. Chris baked an apple pie.

5. Luke wore a warm jacket yesterday.

6. Sofia played computer games after dinner.

7. Everyone played, sang, and danced happily.

8. Daniel wakes up at seven o'clock every day.

9. My dad finished all the soup in the big bowl.

10. Please remind Samuel and me again tomorrow.

C. Put the words in order to write the subjects and the objects of the verbs. Then write "S" in the boxes if they are subjects and "O" if they are objects.

Allen the Chipmunk

1. ________________ ☐ lives in
Chipmunk Allen the

the forest with his family.

2. ________________ ☐ provide
trees the in forest The

3. ________________ ☐ for them.
and food shelter

Allen loves 4. ________________ ☐. He also likes
nuts seeds and

5. ________________ ☐. He can very easily and
fruit fresh

quickly climb 6. ________________ ☐. He likes playing
trees tall

7. ________________ ☐ with his friends in the trees
fun various games

every day. 8. ________________ ☐ always remind
parents Their

9. ________________ ☐ to be careful outside, so they
and Allen friends his

would warn 10. ________________ ☐ of danger
another one

whenever they play out there in the forest. They

make 11. ________________ ☐ to do this.
sounds different

D. Write sentences of your own using each word as the subject of a verb in one sentence and as the object in another sentence.

<u>Flowers</u> are beautiful.
subject

flowers

sun

Subject: ____

Object: ____

photos

Subject: ____

Object: ____

children

Subject: ____

Object: ____

Words that I Have Learned

____

____

____

UNIT 11

Types of Sentences

A **telling sentence** tells about someone or something. It ends with a period (.).

An **asking sentence** asks about someone or something. It ends with a question mark (?).

A. **Read the sentences and put the correct punctuation marks in the circles. Then write the letters in the correct boxes.**

A Plants need sunlight and water ◯

B There are lots of flowers in the garden ◯

C What do you want for dinner ◯

D This is an ice cream parlour ◯

E What's that in your hand ◯

F Is that what you want ◯

G Isn't it amazing ◯

H Curry is spicy ◯

B. Put the words in order to write telling sentences.

1. on   is   the   nine   news   at   o'clock

____

2. the   it   winter   in   snows

____

3. made   glass   this   of   is   vase

____

4. are   the   sitting   they   at   table

____

C. Match the two parts to form asking sentences.

1. When •   • has left the scarf here?

2. Why •   • is your birthday?

3. What •   • you solve the puzzle?

4. Did •   • can't penguins fly?

5. Who •   • is that building?

6. How tall •   • is under the chair?

An **exclamatory sentence** shows a strong emotion like fear, anger, or excitement. It ends with an exclamation mark (!).

An **imperative sentence** tells someone to do something. It ends with a period (.) or an exclamation mark (!).

Examples

Exclamatory Sentence

The cookies are so yummy!

Imperative Sentence

Please give me some more.

D. Check the circles to show whether the sentences are exclamatory or imperative.

	Exclamatory Sentence	Imperative Sentence
1. How lovely this flower is!	◯	◯
2. Pass me the book, please.	◯	◯
3. Never ever give up!	◯	◯
4. Oh no, I forgot my key!	◯	◯
5. Tell me the truth.	◯	◯
6. You look great!	◯	◯
7. Watch out!	◯	◯
8. Write your name here.	◯	◯
9. What a gorgeous view!	◯	◯
10. The fireworks are awesome!	◯	◯

E.   Write what the children are saying.

A	**Imperative Sentence**	

B	**Surprising Sentence**	

C	**Telling Sentence**	

D	**Asking Sentence**	

Words that I Have Learned

UNIT 12 Punctuation and Capitalization

All sentences end with punctuation marks.

Type of Sentence   **Punctuation Mark**

Examples

- Telling Sentence (.)
- Asking Sentence (?)
- Exclamatory Sentence (!)
- Imperative Sentence (. or !)

A. Circle the correct punctuation mark for each sentence.

1. What a wonderful show   **. / !**

2. Nobody is allowed to go there   **. / ?**

3. Are you excited to go shopping   **! / ?**

4. Emily screamed with delight   **. / ?**

5. Drive slowly around schools   **. / ?**

6. Could you pass me the salt   **? / !**

7. Pugs have big eyes   **. / ?**

8. How lovely   **? / !**

9. Help **? / !**

B. **Put the correct punctuation marks in the boxes.**

1. Keep going ☐

2. Am I going to beat him ☐

3. I won't give up ☐

4. We ran the race last Friday ☐

5. How many of you joined the race ☐

6. What an exciting race ☐

7. Who won at last ☐

8. How lucky he is ☐

9. Never run right after lunch ☐

C. **Check if the sentences end with the correct punctuation marks. If not, put the correct punctuation marks on the lines.**

1. How amazing this is? ______

2. Run faster! ______

3. Are you good at painting! ______

4. Ouch, I'm hurt. ______

5. The clinic is on the second floor. ______

6. What good timing? ______

All sentences begin with **capital letters**. All proper nouns begin with capital letters too. Names of people, pets, places, days, months, festivals, and titles of books, songs, and movies are all proper nouns.

Example

Jamie and I watched "The Lion King" at the Princess of Wales Theatre.

D. **Colour the books that have titles with proper capitalization.**

beauty and the beast

The Prince and the Pauper

The Emperor's New Clothes

Goldilocks and the Three Bears

anne of green gables

Jack and the Beanstalk

E. Rewrite the sentences with proper capitalization and correct punctuation.

1. last year's halloween was a friday

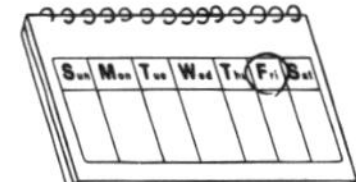

____

2. was mrs. jevon at home on new year's day

____

3. jennifer, ray, and i loved our picnic lunch

____

4. the concert was held in edmonton last august

____

5. "we are the world" is such a great song

____

Words that I Have Learned

____

____

____

UNIT
13 Forming Negative Sentences

The word "**not**" can be added to a sentence to form the negative.

Use "am/is/are not" to tell about something in the present.

Use "am/is/are not" and the "ing" form of a verb to tell about what is not going on.

Examples

- The boots <u>are not</u> new.

- It <u>is not raining</u>.

Negative Sentences

A. **Read the sentences. Check the circles if they are negative sentences. Put a cross if they are not.**

1. It is not very cold. ◯

2. Alaia is playing the piano beautifully. ◯

3. We are not invited to the party. ◯

4. The boys are not cleaning their room. ◯

5. I am not thirsty. ◯

6. ◯

Use "was/were not" to tell about a past state.

Use "was/were not" and the "ing" form of a verb to tell about what was not going on at a past time.

- He <u>was not</u> on our team last year.
- They <u>were not playing</u> outside when it rained.

B. Use ∧ to add "not" in the correct places to make the sentences negative.

1. Dad was using the computer earlier.

2. Zoey and Dennis were at the party last night.

3. They were singing when the bell rang.

4. Jacky was waiting for the bus at two o'clock yesterday.

5. We were looking when the clown came out.

6. Rachel and Percy were classmates last year.

7. The cherry pie we had this morning was very delicious.

8. Rhonda was at home when Jane called.

9. Sophia noticed that the machines were functioning well.

To form a negative sentence with a singular subject except "I" and "you", add "does not" before the base form of a verb to talk about the present.

For a plural subject, "I", and "you", add "do not" before the base form.

Examples

- She <u>does not live</u> near her school.
- Penguins <u>do not fly</u>.

C. Fill in the blanks to form negative sentences with the correct verbs.

sleep	grow	stop	go
like	want	know	

1. The bus _______________ here.

2. Jamie _______________ fishing with his dad.

3. We _______________ vegetables in our backyard.

4. Our pet dog _______________ in my bedroom.

5. Check the map if you _______________ where the arena is.

6. Mr. and Mrs. Moore _______________ to live in the crowded city.

7. I _______________ playing baseball.

 To form a negative sentence to talk about the past, add "did not" before the base form of a verb with any subject.

- Jill <u>did not sing</u> at the party.
- They <u>did not watch</u> yesterday's game.

D. Rewrite the sentences as negative by changing the underlined verbs.

1. 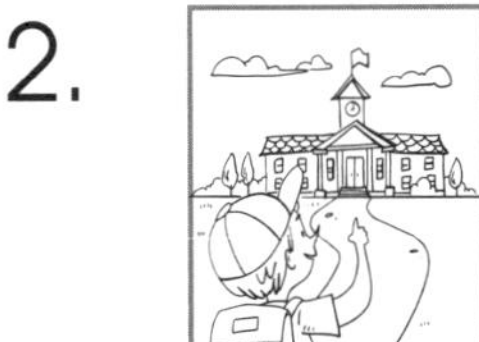 Mom <u>went</u> to work last Saturday.

   ____

2. I <u>studied</u> in this school last year.

   ____

3. Macy and Samuel <u>played</u> in the pool yesterday.

   ____

4. Jason <u>played</u> video games last night.

   ____

Words that I Have Learned

____

____

____

UNIT 14

Contractions

A **contraction** is a short way of writing two words. One or more letters are replaced with an apostrophe (').

Examples

- you are → you're
- it is → it's

It's pretty.

A. Colour the correct contractions of the words.

1. he is   he's   he'is
2. they are   they're   they'e
3. what is   wha's   what's
4. I have   I've   I'ave
5. there is   ther'is   there's
6. how is   how'is   how's
7. do not   do't   don't
8. they will   they'ill   they'll
9. you have   you've   you'e
10. does not   doesn't   does't
11. did not   didn't   did't
12. should not

    You should'nt shouldn't eat so much candy.

B. Check the circles if the contractions are spelled correctly. If not, cross out the words and write the correct spellings above them.

1. I was'nt sure how I broke the toy. ◯

2. Where'is the box office? ◯

3. Isn'ot this your lunch bag? ◯

4. What's in the basket? ◯

5. Katie cann't finish the whole pizza. ◯

6. Cecil didn't watch TV yesterday. ◯

7. How'is everyone doing? ◯

8. We're waiting for you now. ◯

9. There are'nt any cookies left. ◯

10.
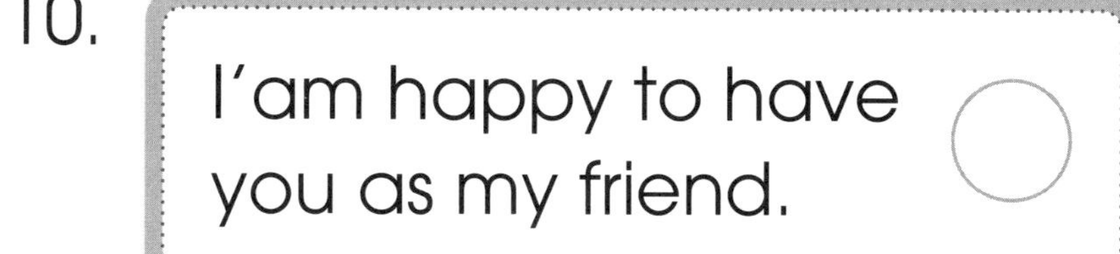

◯

C.   Circle the contractions. Then fill in the blanks with the correct contractions.

Contractions

couldn't	here's	Lily's	she's	we'd
weren't	James's	hasn't	to-do	
cat's	by-law	they'll	Dr.	why's

1. ______________ very excited because she ______________ seen such a big teddy bear before.

2. ______________ a hint to help you crack the code.

3. The children ______________ sleeping when their parents got home.

4. ______________ better do some research before we build the model.

5. ______________ finish the preparation by next Monday.

6. Jerry ______________ see anything because there was no light in the room.

7. ______________ it so very noisy outside?

D. Rewrite the sentences using contractions.

1. It is chasing a rat.

    ____

2. We will have fun at the pool.

    ____

3. That is the book I told you about.

    ____

4. Let us take a rest under the tree.

    ____

5. The children must not swim in the lake when no adults are around.

    ____

    ____

Words that I Have Learned

Contractions

____

____

____

A. Circle the answers.

1. "_____" is a common noun.

   City

   Vancouver

   Toronto

2. The plural of "box" is "_____".

   boxs

   boxies

   boxes

   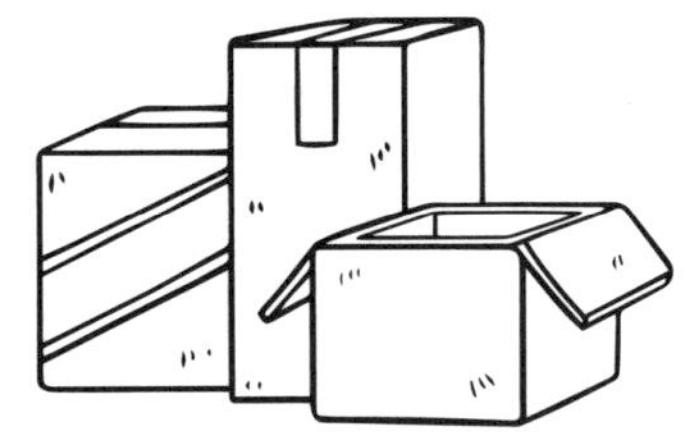

3. Which is correct?

   The girls are eating honey.

   The girls are eating honeys.

   She is eating honeys.

4. Which phrase uses the correct article?

   a sun

   an sun

   the sun

5. Which pronoun is correct?

   _____ want popcorn.

   We

   Them

   Us

6. Which sentence is in the present tense?

   The boy played.

   The boy is playing.

   The boy was playing.

7. Which adjective describes the picture?

   round

   square

   tall

8. The tree is _____ the fence.

   behind

   beside

   in

9. Which preposition is correct?

> Canada Day is ___ July.

on

in

at

10. Which one uses the correct joining word?

Are you staying or leaving today?

Are you staying and leaving today?

Are you staying but leaving today?

11. Which sentence has the predicate underlined?

<u>Ada</u> loves animals.

Ada <u>loves animals</u>.

Ada <u>loves</u> animals.

12. Which one below is an exclamatory sentence?

Do your homework!

We rock!

It is raining.

13. Which punctuation mark can an imperative sentence have?

. or !

! or ?

. or ?

14. The negative sentence for the sentence below is "______".

> I like singing.

I doesn't like singing.

I do like singing.

I do not like singing.

Nouns and Pronouns

B.   **Write the underlined words in the correct boxes.**

Long ago, there was a <u>kingdom</u> called <u>Colourland</u>. The <u>king</u>, <u>King Edwin</u>, and his people made sure it was a happy and colourful place. Their only problem was a naughty little <u>elf</u> named <u>Coby</u>.

One day, Coby took away all the colours! The people woke up to find that everything was in black and white. Everyone tried in vain to look for Coby.

Common Noun

____

____

____

Proper Noun

____

____

____

C.   **Underline the subject pronouns and circle the object pronouns.**

Then someone said, "Look what we have found! It is a note left for us by Coby."

To get all the colours back, Princess Lilian and Prince Ned have to search for one thing in each colour. When they have found it, he or she needs to touch it and say its colour! Then that colour will return to the kingdom. I will be hiding somewhere nearby to make sure they follow the rules.

Coby

D.   Circle the correct present tense and past tense verbs.

King Edwin carefully **studyied** / **studied** Coby's note.   Then he said, "My children **are** / **am** very brave. I **am allow** / **am allowing** them to begin the search today!"

The king asked Wilkin to accompany the children. Wilkin had an idea, "We **are going** / **is going** to look all over the woods just outside Colourland before we **go** / **went** any farther."

E.   Fill in the blanks with the correct prepositions and joining words.

1. The children came to a grassland __________ Colourland and the woods. Lilian touched the grass __________ said, "Green!" They got back the first colour.

2. They searched the woods. Tired, they rested __________ a tree. Ned touched the tree trunk __________ the colour brown returned.

3. Then a blue jay sat __________ Ned's shoulder. He touched it and got back the colour blue.

The Sentence, Subjects, and Objects

F. **Look at the picture. Then complete the sentences with the correct subjects or predicates.**

1. ________________ found the colour orange!

2. ________________ said "Pink!" as he ate a peach.

3. Wilkin ________________________________.

4. The children ________________________________.

G. **Circle the subjects and underline the objects of the verbs.**

The children gathered some fruits. They ate the oranges, peaches, and grapes. Lilian said, "I love fruits! But I am worried. How are we going to find yellow?"

"Look!" said Ned. They saw some roses. "Maybe they are yellow."

"But roses can be pink, red, or white," said Wilkin.

"That reminds me! We have to find red as well!" Lilian said in a panic.

H. Identify the types of sentences. Write the letters.

Sentences

A
What can we use to find red?

B
A ripe strawberry is always red.

C
I found a strawberry!

D
Touch it!

○ Telling

○ Asking

○ Exclamatory

○ Imperative

I. Cross out the letters with the wrong capitalization and write the correct ones above them. Then put the appropriate punctuation in the circles.

after they had found the colour red, the children retrieved the colour yellow with a sunflower and returned to colourland ○

"let's celebrate ○ " cheered the people ○

"how have you been ○ " asked king edwin ○

"we are good ○ we had fun ○ " replied ned ○

"look ○ " said lilian as they saw coby disappear into thin air ○ he left behind a book titled *magic spells* ○

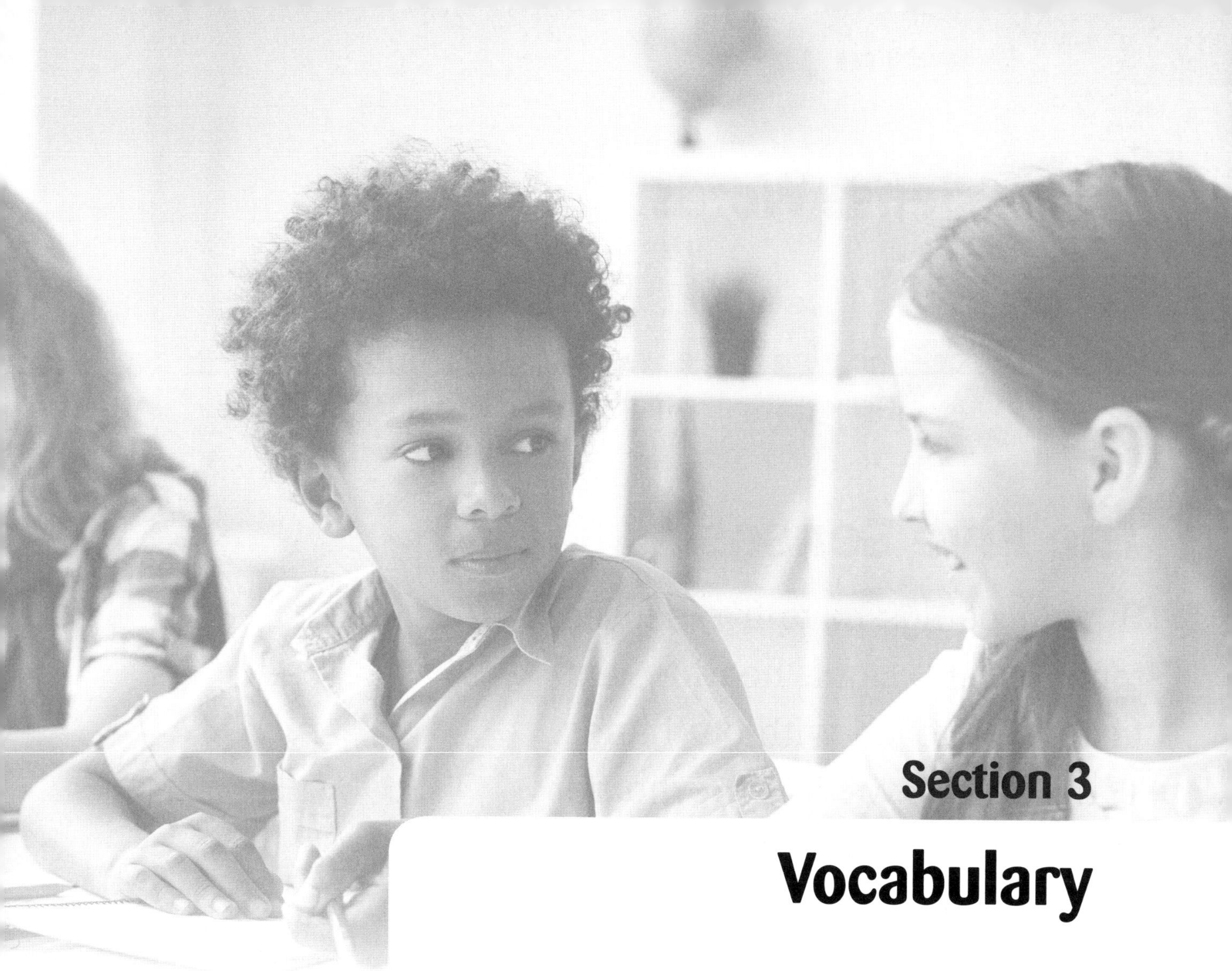

Vocabulary

UNIT
1

Sense Words

hear   hearing   see   sense   **smell**
sight   taste   touch

The Five Senses

Human beings have five senses: touch, smell, sight, hearing, and taste. We <u>touch</u> with our <u>hands</u>. That is how we know whether something is hot or cold, or hard or soft. We <u>smell</u> with our <u>nose</u>. We can tell whether something smells pleasant, like flowers, or unpleasant, like garbage. We <u>see</u> with our <u>eyes</u>, <u>hear</u> with our <u>ears</u>, and <u>taste</u> with our <u>tongue</u>.

A. **Fill in the blanks with the underlined words.**

1. I _____________ with my 👀 _____________ .

2. I _____________ with my _____________ .

3. I _____________ with my _____________ .

4. I _____________ with my _____________ .

5. I _____________ with my _____________ .

B. **Write the five senses. Then draw lines to match.**

| The Five Senses | You can use more than one sense for some situations. |

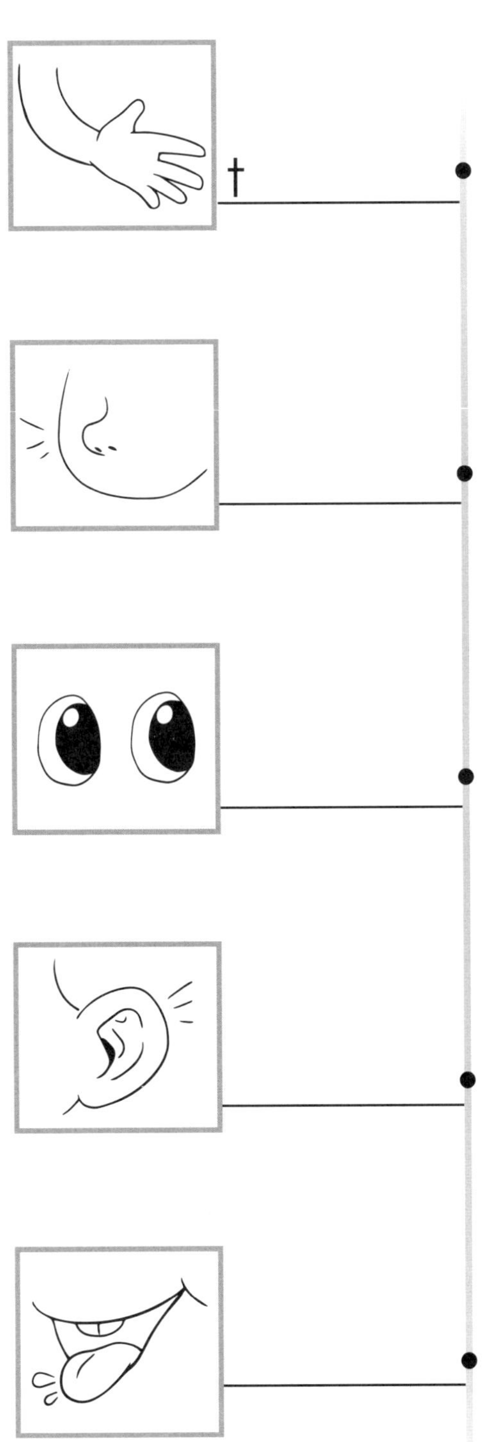

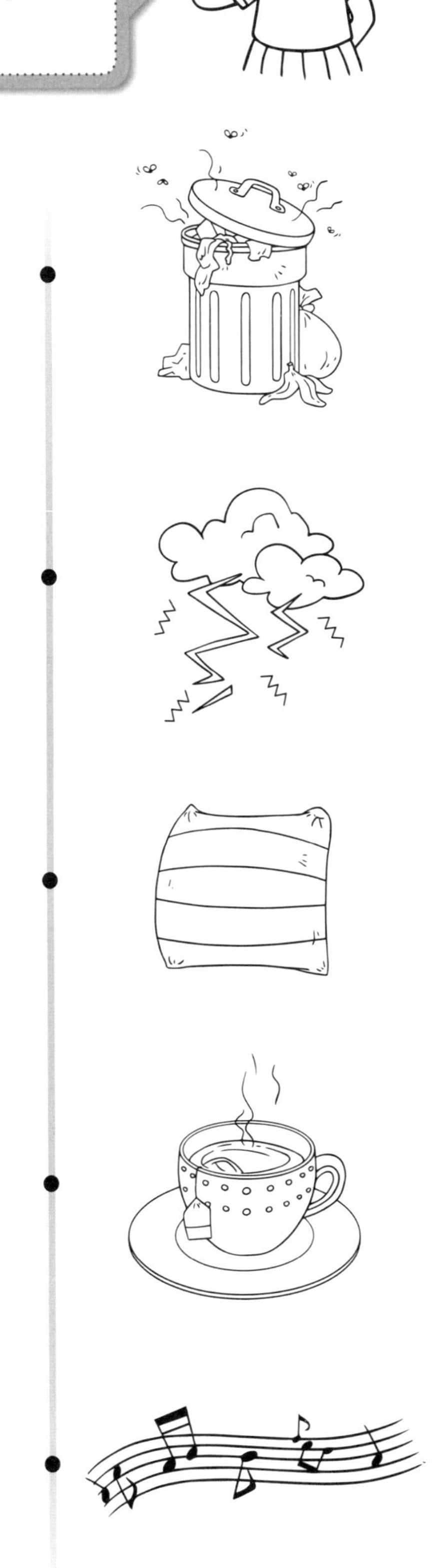

C.   Write the correct words under the pictures.

Adjectives for the Sense of Touch

hot	cold	sticky	sharp	fluffy
hard	soft	smooth	rough	

1.

h _______________

2.

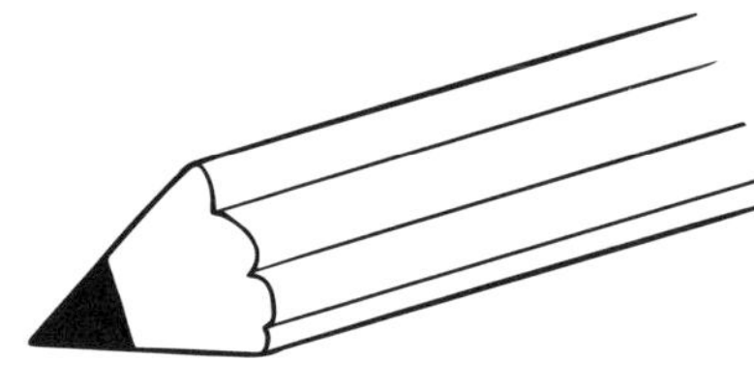

s _______________

3.

f _______________

4.

s _______________

5.

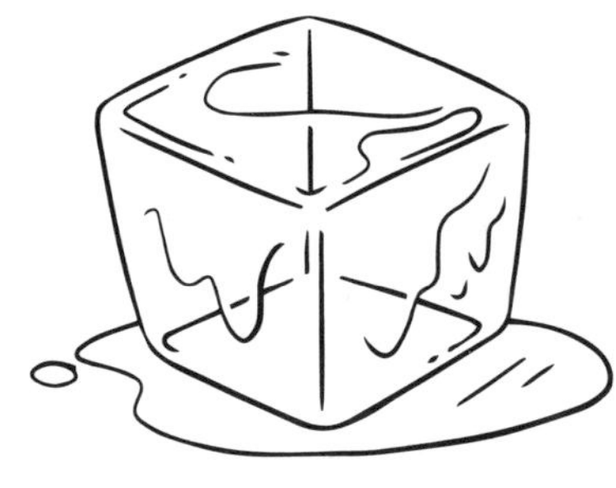

c _______________

6.

h _______________

7.

r _______________

8.

s _______________

9.

s _______________

D. Write the correct adjective for each food item. Then draw one more example.

1.

2.

3.

4.

5.

Words that I Have Learned

Sense Words

____

____

____

UNIT 2 Season Words

spring   summer   fall   winter

cold   cool   hot   warmer

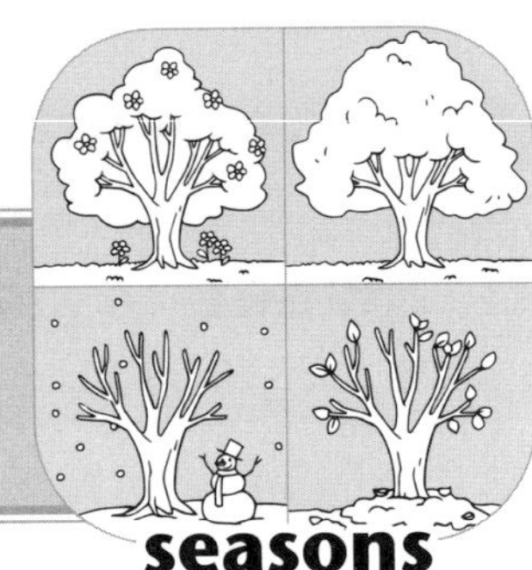

seasons

Different Seasons

There are four seasons in a year: spring, summer, fall, and winter.

Spring is the season when it gets warmer and rains more. Trees begin to bud in spring.

Summer is the season when the temperature gets high and it is hot. Leaves on trees are green in summer.

Fall is the season when leaves change colour. Some leaves change from green to orange, yellow, red, and brown. The temperature drops and it is cool in fall.

Winter is the season when there is a lot of snow in most parts of Canada. It is very cold and there are no more leaves on most trees in winter.

A.   Name the seasons.

1. _______________

2. _______________

3. _______________

4. _______________

B. Fill in the blanks with the correct season words.

1. **Spring**

The temperature gets higher and it is _____________ outside. It is also a wet and _____________ season.

2. **Winter**

The temperature drops below zero and it is very _____________ . It is _____________ and everything is covered in white.

3. **Fall**

The temperature gets lower and it is _____________ outside. It is a _____________ season for flying kites.

4. **Summer**

The temperature gets very high and it is _____________ . It is a _____________ season for playing at the beach.

C.   Match the words with the same or similar meanings. Then find all the words in the word search.

More Season Words

autumn •   • breezy

chilly •   • warm

windy •   • sunny

cozy •   • fall

scorching •   • cold

cloudless •   • hot

f	e	l	e	d	m	c		i	s	y	e	a	j	g
b			k	h	l	l		a	u	t	u	m	n	o
j			c	o	g	o	a	q	s	n	j	r	g	l	p
w	a	r	m	f	n	e	v	h	w	n	d	y	n	
i	u	h	p	a	q	s	c	o	z	y	m	t	u	
d	t	c	o	l	d	u	h	t	i	o	a	v	a	m	f
g	n	h	c	l	o	u	b	d	o	p	l	b	s	w	o
k	u	i	s	s	c	o	r	c	h	i	n	g	c	i	l
a	l	l	c	b	e	j	e	t	g		h	d	n	r
m	c	l	o	u	d	l	e	s	s		o	q	d	h
h	u	y	h	t	e	b	z	c	w	g	b	e	z	y	w
r	p	l	i	f	t	z	y	j	a	x	n	b	m	i	f

D. **Name your favourite season and draw a picture of it. Then fill in the blank and write two more sentences about it using season words.**

my favourite season

My favourite season is ______________ .

____

____

Words that I Have Learned

Season Words

____

____

____

UNIT

3 | Camping Words

backpack   barbecue   binoculars   blanket
camping   campsite   first aid kit   flashlight
rope   sleeping bag   s'more   tent

campfire

Family Camping

My family loves camping. Every summer, my sister and I pack our own backpacks for the camping trip. Dad makes sure to bring the tent, flashlights, binoculars, and a first aid kit. Mom packs our sleeping bags, blankets, ropes, and food for a barbecue.

When we arrive at the campsite, we all help set up the tent. Then we may swim, hike, or look at the wildlife with our binoculars. We then collect dry wood for the campfire.

At night, we have fun barbecuing, eating s'mores, and telling jokes by the fire.

A. Name the camping items.

A ______________________________

B ______________________________

C ______________________________

B. **Match the camping words with the pictures.**

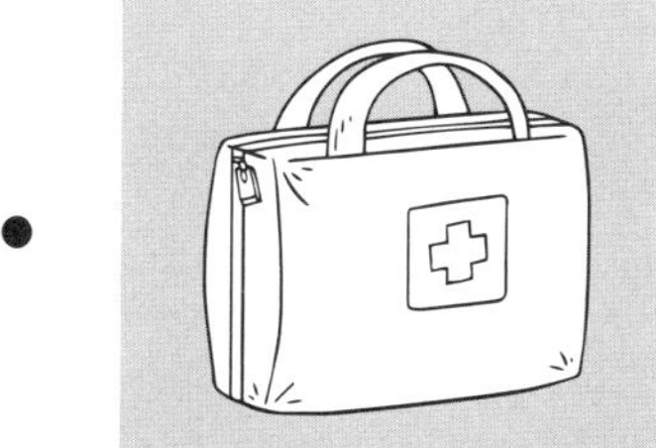

Camping Words

backpack

barbecue

binoculars

blanket

first aid kit

s'more

tent

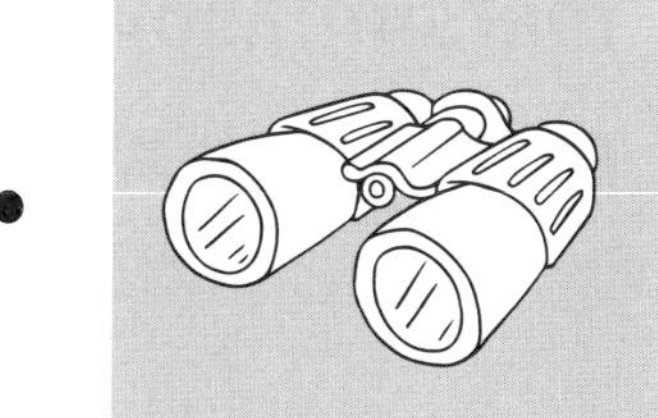

C.   Circle the correct spellings of the camping items.

More Camping Words

1.
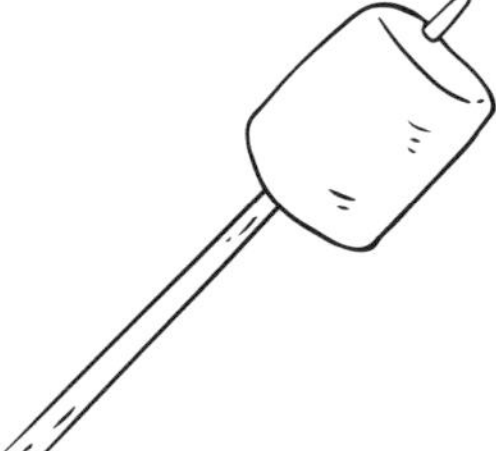

marshmallo
marshmallow
marshmellow

2.

charcoal
chacoal
charcole

3.

compas
comppas
compass

4.
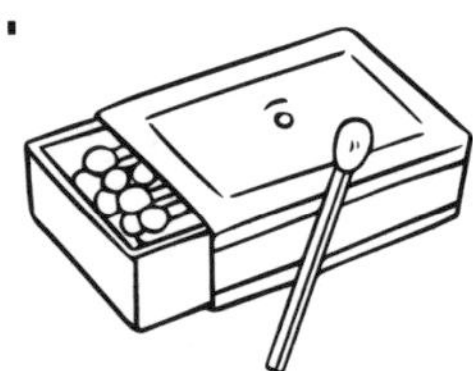

matchs
matches
mattchs

5.

boots
booots
bootes

6.
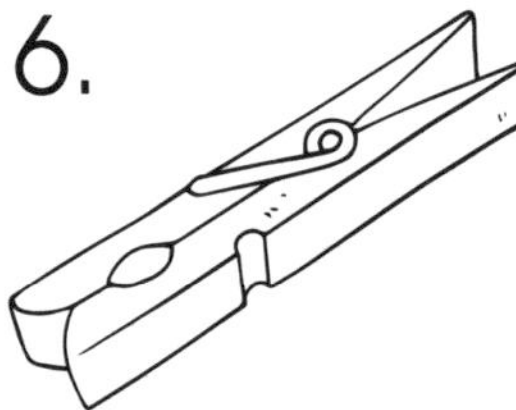

clothspin
clothpin
clothespin

7.

flaske
flask
fllask

8.

aex
axe
axx

9.

sunscreene
sunscrin
sunscreen

10.

lanten
lantern
lenten

D. Fill in the blanks with the correct words.

Camping Activities

wildlife watching   **canoeing**

stargazing   **hiking**

1. Many campsites are far away from city lights so they are perfect places for _____________ .

2. _____________ lets us learn about animals and plants in nature.

3. It is important to wear a pair of comfortable boots when _____________ .

4. _____________ was a way of travelling across water in the past but today it has become a common camping activity.

Words that I Have Learned

Camping Words

____

____

____

UNIT
4 Community Words

apartment building   bakery
bungalow   hospital   library
police station   school   supermarket
swimming pool   townhouse

My Community

There are many different places in my community. My family and I live in a townhouse but there are other types of homes, such as bungalows and apartment buildings.

There are schools and libraries where we learn about the world. A police station and a hospital provide us with emergency services. There are supermarkets, bakeries, and flower shops where we buy things to meet our daily needs. There are also eating places where we can enjoy dishes from around the world.

My favourite fun places to go with my family and friends are the park and the swimming pool.

A.   **Name the three types of living places.**

1. _______________   2. _______________   3. _______________

B. Identify the community places. Name them or write the letters.

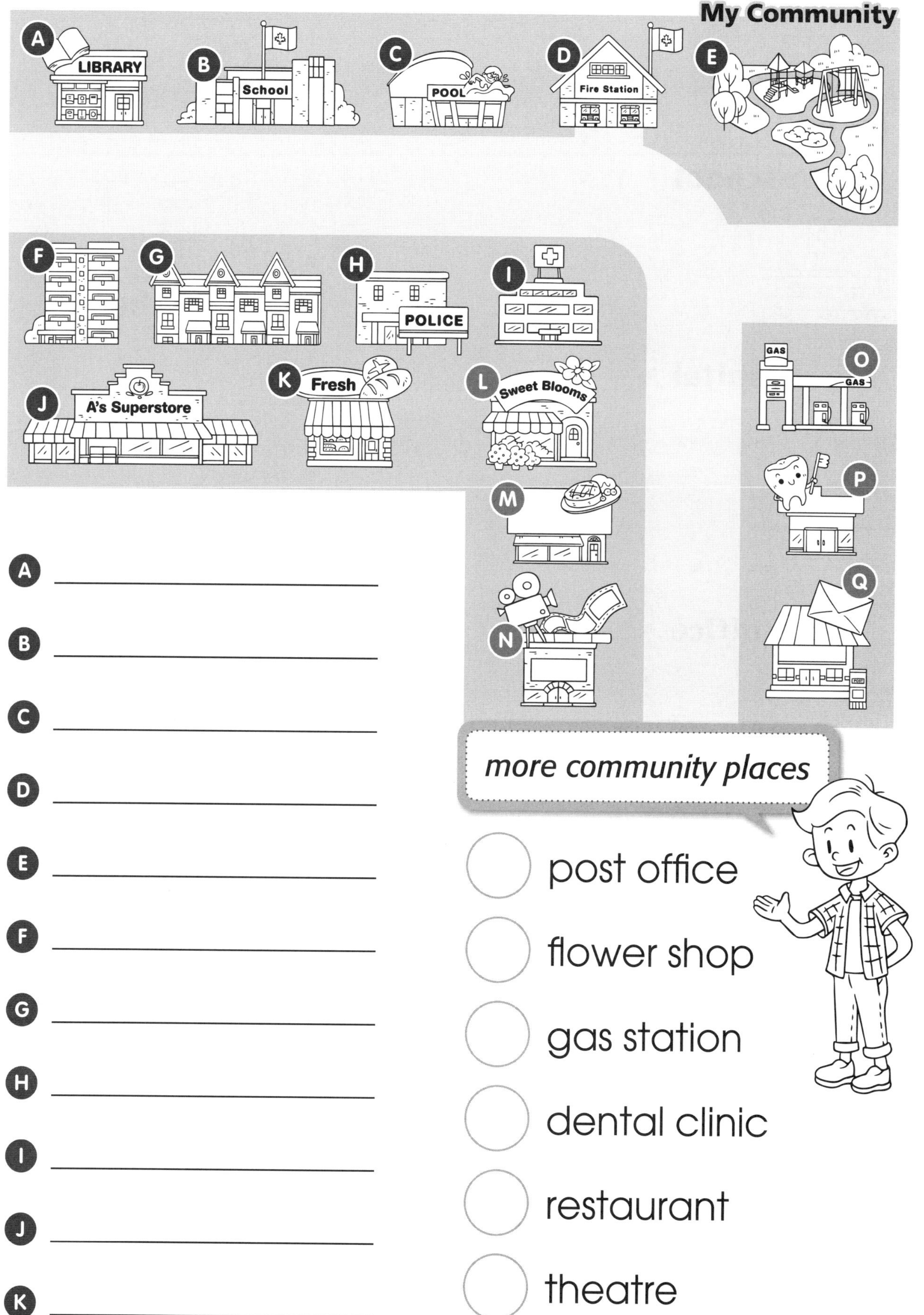

A _______________________

B _______________________

C _______________________

D _______________________

E _______________________

F _______________________

G _______________________

H _______________________

I _______________________

J _______________________

K _______________________

C. Match the community workers with the places.

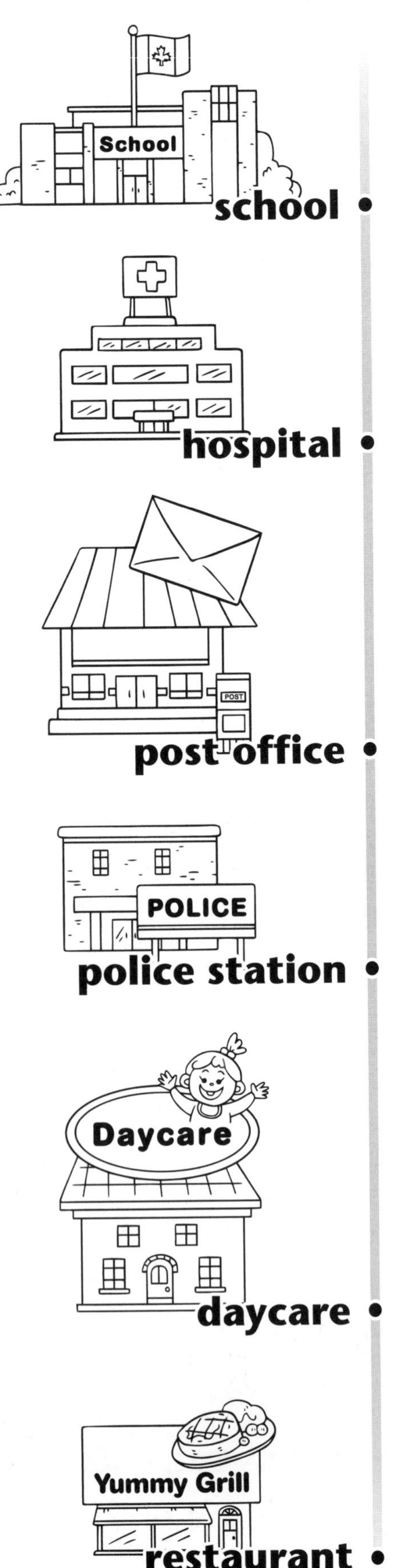

D. Fill in the blanks with the correct community words.

Community Place	Community Worker
convenience store	mail carrier
library theatre	chef doctor

1. The ____________ of this restaurant makes award-winning desserts.

2. You have to see the ____________ when you feel sick.

3. There is a ____________ near the cottage so we can buy some of the things we need there.

4. Maggie and her friends went to the ____________ and saw an interesting movie last night.

5. Mom is waiting eagerly for the ____________ to come and deliver a parcel from Aunt Daisy.

6. Oh no, I forgot to return these books to the ____________ !

Words that I Have Learned

Community Words

____

____

____

UNIT 5 Polygon Words

heptagon   hexagon   octagon
pentagon   quadrilateral   shape
triangle   two-dimensional

polygons

Polygons

A polygon is a closed two-dimensional shape with three or more straight sides. Circles and other shapes with curves are not polygons.

Polygons are named according to the number of sides they have. A polygon with three sides is called a triangle, one with four sides is called a quadrilateral, and one with five sides is called a pentagon. A six-sided polygon is a hexagon, a seven-sided one is a heptagon, and an eight-sided one is an octagon.

You can find polygons in many things around you. For example, a kite is a quadrilateral and a stop sign is an octagon.

A.   Name the shapes. Then colour the polygons.

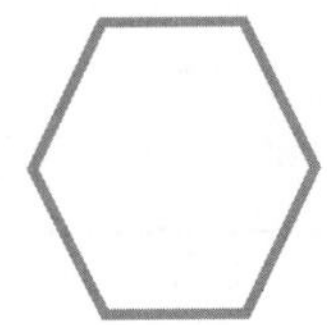

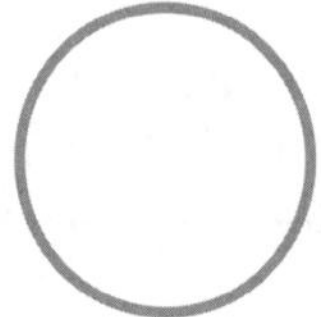

1. _______________

2. _______________

3. _______________

B. Check the correct letters to name the polygons.

1. 

- (A) quadrilateral
- (B) hexagon
- (C) heptagon

2. 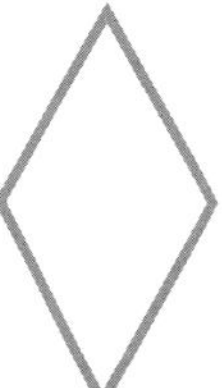

- (A) hexagon
- (B) triangle
- (C) quadrilateral

3. 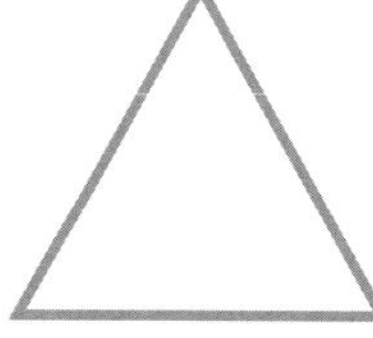

- (A) heptagon
- (B) octagon
- (C) triangle

4. 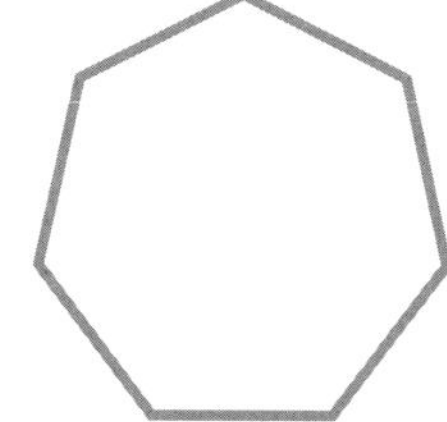

- (A) heptagon
- (B) hexagon
- (C) octagon

5. 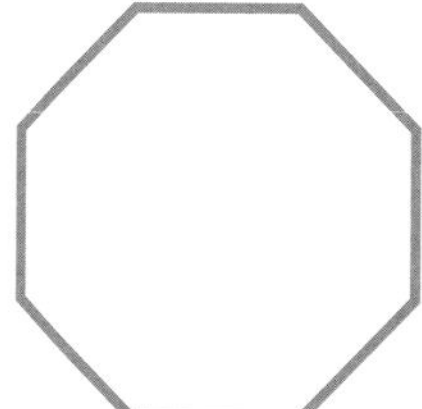

- (A) pentagon
- (B) hexagon
- (C) octagon

6. 

- (A) triangle
- (B) pentagon
- (C) hexagon

- (A) pentagon
- (B) hexagon
- (C) octagon

C. Trace the polygons. Then write the number of sides and name the polygons.

1.

___________ sides

Name of Polygon

2.

___________ sides

Name of Polygon

3.

___________ sides

Name of Polygon

4.

___________ sides

Name of Polygon

5.

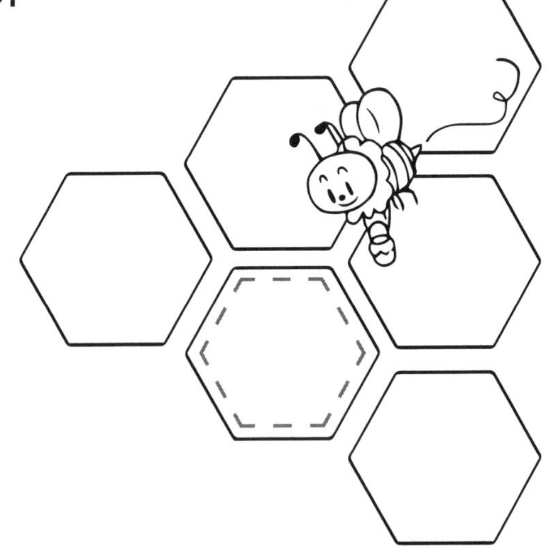

___________ sides

Name of Polygon

D. Look at each four-sided polygon. Draw a bigger one on the side and then name the polygon.

Name

Name

Name

Name

Name

Polygon Words

____

____

____

UNIT 6

Computer Words

The Computer

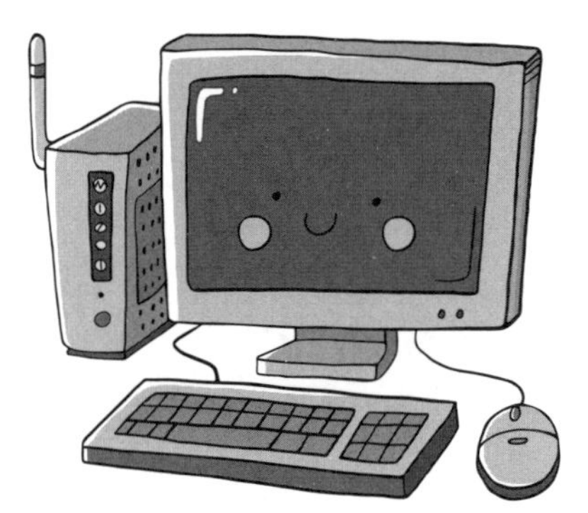

Computers are used everywhere – at home, at school, at the doctor's, at the dentist's, and in department stores. It is important to know the main parts of the computer. The CPU is short for "Central Processing Unit", which is like the brain of the computer. The monitor is the screen that displays words and pictures. When you type on a keyboard, your words appear on the monitor. A mouse allows you to control a pointer on the screen to get your task done. If you want a paper copy, you can use a printer to print the words or pictures. If you add a modem to your computer, you can have access to the Internet.

A.   **Unscramble the words to name the parts of a computer.**

1. imonrto _______________

2. rcnese _______________

3. domme _______________

B.   Name the parts of the computer.

C. Match the computer icons with their functions.

Functions

(A) play/pause

(B) stop

(C) power on/off

(D) volume control

(E) brightness control

(F) battery level

(G) headphone jack

(H) music

(I) USB port

(J) settings

(K) mute

(L) tools

D. Fill in the blanks to show the uses of a computer.

Uses of a Computer

music   communicate   buy   photos   information

1. We can listen to ______________ on the computer.

2. We can search for all kinds of ______________ on various websites.

3. We can use the computer to ______________ or sell things.

4. We can ______________ with other people through e-mail and social networks.

5. We can share ______________ with our family and friends.

Words that I Have Learned

Computer Words

____

____

____

Section 3

Vocabulary

UNIT 7

Water Words

brook   creek   lake   ocean
river   sea   stream

Bodies of Water

There are different types of water bodies. The largest are oceans, which are large open areas of salt water. Many people refer to oceans as seas, but seas are in fact smaller than oceans and are connected to oceans. They are typically partially enclosed by land. Lakes are large bodies of water surrounded by land. Most lakes are freshwater. Ponds are also surrounded by land but they are smaller than lakes.

There are flowing bodies of water, like rivers. Rivers flow into other rivers, lakes, or seas. Streams, creeks, and brooks are also flowing bodies of water but they are narrower and shallower than rivers.

A.   Unscramble the letters to name the water bodies.

1. ______________
   eas

2. ______________
   dopn

3. ______________
   korbo

4. ______________
   tearms

5. ______________
   keal

6. ______________
   rceke

7. ______________
   virre

8. ______________
   coane

The Five Oceans of the World

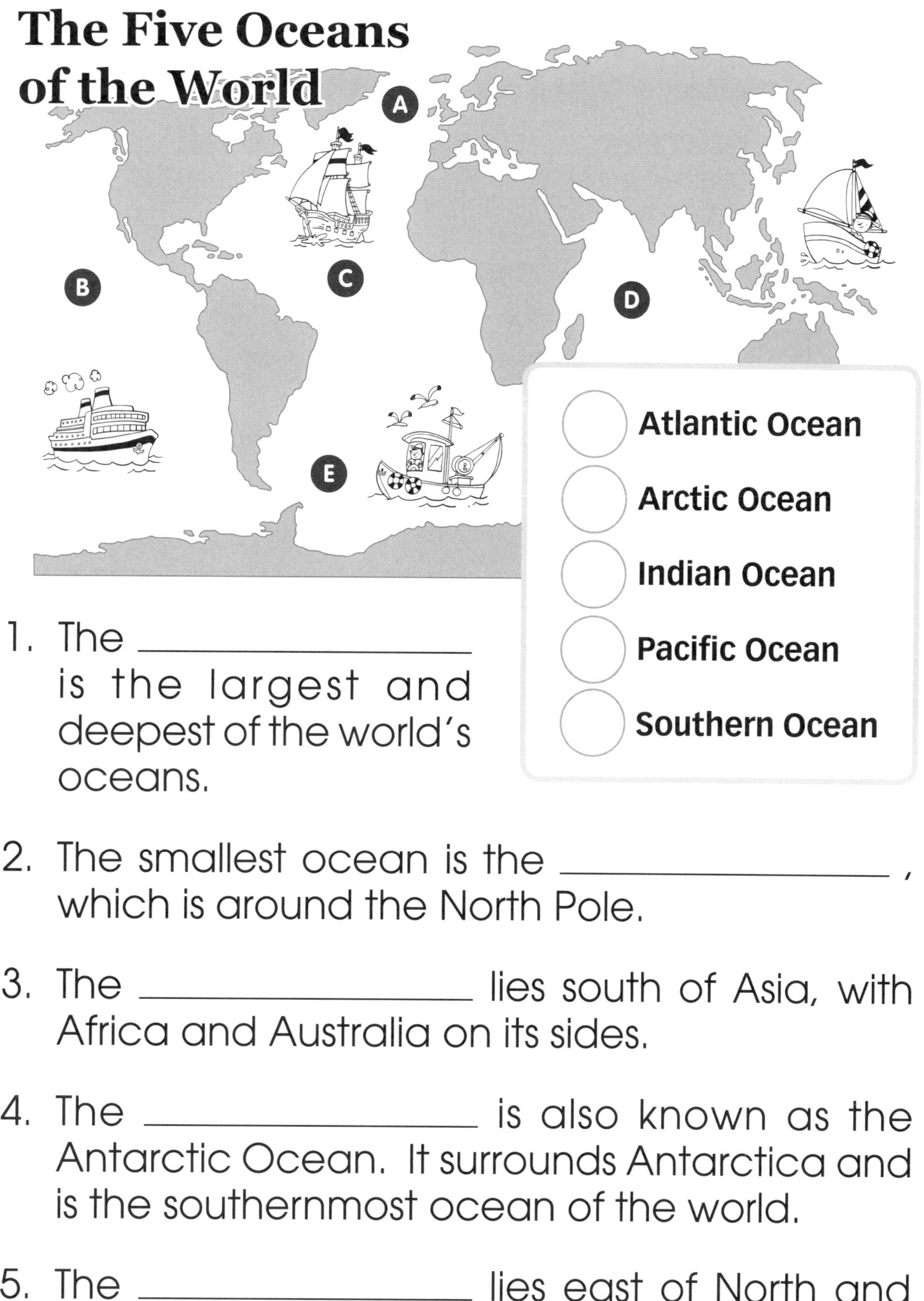

1. The ______________________ is the largest and deepest of the world's oceans.

2. The smallest ocean is the ______________________, which is around the North Pole.

3. The ______________________ lies south of Asia, with Africa and Australia on its sides.

4. The ______________________ is also known as the Antarctic Ocean. It surrounds Antarctica and is the southernmost ocean of the world.

5. The ______________________ lies east of North and South America.

C.   **Look at the pictures and name the bodies of water.**

More Bodies of Water

delta	fjord	geyser	glacier
reservoir	swamp	waterfall	

1.

2. ______________

3. ______________

1. ______________

4. ______________

5.

6. ______________

7. ______________

5. ______________

D. Identify the shadows. Circle the correct names of the animals. Then draw lines to match if they are aquatic animals.

 whale / shark •

 octopus / jellyfish •

 cat / rabbit •

 crab / turtle •

 owl / squirrel •

 seal / crocodile •

• **Aquatic Animals**

Words that I Have Learned

Water Words

____

____

____

UNIT 8 Synonyms

Synonyms are words with similar meanings.

beautiful – pretty   big – large
chose – picked   delicious – tasty – yummy
Mom – mother   sad – unhappy

glad – happy

Tasty Cupcakes

Dory was unhappy. She had lost her favourite dress. It was a beautiful red dress with a big, pretty bow. Her mother wanted to make her happy so she baked a batch of delicious cupcakes for Dory. Dory picked a large cupcake and then she chose one more. As soon as she tasted them, she said, "Thank you, Mom! They are so yummy!" Her mother was glad that Dory liked the cupcakes and that she was no longer sad.

A. Write the synonym(s) of each word.

tasty

sad

pretty

big

happy

Mom

picked

B. Write synonyms to describe the pictures.

> hungry   frightened   shiny
> drowsy   tiny

1. 
scared

____

2. 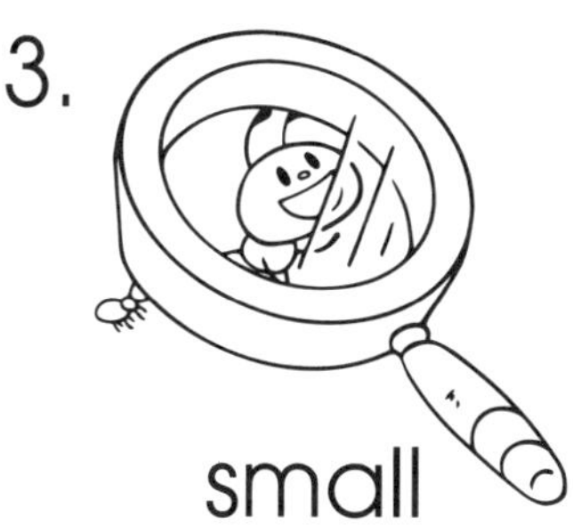
sparkly

____

3. 
small

____

4. 
sleepy

____

5.
starving

____

C. Circle the synonyms of the words in the boxes.

1. **friend**   buddy   neighbour   pal

2. **jump**   spin   leap   hop

3. **angry**   furious   patient   mad

4. **clever**   smart   intelligent   kind

5. **brave**   cautious   courageous   bold

D.   Fill in the blanks with the synonyms of the words under the lines.

fast	breezy	damp	hard	little
store	tired	huge	dirty	crying

1. Cindy was _____________ because she fell down.
    weeping

2. It was a _____________ day in the city.
    windy

3. Mom was _____________ after her trip.
    exhausted

4. The _____________ child held on to the balloon.
    small

5. The weather was _____________ and warm.
    humid

6. This _____________ does not open on Sundays.
    shop

7. The kiwi fruit was _____________ and green.
    firm

8. Becca ran _____________ toward the finish line.
    quickly

9. The bike tires were _____________ after they went
    grimy

    through the mud.

10. Mike found a _____________
     giant

     zucchini in the garden.

E. Rewrite the sentences using the correct synonyms for the underlined words.

pails	bunny	shut	weird	awesome

1. Little Ryan loves the fluffy <u>rabbit</u>.

   ____

2. Please <u>close</u> the door behind you.

   ____

3. Did you hear that <u>strange</u> noise?

   ____

4. Hana's performance was <u>amazing</u>.

   ____

5. Let's fill the <u>buckets</u> with water.

   ____

Words that I Have Learned

Synonyms

____

____

____

UNIT 9

Antonyms

cold – hot	day – night	dry – wet
less – more	long – short	

The Cactus

The cactus plant grows in the desert where it is hot in the day and cold at night. There is more sunshine and less rainfall in the desert than many other places in the world. When it does rain for short periods of time, the shallow plant roots soak up rainwater from the wet ground. The stem of the cactus plant is thick with thin prickly thorns on it. This means that the plant can store water for when the ground is dry for long periods of time.

A.   Colour the pairs of antonyms with different colours.

hot   thick   wet   thin   day   short

night   less   cold   long   dry   more

B. For each group of words, cross out the one that is not an antonym of the word on the left.

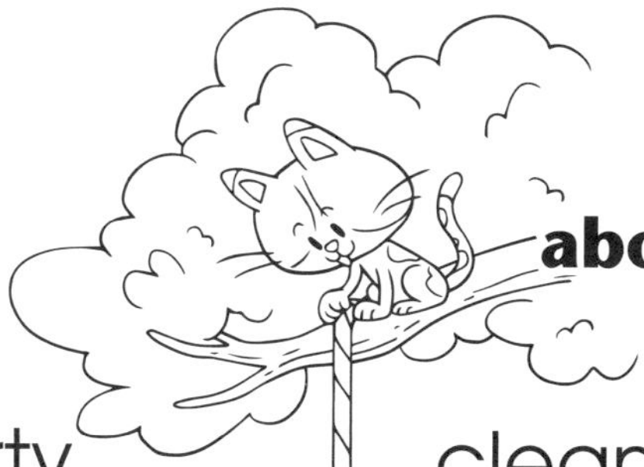
above

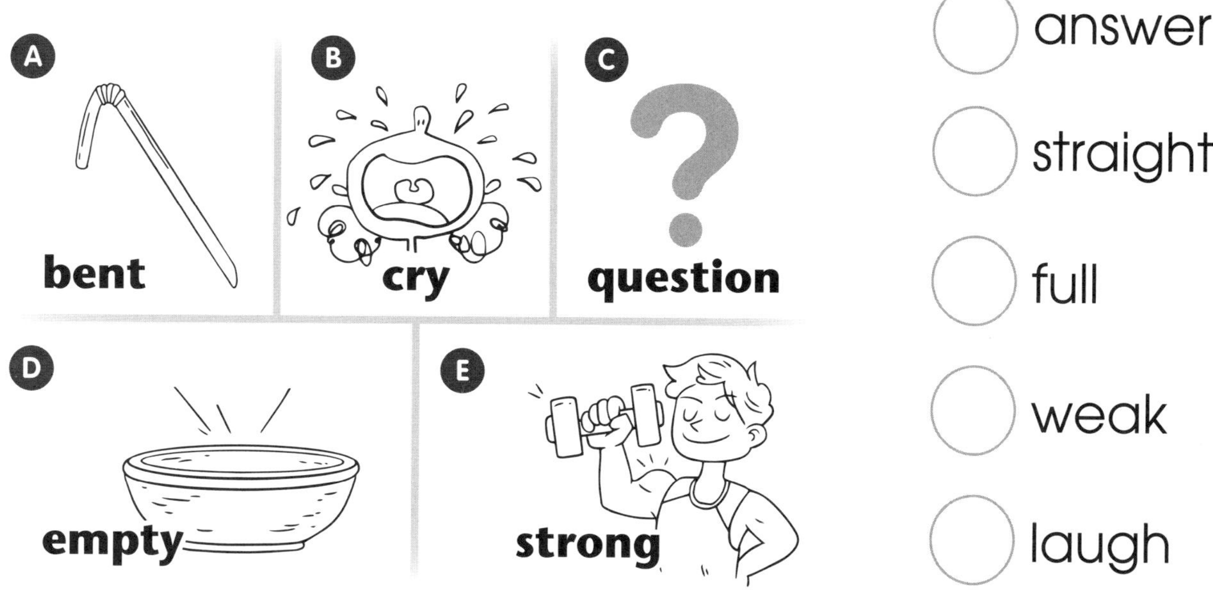

1.	dirty	clean	messy	tidy
2.	give	take	provide	receive
3.	scared	bold	brave	afraid
4.	end	start	begin	open
5.	short	large	tall	high
6.	smooth	rough	rugged	plain

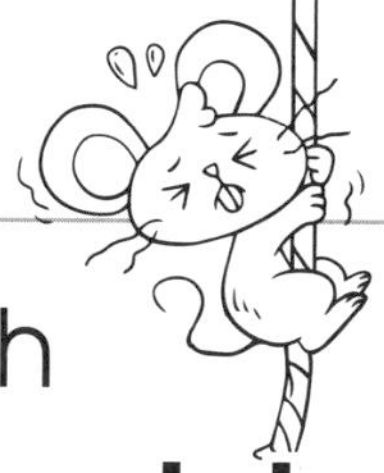
below

C. Match the antonyms. Write the letters.

A
bent

B
cry

C
question

D
empty

E
strong

◯ answer
◯ straight
◯ full
◯ weak
◯ laugh

D. Write each word in the box with its antonym.

go   fast   depart   difficult   glad   hard
correct   happy   swift   right   speedy
leave   proper   jolly   challenging

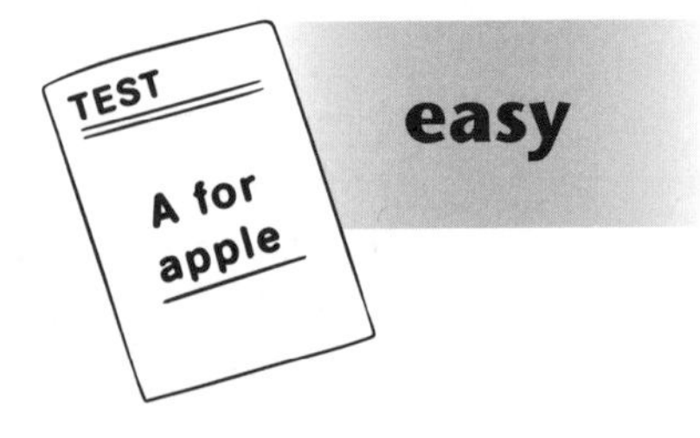

E. Circle the antonyms in the sentences. Then write them on the lines.

Antonym

1

1. Betsy left home early so that she would not be late for the fun event.

2

2. The best time to fly a kite is on a calm day and the worst time is on a windy day.

3

3. Derek opened his eyes when the hot-air balloon went up but he closed them when it came down.

Words that I Have Learned

Antonyms

UNIT 10 Homophones

> Homophones are words that sound the same but have different spellings and meanings.

blew – blue	dear – deer
road – rode	sea – see
son – sun	tail – tale	too – two

Amar and His Son

Amar and his son had a lot of fun on Sunday. In the morning, they got up early to see the sun rise in the mountains. Then they each had two eggs for breakfast. They had sausages too. In the afternoon, they rode their bikes along a trail away from the road. They were excited to come across a deer. Then they sat by the sea under the blue sky. The wind blew lightly as Amar told his son a tale about a tiger with a soft, fluffy tail. At night, Amar said to his son, "Good night, my dear, brave knight!" And he switched off the lights and went to sleep.

A.   Write the homophones of the words.

1. road _____________

2. two _____________

3. blue _____________

4. son _____________

5. tail _____________

6. see _____________

7. night _____________

8. dear _____________

reign

flour

plain

meet

quay

pair

male

won

C. Write the correct homophones of the words under the lines.

1. The ___________ lives in the woods.
   bare

2. We ___________ the corn.
   eight

3. Mary walked ___________ the car.
   buy

4. It takes 100 ___________ to make a dollar.
   sense

5. The doctor checks my ___________ .
   wait

6. She ___________ the answer.
   new

7. Can you ___________ the music?
   here

8. The girl took ___________ nuts.
   sum

9. Judy picked the ___________ .
   flour

10. Will she ___________ the candy to me?
    cell

11. I got stung by a ___________ !
    be

12. I will ___________ my name
    right
    on the card.

D. **Rewrite the sentences by replacing the underlined words with the correct homophones.**

1. Kelly taught us how to tie a <u>not</u>.

____

____

2. I picked berries on my <u>weigh</u> to Grandma's house.

____

____

3. Ricky played basketball for an <u>our</u>.

____

____

4. The <u>hair</u> hopped away when we got closer.

____

____

Words that I Have Learned

Homophones

____

____

____

Section 3

Vocabulary

A.   Circle the answers.

1. We use our sense of _____ to see.

   hearing

   touch

   sight

2. In which season does the snow fall?

   summer

   fall

   winter

3. Which camping word is spelled correctly?

   compase

   compass

   compas

4. Which is not a community word?

   apartment

   building

   townhouse

   flask

5. Where does a baker work in a community?

   in a bakery

   in a library

   in a hospital

6. Which polygon is this?

   hexagon

   octagon

   pentagon

7. What is the function of this computer icon?

   volume control

   power on/off

   brightness control

8. To which category does the word "information" belong?

   a community word

   a polygon word

   a computer word

9. Which is a frozen body of water?

a glacier

a swamp

an ocean

10. What body of water is this?

a fjord

a delta

a geyser

11. The synonym of "sleepy" is ____ .

relaxed

drowsy

active

12. Which is not a synonym of the word "friend"?

neighbour

pal

buddy

13. The antonym of "scared" is ____ .

brave

frightened

afraid

14. The antonym of "stay" is ____ .

stayed

left

leave

15. The words "hour" and "____" are homophones.

our

flower

hours

16. The words "weight" and "____" are homophones.

wheat

eight

wait

Sense, Season, and Camping Words

B. Read the story. Then write the underlined words in the correct boxes.

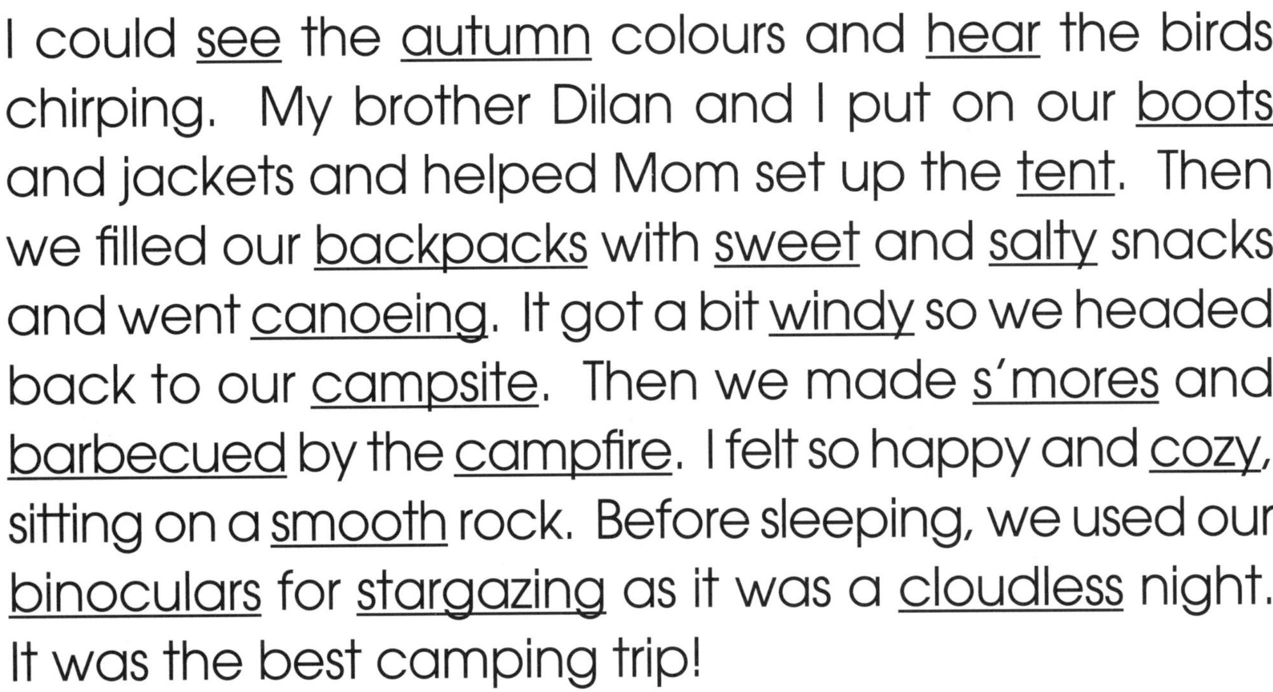

We went <u>camping</u> in the middle of <u>fall</u>. It was a beautiful but <u>chilly</u> day. I could <u>see</u> the <u>autumn</u> colours and <u>hear</u> the birds chirping. My brother Dilan and I put on our <u>boots</u> and jackets and helped Mom set up the <u>tent</u>. Then we filled our <u>backpacks</u> with <u>sweet</u> and <u>salty</u> snacks and went <u>canoeing</u>. It got a bit <u>windy</u> so we headed back to our <u>campsite</u>. Then we made <u>s'mores</u> and <u>barbecued</u> by the <u>campfire</u>. I felt so happy and <u>cozy</u>, sitting on a <u>smooth</u> rock. Before sleeping, we used our <u>binoculars</u> for <u>stargazing</u> as it was a <u>cloudless</u> night. It was the best camping trip!

Sense Word	Season Word	Camping Word

C. Read what the people say and draw lines to show where they should go.

1. 

2.

3.

4.

- hospital
- daycare
- post office
- flower shop

D. Look at the pictures and write the correct polygon words.

octagon   triangle   pentagon   rhombus   rectangle

1. 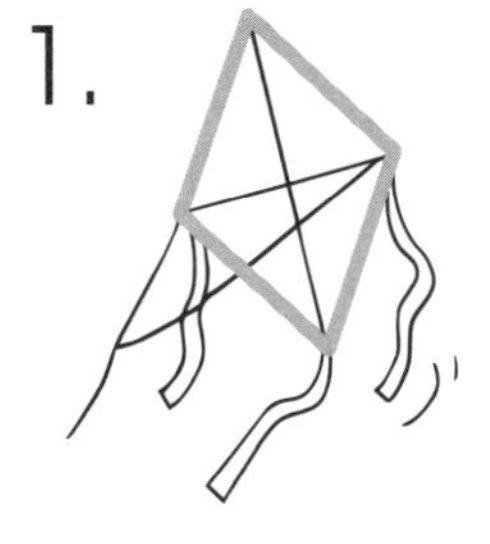

____

2.

____

3. 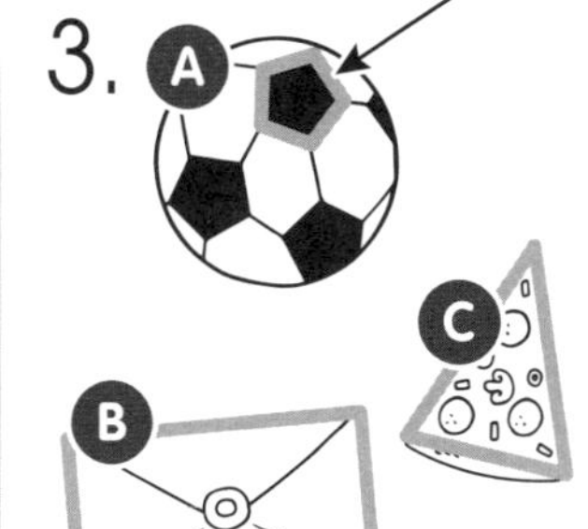

A ________________

B ________________

C ________________

Computer Words

E.   Fill in the blanks to complete the sentences.

1. The ____________ displays words and pictures.

2. The ____________ is the "brain" of the computer.

3. You can use a ____________ to type.

4. The ____________ allows you to control the pointer on the screen.

Water Words

F.   Label the picture with the correct water words.

waterfall   pond   delta   turtle   river

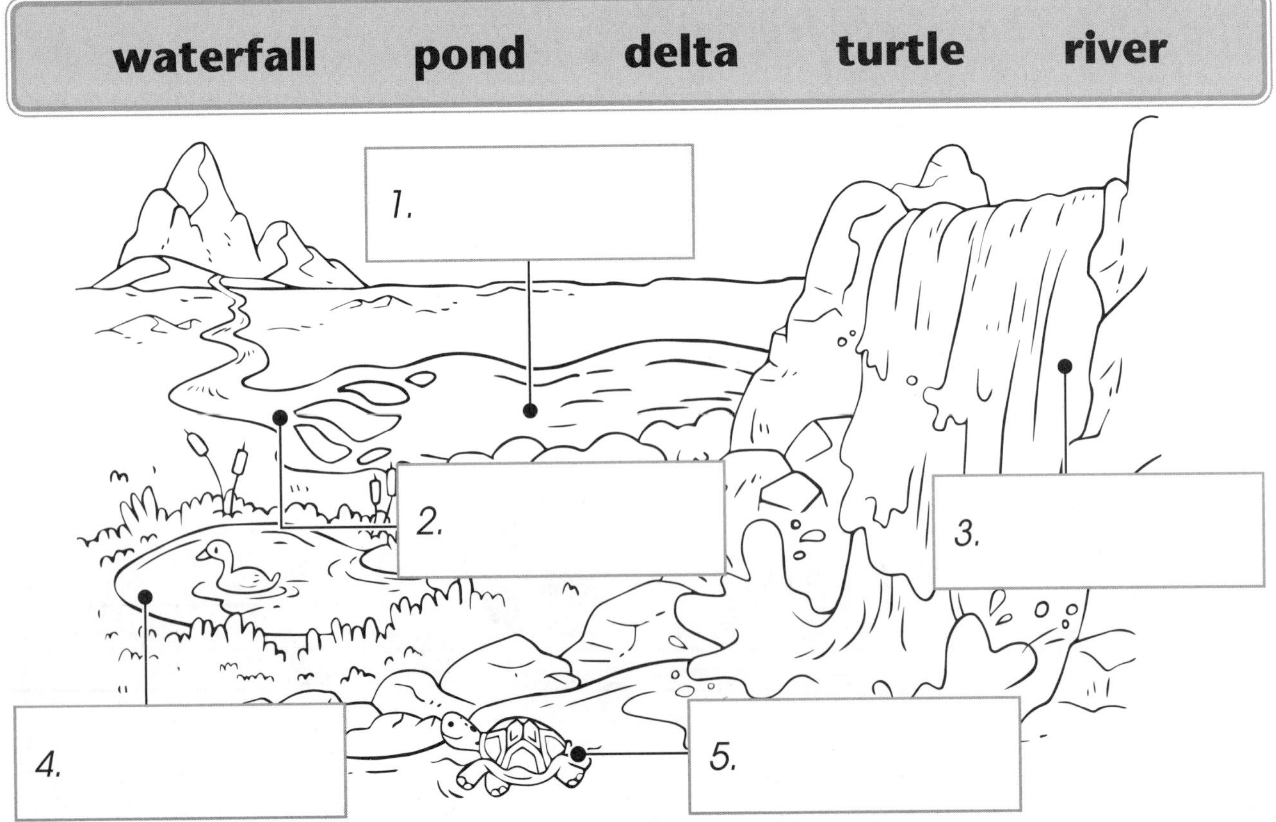

G. **Complete the crossword puzzle with the synonyms or antonyms of the clue words.**

Across

Synonyms

- Ⓐ quickly
- Ⓑ clever
- Ⓒ scared
- Ⓓ little
- Ⓔ sad
- Ⓕ hungry

Down

Antonyms

- ❶ rough
- ❷ easy
- ❸ empty
- ❹ day
- ❺ slow
- ❻ question

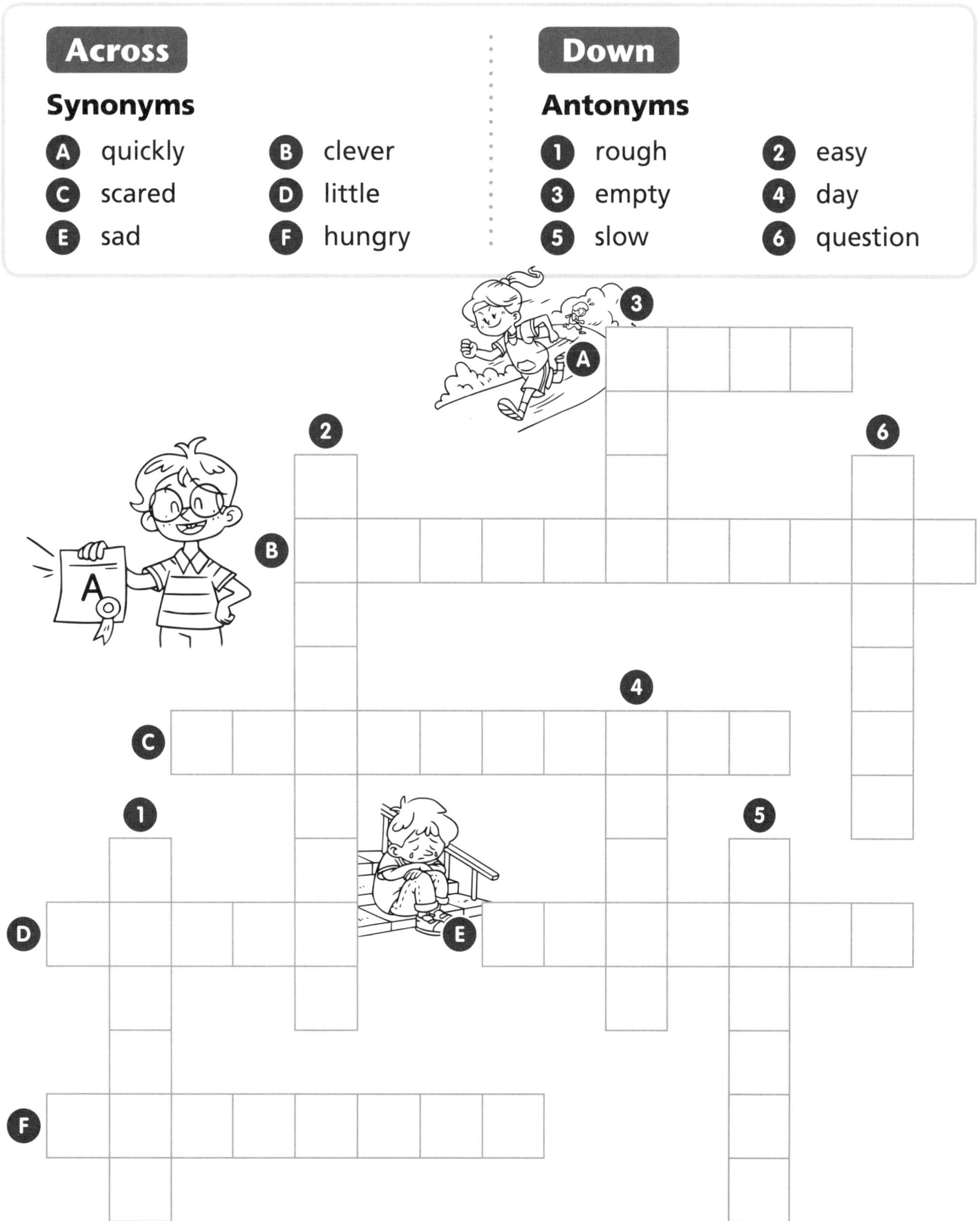

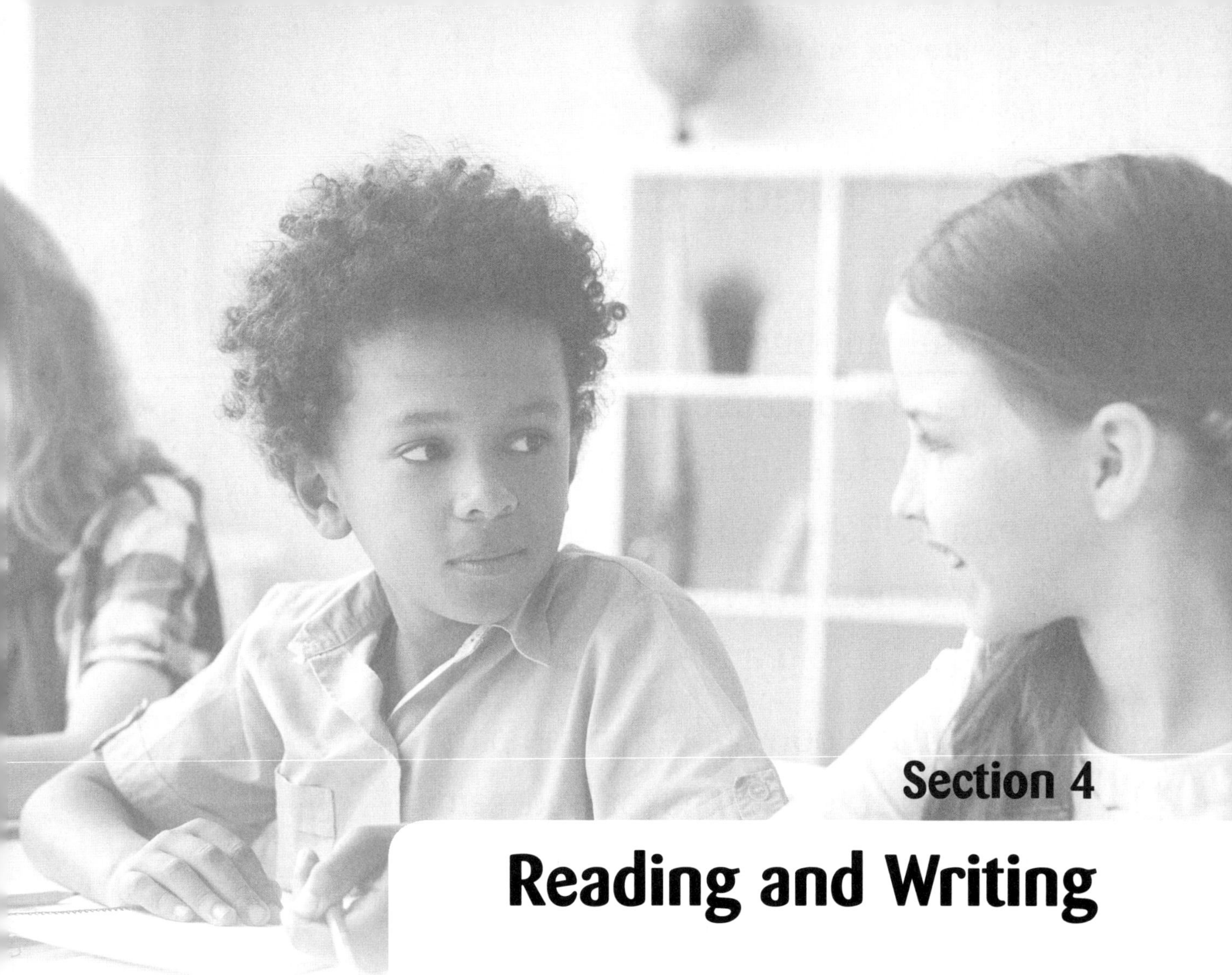

Section 4

Reading and Writing

UNIT 1

A Balloon Ride

It was a sunny morning. Janet got out of bed early because she was going for a ride in a hot-air balloon. "I'm so excited!" she said. "Get ready quickly!" her mom told her. Then they left home for the big adventure.

The colourful balloon waited in the park. Janet jumped into the basket and said, "I'm ready to fly!" The man in the basket used a burner to make the air hot. The balloon began to lift off slowly and up they went into the sky. Janet felt like a bird flying over the tops of trees and houses!

A.   Draw lines to match who said what.

• "Get ready quickly!"

• "I'm ready to fly!"

• "I'm so excited!"

B. Circle the answers.

1. How does Janet feel?

   scared

   sad

   excited

2. What does Janet ride in?

3. Who is with Janet?

   her mom

   her dad

   her brother

4. What does the balloon fly over?

   clouds

   birds

   trees

C. Answer the questions.

1. What is the setting of the story?

The setting of a story is the place and time of the events.

____

2. What is the big adventure?

____

3. Describe the hot-air balloon.

____

D. Read the story on page 182 again. Then write the information and circle the correct picture and word.

1. Title: _________________________________

2. Characters: _____________________________

    ____

3. Place:

4. Time of the Day: **morning / afternoon / night**

E. Read the text and cross out the sentences that do not belong.

Sentences in a text have to be related to make sense.

Hot-air Balloon

There is a burner in the hot-air balloon. The burner has to be lit. You can light candles with matches. It heats up the air in the balloon. The children played a ball game. The hot air makes the balloon rise into the sky.

F. **Read the sentences and cross out the ones that do not belong. Then write the sentences in order and use sequence words to link them.**

You can use words such as "before", "after", and "then" to show the sequence of the events.

A Janet got up early.

B She had a nightmare.

C _______ she got ready and went to the park.

D _______ the man lit the burner, Janet jumped into the basket.

E _______ the balloon lifted off, Janet felt like a bird flying.

F Some birds have wings but cannot fly.

____

____

____

____

____

Words that I Have Learned

____

____

____

UNIT 2
The Sun and the Ocean

"Grandpa, why does the rain fall?" asked Toby. His Grandpa said, "I asked my grandma the same question. Here is what she told me. The rain falls because of something that happened a long time ago. The Sun and the Ocean were best friends. One day, the Ocean wanted to visit the Sun on

the tall mountain. So he turned himself into clouds and rose to the mountain. The Ocean stayed with his friend there, but every time the Ocean misses his home, he turns into water again and falls down as rain to the earth below."

A.   Check if the sentences are true. If not, put a cross.

1. Toby wants to know why the rain falls.

2. Toby's grandma tells him the story.

3. The Sun and the Mountain are best friends.

4. The Ocean turns into clouds.

5. The Ocean's home is on the mountain.

B. Circle the answers.

1. Who told Grandpa the story?

    Toby

    Toby's grandma

    Grandpa's grandma

2. The Sun and the Ocean are ____ .

    brothers

    cousins

    friends

3. Who visits the Sun?

    the Ocean

    the Sun

    the rain

4. Who are the main characters of the story?

C. Answer the questions.

1. Is "The Sun and the Ocean" a folk tale?

    ____

A folk tale is a story passed on by people through speech.

2. Where does the rain fall?

    ____

3. When does the Ocean turn into rain?

    ____

D. Match the sentences with the pictures. Then put the sentences in order. Write the letters in the circles.

A The clouds rain onto the earth below.

B The Ocean turns into clouds.

C The Sun and the Ocean are best friends.

D The clouds rise up to where the Sun is on the mountain.

In order:

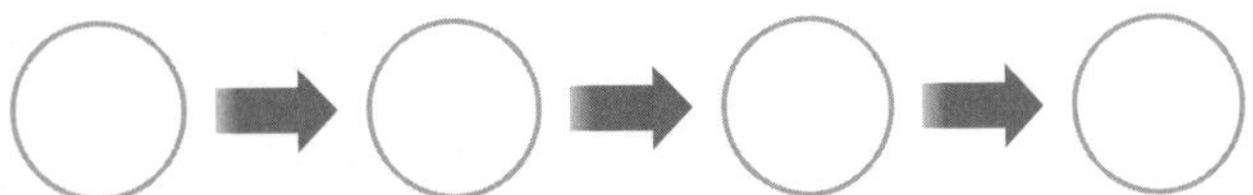

◯ ➡ ◯ ➡ ◯ ➡ ◯

E. **Write the sentences in order to continue the story "The Sun and the Ocean". Then draw a picture to go with it.**

- Then the Sun wants to visit the Ocean.
- The Ocean becomes himself again.
- The next morning, the Sun leaves his friend.
- The rain falls down to the earth.
- He rises high up in the sky again.
- He sets at dusk to meet his friend.

The rain ____

____

____

____

____

____

Words that I Have Learned

____

____

____

UNIT 3

The Museum Trip

Dear Grandpa and Grandma,

I hope you are doing well.

Yesterday, our class went on a trip to the ROM (Royal Ontario Museum). We left school at nine o'clock in the morning and returned at three o'clock in the afternoon.

When we got to the museum, we visited the Bat Cave, the dinosaurs, and the Egyptian mummies. We had a fun time there.

Today, when we got back to school, we drew and wrote about what we saw in the museum. I have learned a lot from this trip. Let's go to the ROM the next time you visit us in Toronto.

Take care.

Sincerely,

George

A.   **Write what George saw in the museum.**

1. 

2. 

3. 

___________________   ___________________   ___________________

B. Circle the answers.

1. What is the ROM?

   a school

   a library

   a museum

2. Who goes on the trip with George?

   his classmates

   his parents

   his grandparents

3. Where will George take his grandparents the next time they visit?

   to the ROM

   to his school

   to Toronto

4. What time does the trip end?

C. Answer the questions.

1. Write the answers.

   Sender: ___________________

   Receivers: _______________________________________

A letter begins with "Dear ____" to tell who receives it. The sender's name appears at the bottom of the letter.

2. What is the full name of the ROM?

   ____

3. What does George do in school after the trip?

   ____

D. Fill in the blanks to complete the letter about a trip. Then draw your face in the circle.

My Letter

Dear ____________________ ,

receiver

I hope you are doing well. I am writing to

tell you about my trip to __________________ .

name of place

I went there on ________________ with

date and month

________________ . Some of the things we

people you went with

did there were _____________________

____

________________________________ .

I cannot wait for you to visit me. Then we can

go on a trip together!

Sincerely,

____

your name

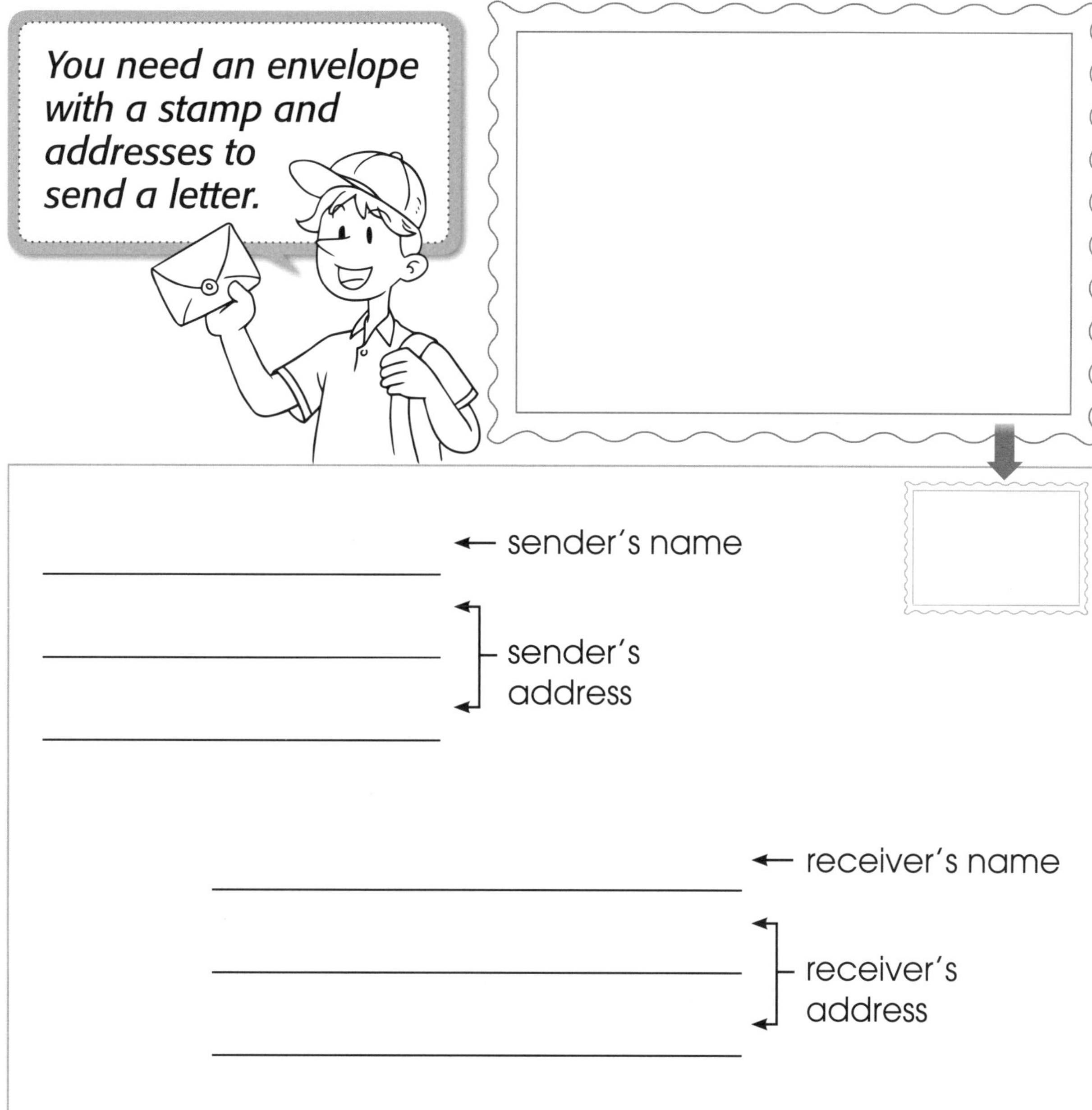

Words that I Have Learned

UNIT 4

Alphabet Rhyme

A is for ape.

B is for bike.

C is for cape

And **D** is for dike.

I is for inn.

J is for jam.

K is for kin

And **L** is for lamb.

E is for ear.

F is for five.

G is for gear

And **H** is for hive.

M is for more.

N is for net.

O is for oar

And **P** is for pet.

A.   Write what the pictures are with words from the rhyme.

1.

____

2.

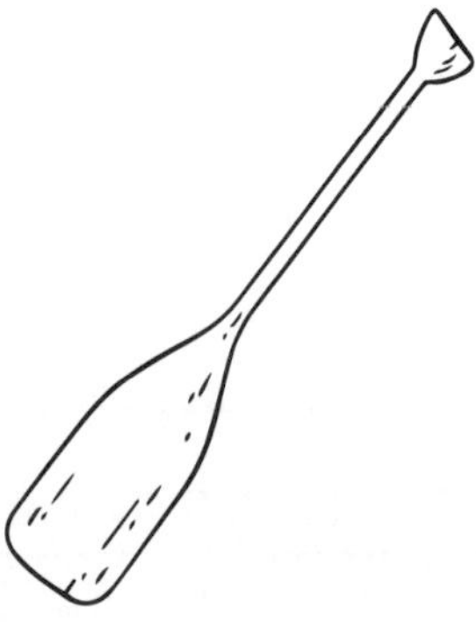

____

3.

____

B. Circle the answers.

1. How many rhyming pairs are there?

    four

    six

    eight

2. There are ____ lines in the poem.

    12

    16

    26

3. Which word rhymes with "inn"?

    kin

    dike

    hive

4. Which one rhymes with "ear"?

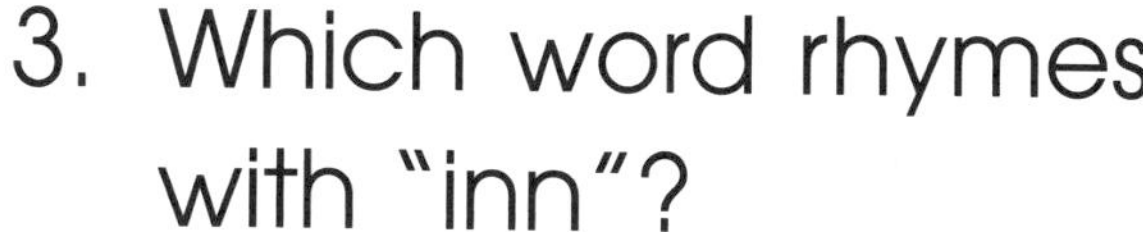

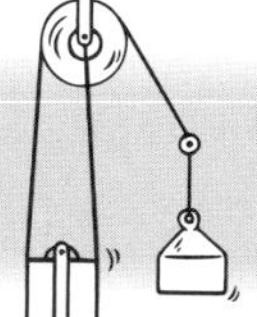

A rhyme is a poem with lines ending with words that rhyme. It can be written in stanzas, which are like paragraphs in a written text.

C. Answer the questions.

1. What type of text is this?

    ____

2. How many stanzas are there in this rhyme?

    ____

3. List the rhyming pairs.

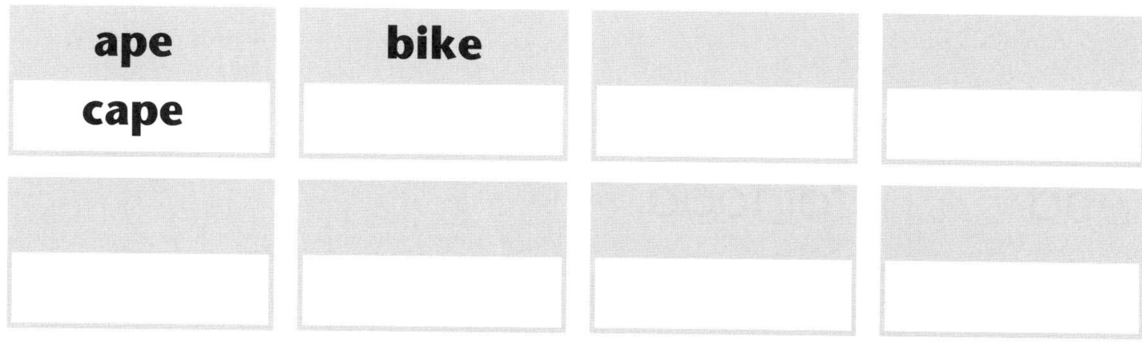

ape	bike		
cape			

Stanzas in a rhyme follow a rhyme scheme. A stanza has the ABAB scheme when:

- the first and the third lines rhyme, and
- the second and the fourth lines rhyme.

e.g.   A is for <u>ape</u>. ← A
       B is for bike. ← B
       C is for <u>cape</u> ← A
       And D is for dike. ← B

D. Complete the stanza following the ABAB scheme. Then draw pictures to go with it.

☐ is for quail. ←

R is for _________ . ←

S is for _________ . ←

And ☐ is for toad. ←

E. Complete the rhyme from A to H following the AABB scheme.

Alphabet Rhyme

 A _______________________________

 B _______________________________

C _______________________________

And  D _______________________________

 E _______________________________

F _______________________________

 G _______________________________

And H _______________________________

Words that I Have Learned

____

____

____

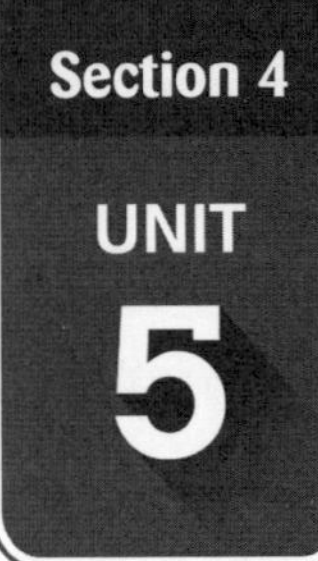

UNIT 5

Today Is My Birthday!

Hooray!

Today is my seventh birthday!

I will help my mother bake

A big pink strawberry cake!

All my friends will sing.

And I will be like a king!

We will eat, play, and run.

And have lots of birthday fun!

A. **Read the poem. Then colour the correct cake using the colour mentioned in the poem and draw the correct number of candles.**

B. Circle the answers.

1. When is the writer's birthday?

    yesterday

    today

    tomorrow

2. How old is the writer?

    five years old

    six years old

    seven years old

3. Who will sing at the party?

    the writer

    the writer's mother

    the writer's friends

4. With whom will the writer bake a cake?

C. Answer the questions.

1. Why is the writer happy?

    ____

2. What will the children do at the birthday party?

    ____

3. List the rhyming pairs in the poem.

    _____________________   _____________________

    _____________________   _____________________

D.   Read the poem. Then colour the boxes to show its characteristics.

My Birthday

This year my birthday

Falls on a Sunday!

I will be very glad

To spend time with my dad.

And Mom will be there

With us in the open air.

We will play in the sun

And have lots of fun!

Characteristics of the Poem

This poem has a title.

This poem has short sentences.

This poem has rhyming words.

This poem follows the ABAB scheme.

This poem follows the AABB scheme.

This poem describes items.

This poem describes feelings.

E. **Look at the picture and write a short poem about it. Give your poem a title and make sure it follows a rhyme scheme.**

Some Words You May Use

stars	clown	balloons
dots	happy	shiny

____

Title of Poem

____

____

____

____

____

____

____

Words that I Have Learned

____

____

____

UNIT 6

The Butterfly's Life Cycle

All living things have a life cycle. They are born, they grow up, they lay eggs or have babies, and they die. Butterflies have an interesting life cycle.

Egg

A tiny egg is laid on a leaf.

Caterpillar

The egg hatches and becomes a caterpillar. The caterpillar eats a lot and becomes big.

The Butterfly's Life Cycle

Pupa

It forms a cover around itself and becomes a pupa.

Butterfly

After a few weeks, the pupa hatches and becomes a butterfly.

A. Write 1 to 4 to put the events in order.

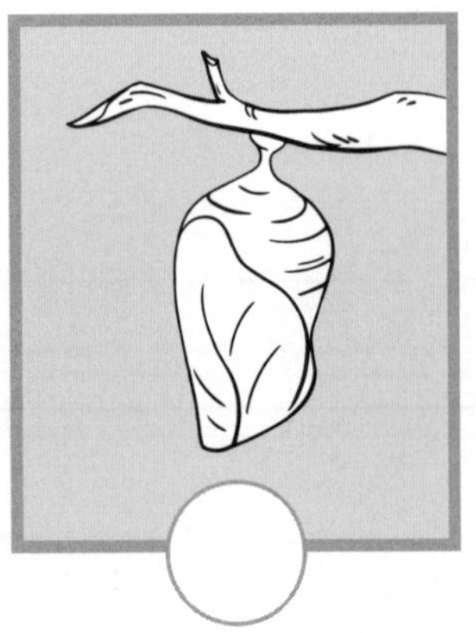

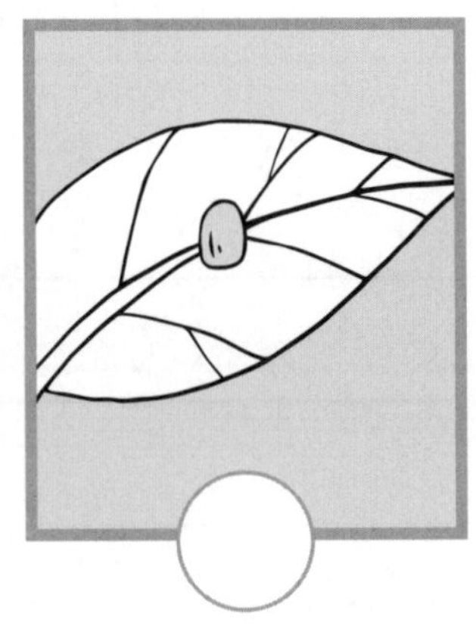

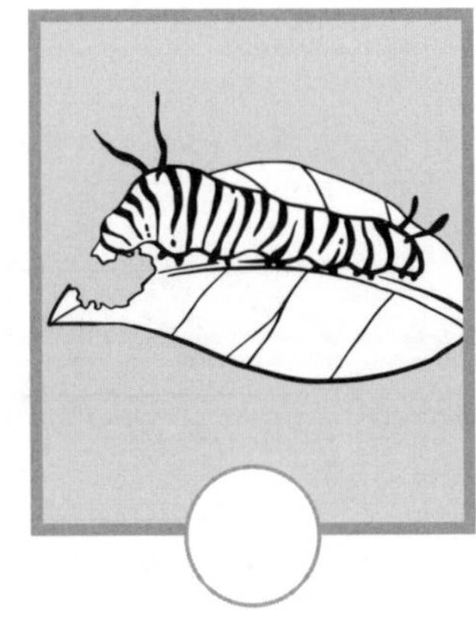

B. Circle the answers.

1. What does the egg hatch into?

    a caterpillar

    a pupa

    a butterfly

2. The caterpillar is covered when it becomes _____ .

    an egg

    a pupa

    a butterfly

3. The caterpillar eats a lot before becoming _____ .

    a pupa

    an egg

    a butterfly

4. What turns directly into a butterfly?

C. Answer the questions.

1. What is the title of the graphic text?

    ____

A graphic text uses diagrams/pictures and words to show information.

2. What is the text about?

    ____

3. How many pictures are there? What do they show?

    ____

D. **Write a title for the diagram. Colour, label, and draw arrows to complete it. Then identify its characteristics and check the circles.**

Title: ____

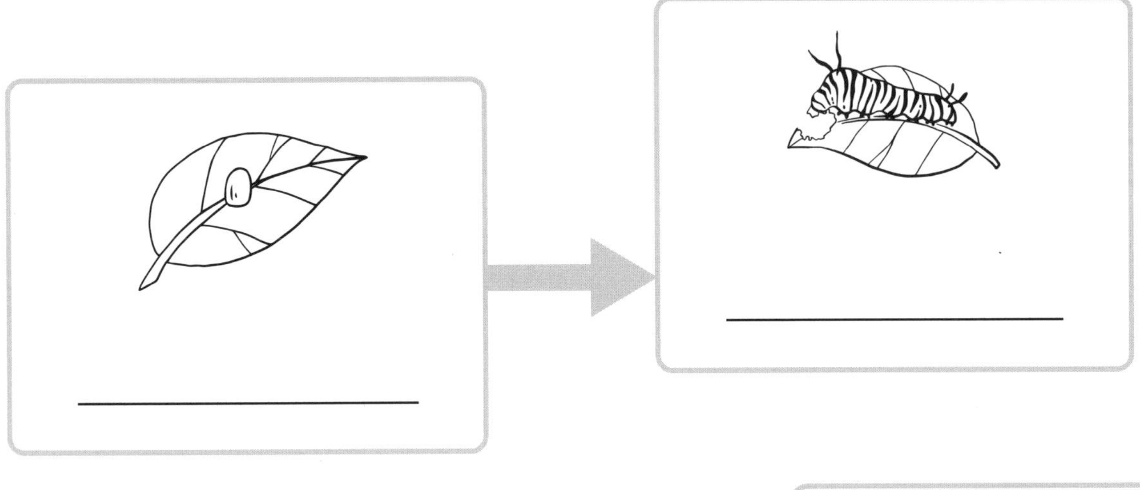

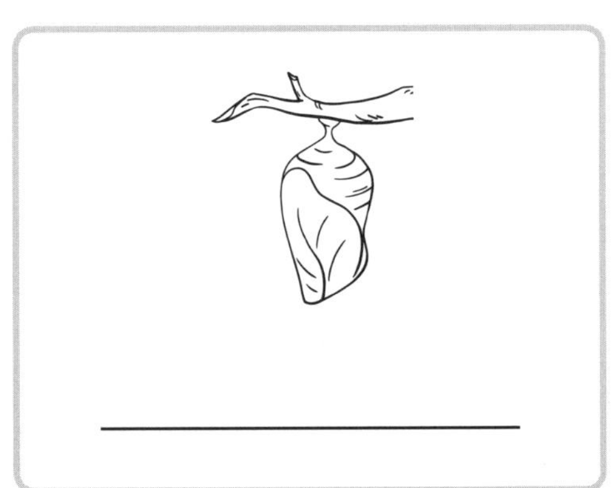

Characteristics of a Diagram

A diagram is a type of graphic text.

○ legend   ○ arrows

○ compass   ○ text

○ title   ○ colour

○ labels   ○ pictures

E. Read the sentences. Then draw a diagram to show the life cycle of the sunflower.

 A seed falls on the ground.

 Roots come out.

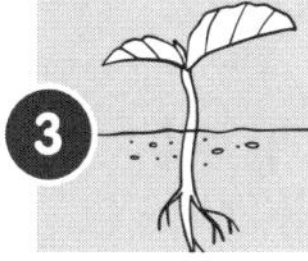 The seed grows into a shoot and leaves appear.

 A bud appears and the flower opens.

 The flower dies and the seeds fall on the ground.

Title: _______________________________

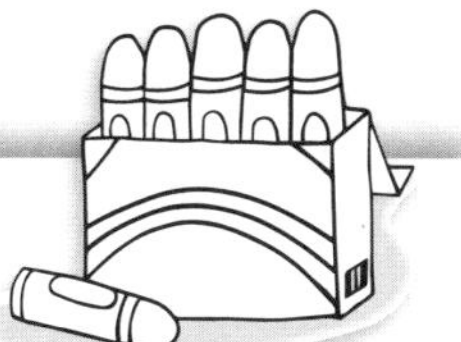

Words that I Have Learned

____

____

____

UNIT 7

Crispy Squares

Crispy Square Recipe

Ingredients

- 5 cups of rice crispies
- 1 packet of marshmallows
- $\frac{1}{2}$ cup of margarine

Directions

1. Melt the margarine in the saucepan; add the marshmallows and keep stirring until they melt.

2. Mix this mixture with the rice crispies in the large bowl.

3. Pat into the greased baking dish and cool it in the refrigerator.

4. Cut into squares.

Utensils

 large bowl

 saucepan

 spatula

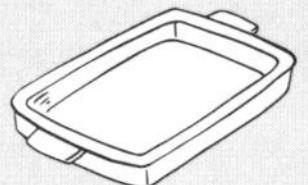 baking dish

 measuring cup

A. Read the recipe. Then write 1 to 4 to put the steps in order.

B. Circle the answers.

1. Which step below requires heat?

    Step 1

    Step 2

    Step 3

2. Which item is used for measuring?

    baking dish

    spatula

    measuring cup

3. "Utensil" means _____ .

    a clothing item

    a kitchen tool

    a furniture item

4. Which item is not an ingredient in the recipe?

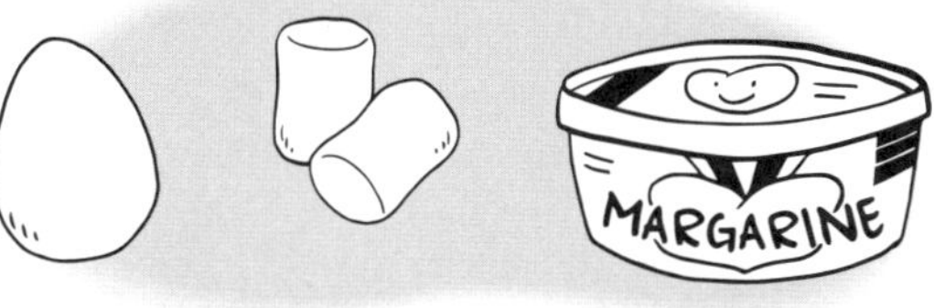

C. Answer the questions.

Instructions are informational texts that provide step-by-step directions to teach you how to do something.

1. Why is this recipe an informational text?

    ____

2. What ingredients are needed to make crispy squares?

    ____

3. What is the use of the spatula in this recipe?

    ____

D.   Look at the diagram. Then complete the recipe.

How to Make a Smoothie

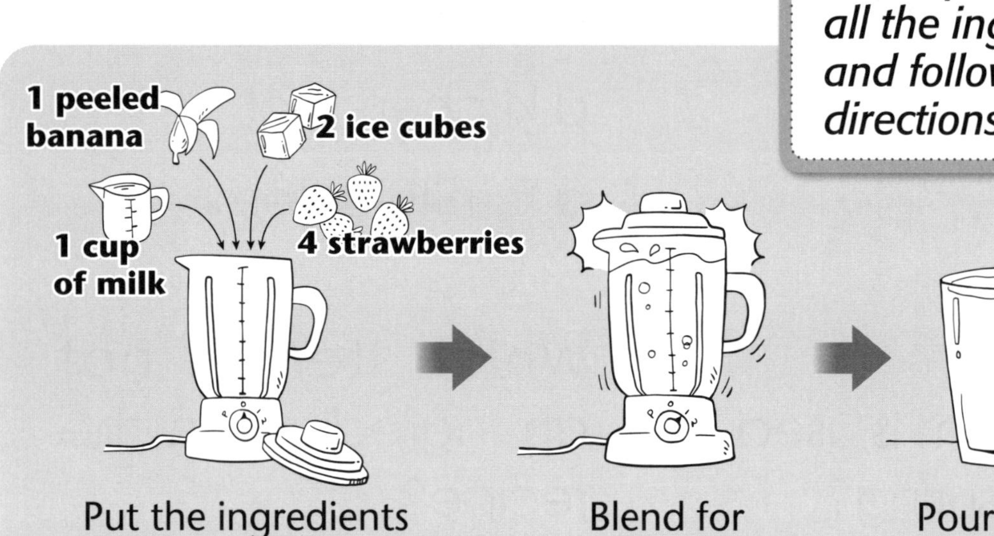

_________________ Recipe

Ingredients

____

____

____

____

Utensils

____

____

____

Directions

1 _________________________________

2 _________________________________

3 _________________________________

E. **Draw a picture of a simple food item. Then write the ingredients, utensils, and directions needed to make it.**

_________________________ Recipe

Ingredients

Directions

Utensils

Words that I Have Learned

UNIT 8 Jumbo the Gigantic Elephant

In the early 1880s, there was an enormous elephant named Jumbo. He was named by a zookeeper of the London Zoo after the Swahili word "jumbe", which means chief. Almost 100 000 children wrote to Queen Victoria to stop him from being sold. However, Jumbo was sold to Barnum and Bailey Circus and became a star of their show. He was so huge that he could carry up to 100 children on his back at one time!

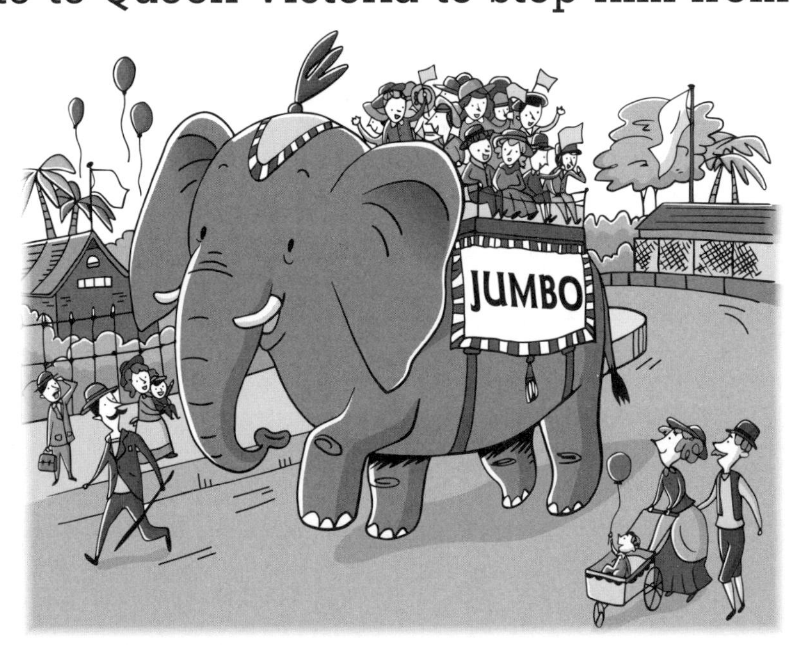

A. Match the words with their meanings.

Word		Meaning
1. jumbe		very big
2. almost		chief
3. enormous		nearly
4. star		famous performer

B. Circle the answers.

1. What was the queen's name?

   Elizabeth

   Alexandra

   Victoria

2. "Jumbe" is a word in the ____ language.

   Swahili

   circus

   English

3. Who was the star of the circus?

   Jamie

   Jumbo

   Jumbe

4. Barnum and Bailey was a ____ .

C. Answer the questions.

1. When was Jumbo kept at the London Zoo?

   ____

   ____

Informational texts contain facts such as dates, numbers, and names.

2. How many children could Jumbo carry?

   ____

3. Who gave Jumbo his name?

   ____

D.   Read the informational text and fill in the facts.

Jumbo's Accident

On one of his trips with Barnum and Bailey Circus, Jumbo was struck by a train in an accident. This happened on September 15, 1885 in St. Thomas, Ontario, Canada. At that time, Jumbo was trying to save the life of a young elephant named Tom Thumb, who had wandered near the train tracks. A life-sized statue of Jumbo was put up in St. Thomas in 1985.

Facts about Jumbo's Accident

Date of the Accident: ________________________________

Place of the Accident: ______________ ______________
                              city   province

____
      country

Whom Jumbo Wanted to Save: ________________

What Jumbo Was Struck by: ________________

When Jumbo's Statue Was Erected: ____________

Where Jumbo's Statue Was Erected: ____________

E. **Complete the facts about yourself. Then draw or paste a picture of yourself in the box.**

Facts about Me

My name is ________________ .

I was born on ____________
date

in ____________ , ____________ . My family and
city   country

I live in ____________ . I am ______ years old.
province   age

I have ____________ eyes and ____________ hair.
colour   colour

I have ______ siblings.
number

Words that I Have Learned

____

____

____

UNIT 9 Bat Facts

Bats are interesting animals. They are the only mammals that can fly. Like other mammals, they give birth to live young.

Habitat

Bats live in almost every country in the world. They live in places with mild temperatures – where it is not very hot or very cold.

Diet

Bats usually eat fruits or insects. Vampire bats eat the blood of dead birds and cattle.

Senses

Bats have good hearing. This helps them find food. They see best in the dark, which is when they hunt for food.

A.   Check the correct sentences.

1. Bats are flying mammals.

2. Mammals can fly and give birth to live young.

3. A "habitat" is the home of an animal.

4. "Diet" means what someone eats.

5. Bats can see best in the morning light.

B. **Circle the answers.**

1. Mild temperatures are _____ temperatures.

   very hot

   very cold

   not very hot or cold

2. What helps a bat find food?

   its hearing

   its flying skills

   its sense of taste

3. When do bats hunt?

   in the morning

   in the afternoon

   at night

4. What do bats usually eat?

C. **Answer the questions.**

An informational text tells you the facts about someone or something. These facts are sometimes put under different subheadings.

1. Does the text contain facts or fiction?

   ____

2. What are the subheadings in the text?

   ____

3. How can you tell that bats are mammals?

   ____

Section **4**

Reading and Writing

D. **Read the text and cross out the sentences that are not facts. Then rewrite the text as an informational text.**

A Bat's Hearing

A bat flies at night without crashing. This is because bats are magical animals. It makes noise and listens for it to bounce back. This noise is called an echo. An echo is created by an enchanted wand. The echo tells a bat where an object is. Then the bat can avoid the object. That is why no bats have crashed into the witch's castle.

A Bat's Hearing

____

____

____

____

____

____

____

E. **Write an informational text about an animal. Then draw a picture to
    go with it.**

_______________ **Facts**

Habitat

____

____

____

____

____

____

Words that I Have Learned

____

____

____

UNIT 10 — Big Red Rescuer

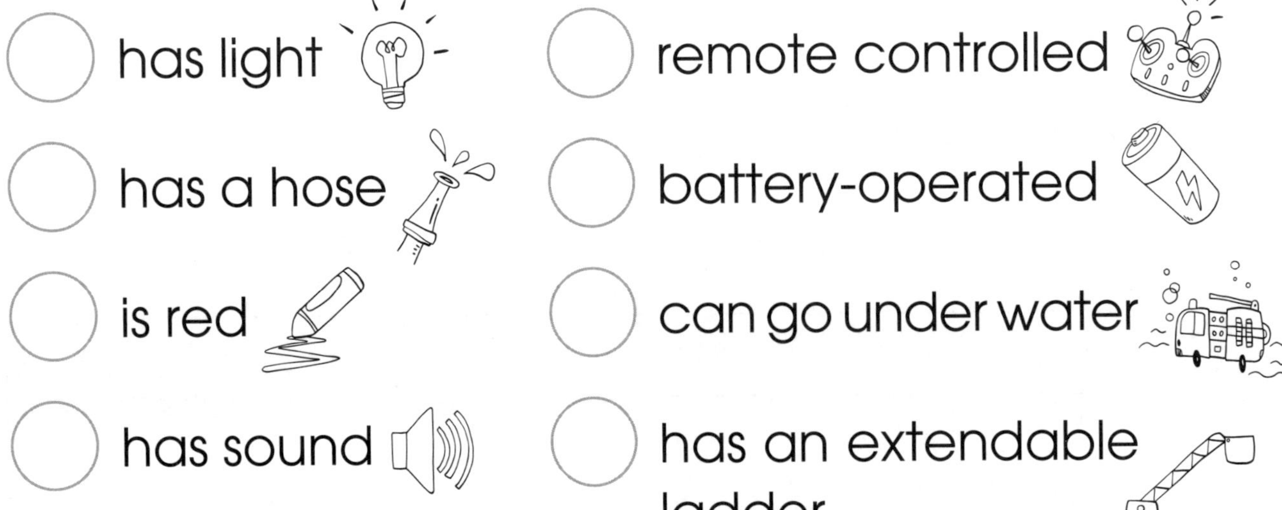

A. **Check the features of the fire truck. Then colour the truck.**

- ( ) has light
- ( ) remote controlled
- ( ) has a hose
- ( ) battery-operated
- ( ) is red
- ( ) can go under water
- ( ) has sound
- ( ) has an extendable ladder

B. Circle the answers.

1. "Splash" refers to the sound of _____ .

   the hose

   the truck

   water

2. The fire truck is _____ .

   a toy truck

   an imaginary truck

   a real truck

3. "Rescue" means "_____".

   play with

   save

   buy

4. Which hat is the boy wearing?

C. Answer the questions.

1. What product is the ad promoting?

   ____

   ____

An ad is a media text that can be used to promote a product to an audience – a group of people the ad is designed for.

2. Who do you think is the audience of this ad?

   ____

3. Why are some words in the ad in bold?

   ____

Section 4

Reading and Writing

D. Look at the ad. Then circle and check the correct answers.

1. Product:
superwoman costume / superwoman figurine

2. Intended Audience:
parents / young boys / young girls

3. Purpose:
to inform / to instruct / to persuade / to entertain

4. Slogan: **Be a Superwoman! / SALE**

5. Price: **$20.99 / $15.99**

6. Overt Message (clear, direct, and obvious message):

   (A) Girls are superwomen.

   (B) Superwomen love this costume.

7. Implied Message (hidden message):

   (A) Superwomen can fly in this costume.

   (B) You will be strong like a superwoman in this costume.

E. Fill in the information about an ad for a product. Then design the ad.

Product: ____

Features of Product: ________________________________

Price: __________   Purpose of Ad: __________________

Intended Audience: ________________________________

Slogan: ____

Overt Message: ____________________________________

Implied Message: __________________________________

My Ad

Words that I Have Learned

____

____

____

A. Circle the answers.

1. A story has _____ .

    characters

    an instruction

    rhyming words

2. Which group of words shows the sequence of events in a story?

    because, after, then

    before, after, then

    and, or, but

3. _____ is a story passed on through speech.

    An ad

    A letter

    A folk tale

4. Whose name appears at the bottom of a letter?

    the receiver's

    the sender's

    the mail carrier's

5. An envelope needs _____ .

    a greeting

    a picture

    addresses and a stamp

6. In a rhyme, the stanzas are like _____ .

    stories

    paragraphs

    poems

7. In the AABB rhyme scheme, the _____ and _____ lines rhyme.

    first ; fourth

    first ; third

    first ; second

8. Which text type has rhyming words?

    a diagram

    a poem

    a letter

9. A diagram is a type of _____ .

   literary text

   graphic text

   poem

10. A diagram has _____ .

   a compass and arrows

   labels and pictures

   text and a compass

11. Which is a recipe?

12. A recipe includes _____ .

   step-by-step instructions

   dates, numbers, and names

   a slogan and price

13. Which is not a characteristic of an informational text?

   contains headings

   contains facts

   contains fictional information

14. The facts in an informational text can be put under _____ .

   different legends

   different titles

   different subheadings

15. Which one is a media text?

   a rhyme

   an ad

   a recipe

B.   Read the text. Then check if the sentences are true. Put a cross if they are false.

The Bumblebee

The bumblebee is an important insect. It is a very good pollinator, which means it helps spread pollen from one plant to another so that other plants can grow.

Physical Characteristics

A bumblebee is yellow and black and has six legs. It has two antennae for smelling, and a female bumblebee has a stinger for defending itself.

Habitat

Most bumblebees live in a nest. Each group or colony has a queen, worker bees, and drones. The queen bee is the leader. It lays 4 to 8 eggs in the nest after a winter in hibernation. The eggs hatch to become worker bees, which are female, and drones, which are male. The colony grows until it has 50 to 600 bees.

Diet

A bumblebee uses the sweet nectar and pollen from flowers for energy. A worker bee makes honey by chewing the pollen and mixing it with its saliva.

1. The bumblebee is a good pollinator.

2. All bumblebees have a stinger.

3. Each colony has a queen, a king, and worker bees.

4. The queen bee lays 4 to 8 eggs in the nest after hibernating.

5. A bumblebee uses the pollen from plants to make honey.

C. Answer the questions.

1. What type of text is this?

____

2. How does a bumblebee help plants grow?

____

3. How does a worker bee make honey?

____

____

4. Do you think the bumblebee is an important insect? Why or why not?

____

____

D. Label to complete the diagram of the life cycle of a bumblebee. Then write a short poem that follows a rhyme scheme about bumblebees.

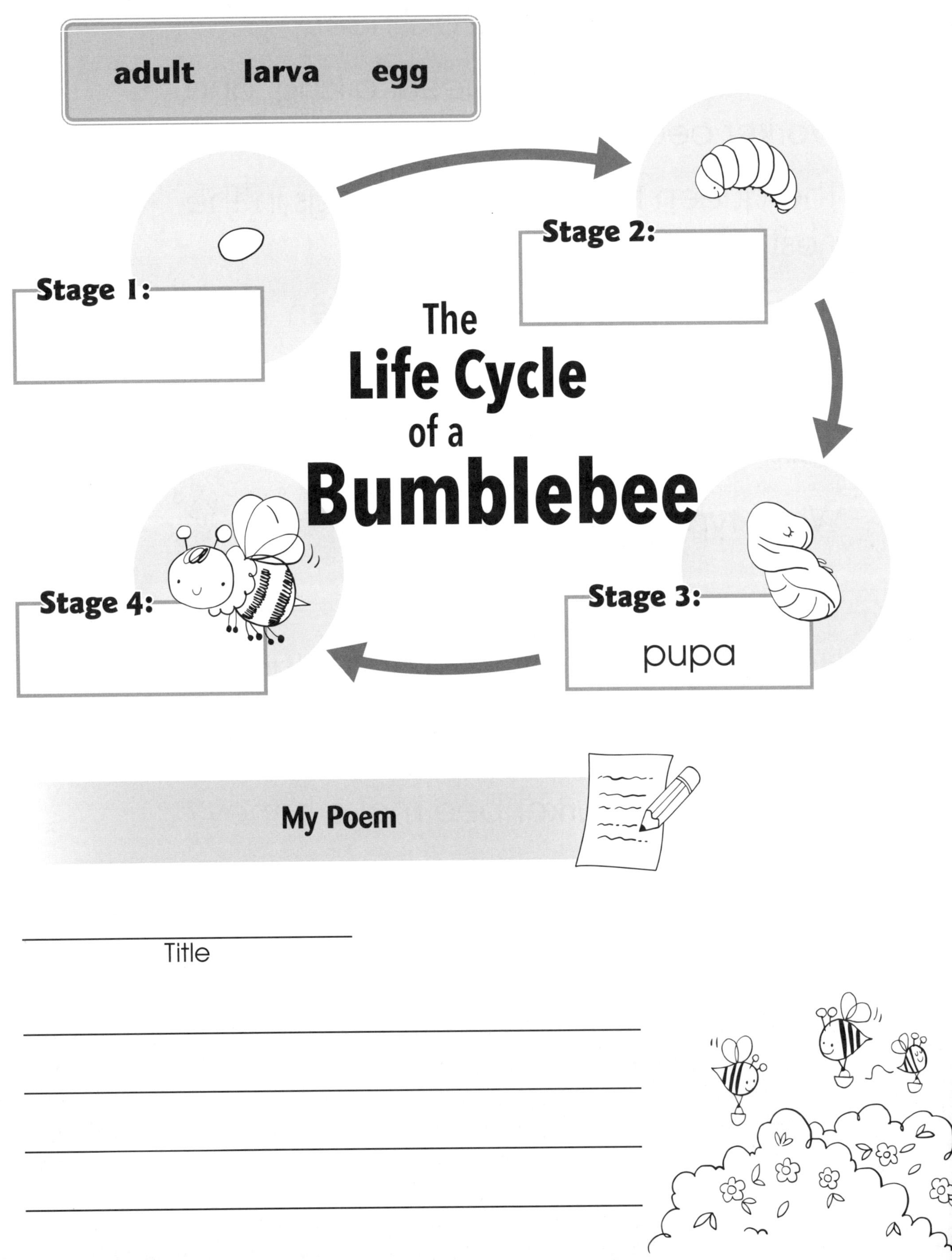

My Poem

____
Title

____

____

____

____

E.   Fill in the information about an ad for a honey product. Then design the ad.

Product: ___________________________

Price

Product Features: _____________________

Purpose of Ad: ______________________

Intended Audience: ___________________

Slogan: ____________________________

Overt Message: ______________________

Implied Message: ____________________

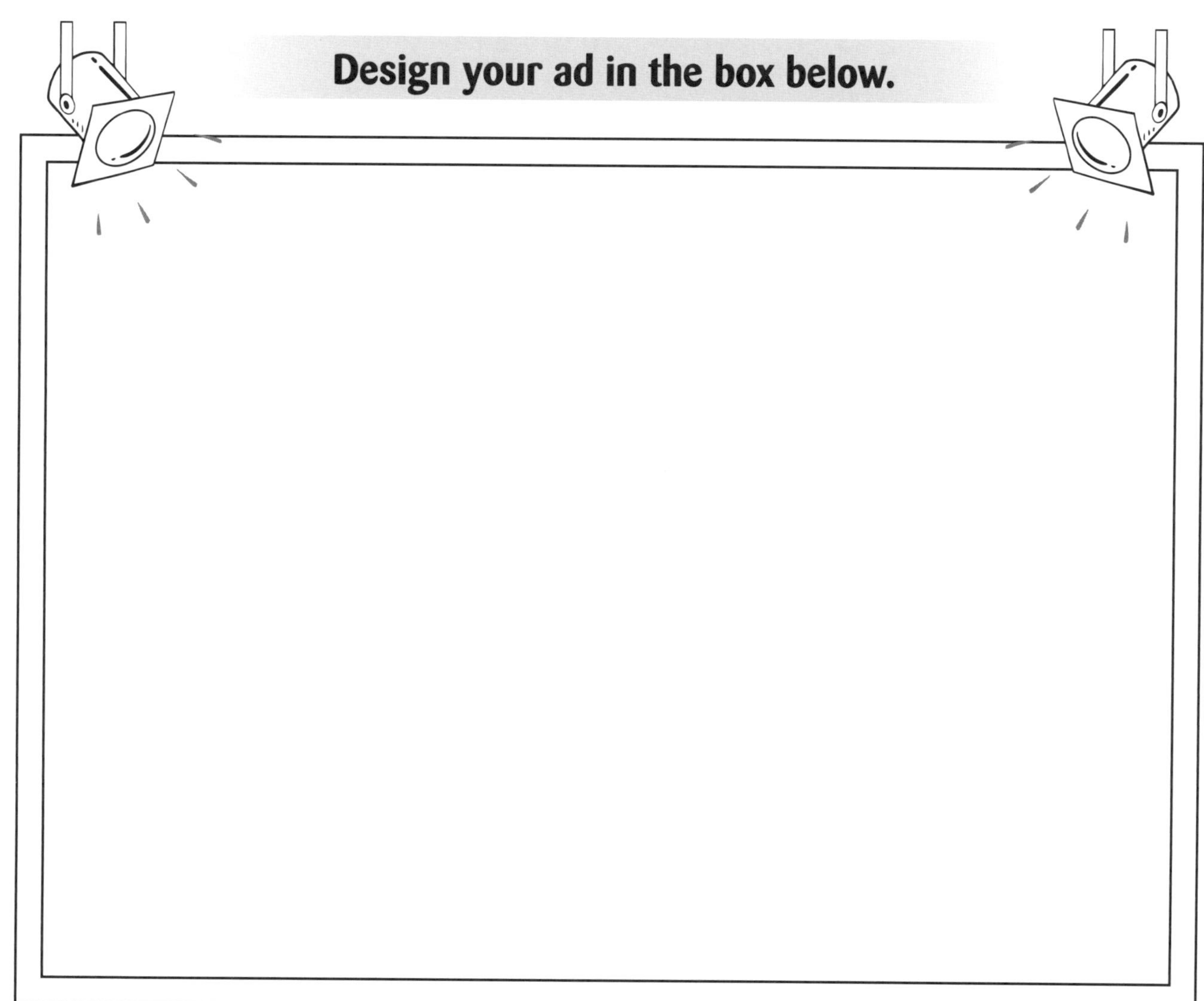

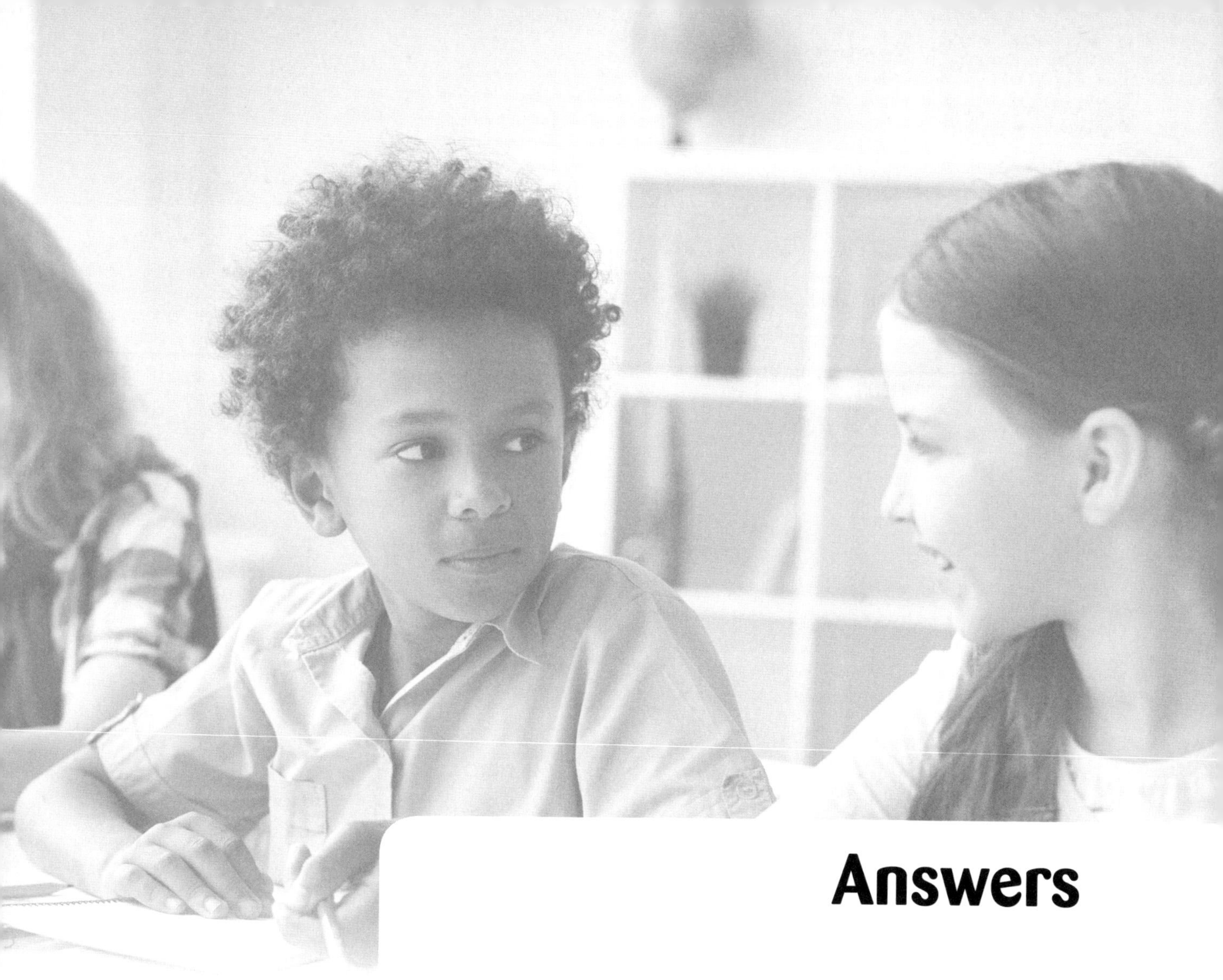Answers

1   Consonants

A. Beginning Consonant: (b)at ; (f)ish ; (d)uck

   Middle Consonant: koa(l)a ; pe(t)al ;

                  ba(n)a(n)a

   Ending Consonant: bu(s) ; pe(n) ; ja(r)

B.

	Beginning Consonant	Middle Consonant		Ending Consonant	
	h	j	p	s	r	b
crab						✓
jam		✓				
star					✓	
hat	✓					
music				✓		
hammer	✓				✓	

C. Beginning Consonant:
queen ; mouse ; turtle ; nurse
Middle Consonant:
hockey ; beaver ; fairy
Ending Consonant:
STOP ; book

D. (N)u(n)avut

(N)u(n)avut is a large territory in the (n)orth of
Ca(n)ada. It is (n)ear the (N)orth Pole. It is very
cold there. (N)ot ma(n)y pla(n)ts grow there

because it is so cold.

In (N)u(n)avut, there are six mo(n)ths of
dark(n)ess and six mo(n)ths of daylight. You
might see the su(n) shi(n)ing at 9 o'clock at
(n)ight in Ju(n)e, just like it does at (n)oo(n)!

2   Hard and Soft "c" and "g"

A. 1.  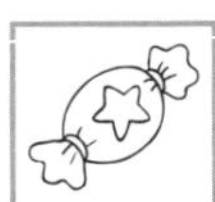
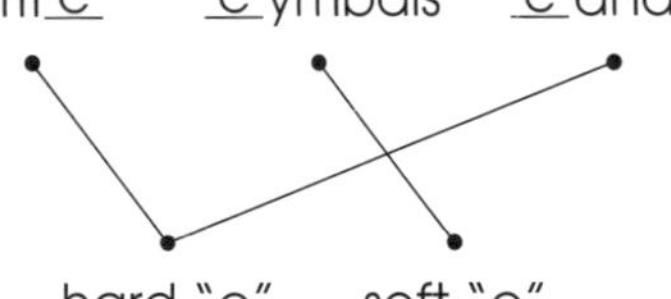

atti c   c ymbals   c andy

hard "c"   soft "c"

2.   

an g el   g irl   fla g

hard "g"   soft "g"

B. 1. Hard c: castle
2. Hard g: gift
3. Soft c: dancer
4. Soft g: giraffe

C. Hard "c": cage, carrot, circus
Soft "c": juice, celery, circus
Hard "g": goose, bag, garbage
Soft "g": cage, garbage, danger, genie

D. Pen(g)uins

Pen(g)uins are birds that (c)annot fly but
are (g)ood swimmers. They live in i(c)y
Antar(c)ti(c)a and off the (c)oast of Afri(c)a
and Australia. The smallest pen(g)uin is
40 (c)entimetres tall. It is (c)alled the Blue
Fairy. The tallest pen(g)uin, the Emperor,
seems hu(g)e in (c)omparison!
The female pen(g)uin lays an e(gg) or two and
(g)oes off in search of food. While she is (g)one,
the male prote(c)ts the e(gg)s from dan(g)er.

3 Silent Consonants

A. 1. ta(l)k   2. sta(l)k
   3. crum(b)   4. (k)ni(gh)t
   5. spag(h)etti   6. clim(b)
   7. (k)not   8. anc(h)or

B. 

C. 1. l   2. k
   3. h   4. b
   5. l

D. (h)onest ; ca(l)m ; (k)nock ; c(h)oir
   1. honest   2. Knock
   3. calm   4. choir

E. Kelvin the (Knight)

Kelvin was an (honourable) (knight). He was charged with capturing the thieving (ghosts) called Creepie and Spook. At first, Kelvin (thought) he (would) lure them with (crumbs) or (salmon) but he (knew) they were not that (dumb). Then he came up with another (scheme). He (knitted) a web and (calmly) waited for the (ghosts) to arrive. They got (caught) in his trap and Kelvin was declared the (heir) to the throne.

4 Consonant Blends: L Blends

A. 1. cl   2. bl
   3. bl   4. fl
   5. pl   6. fl
   7. sl   8. gl

B. 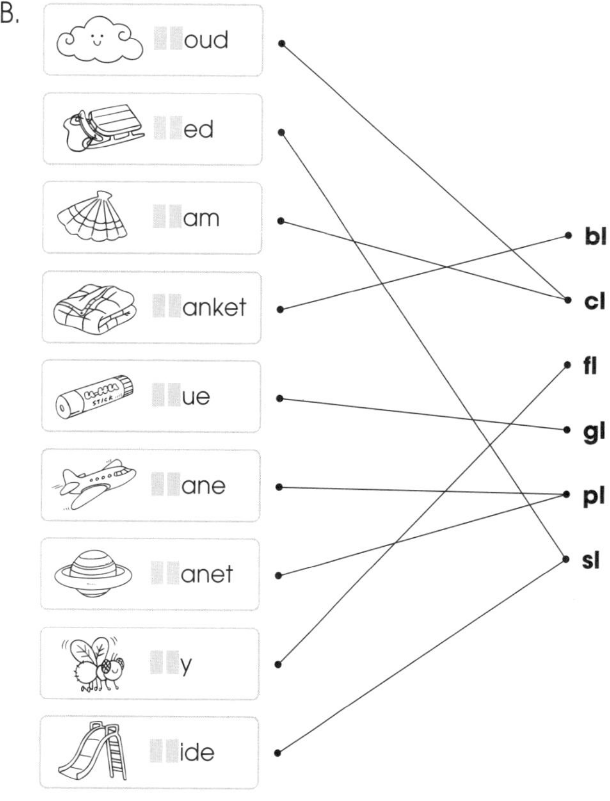

C. 1. gl   2. fl
   3. pl   4. fl
   5. pl   6. Fl
   7. sl   8. sl
   9. bl ; cl

D. Ladybugs

Ladybugs are insects. They are often red with (black) spots. Some are (black) with red spots. In the summer, they live on (flowers), shrubs, and other (plants). In the winter, they live in trees and houses.

Ladybugs are capable of (flying). Although they cannot reach the (clouds), they can reach great heights. On land, they are small enough to crawl on (flowers) and even on tiny (blades) of grass.

5 Consonant Blends: R Blends

A. 1. cr 2. gr
3. dr 4. fr
5. br 6. tr
7.

B.

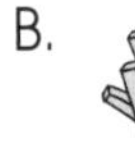
 fr

 gr

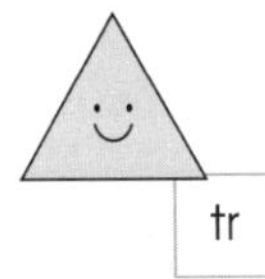 tr
 cr
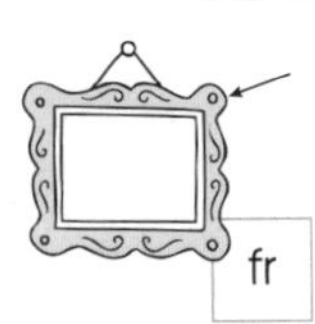 fr
 pr
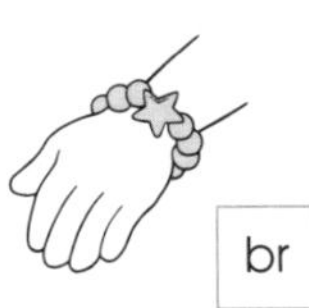 br
 tr

 dr

C. 1. ✔ 2. ✘ ; bread
3. ✘ ; crust 4. ✔
5. ✘ ; brush 6. ✘ ; tray

D. (cr)ops ; (Fr)iday ; (tr)ip ; (pr)esident
1. trip 2. crops
3. Friday 4. president

E. (Trisha's) (Dream)

A few days ago, (Trisha) had a (dreadful) (dream). She was standing under tall (trees) in a scary forest. She suddenly felt huge (drops) of rain on her (dress)! (Trisha) ran in the wet (grass) to hide inside a small (brick) house. It was then that she woke up to realize that in reality there was rain coming in (from) her window!

6 Consonant Blends: S Blends

A. 1. sc 2. sk
3. sl 4. sm
5. sn 6. sp
7. st 8. sw

B.

S-blend Words

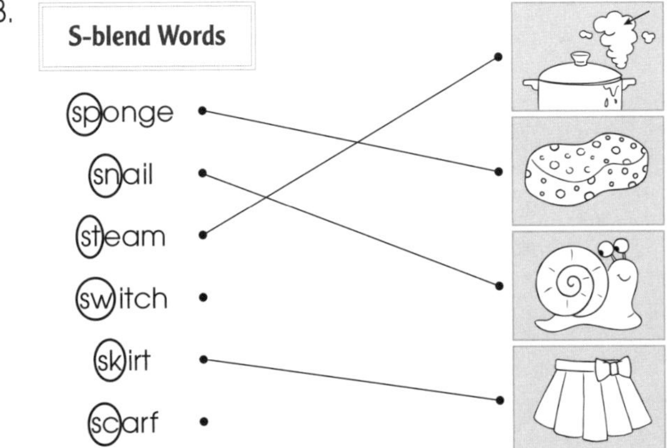

C. 1. sl 2. sl
3. sm 4. sw
5. sm 6. sk

D. 1.

2. smoothie 3. smell
4. spot 5. stairs
6. swan 7. scooter
8. skip

E. Dance Lessons

When (Stella) was three years old, she (started) taking dance lessons. She wore a pink (skirt) with (small) ballet (slippers). She practised the (steps) every day.

By the time she was sixteen, she was very good at ballet. (Stella) was offered the leading role in a play called "(Swan)". She quickly learned many new (steps) and routines. Because of her hard work, (Stella) (spun) in circles and (slowly) bowed as she became the (star) of the (stage)!

7   Consonant Digraphs

A. th ; ch ; wh ; sh ; sh ; sh

B. 1. th   2. sh
   3. wh   4. wh
   5. sh   6. th
   7. ch

C. 1. In orange: (Sh)e sells sea(sh)ells by (th)e [yellow]
        sea(sh)ore.
   2. In blue: (Ch)ester (ch)ewed (th)e [yellow] (ch)ewing
        gum (ch)eerily.
   3. In orange: (Th)e [yellow] (sh)iny (sh)oes in Susie's
        (Sh)oe (Sh)op (sh)immer in (th)e [yellow]
        (sh)ining sun.
   4. In yellow: (Th)eodore (th)ought (th)e
        (th)imble was (th)ick.
   5. In yellow: (Th)e (th)in (th)ief (th)rew (th)e
        (th)read to (th)e o(th)er (th)ree
        (th)ieves.
   6. In green: Willy (th)e [yellow] (Wh)ale (wh)irled (wh)ile
        (th)e [yellow] (wh)eel of (th)e [yellow] (wh)ite
        (wh)aler (wh)istled.

D. (Individual examples)

E. Sheila's Shopping Adventure

Sheila was excited to go shopping with her elder brother, Chandler. She woke up early on Thursday and showered quickly. Then she threw on her favourite pink dress with white shoes. She was going to buy things for everyone: shampoo for her dog, red thread with a shiny thistle for her grandma, delicious cherries for her mom, and a whistle to surprise Chandler.

However, once they started the car, they noticed that its steering wheel was not working. So they took the bus instead, and Sheila saw a big cheese factory, a giant chair, and a whale museum on her way to the mall!

8   Short Vowels

A. 1. n(e)t   2. l(a)mp
   3. t(e)nt   4. s(i)x
   5. b(u)g   6. m(a)p
   7. m(o)p   8. s(u)n
   9. l(i)ps   10. r(o)ck

B. 1. 
   2.
   3.
   4.
   5.

C. 1. i   2. o
   3. e   4. a
   5. u
D. 1. e   2. a
   3. u   4. o
   5. i

E. Jill's Umbrella Hat

(yellow) **Jill** has an umbrella (red) **hat**. It is an umbrella (purple) **but** it is also a hat. It was a (yellow) **gift** from her (green) **mom**. She (red) **can** use it in the rain and also in the (purple) **sun**. She (blue) **wears** it on her (blue) **head**. (green) **Ron** likes her umbrella hat. He thinks it is (purple) **fun** to wear it.

---

9 Long Vowels

A. 1. i   2. o
   3. a   4. i
   5. e   6. u
   7. a   8. u

B. 1. 

2. 

3. 

4. 

5.

C.

Long-vowel Words

sp(i)der
r(u)ler
wh(a)le
gl(o)be
(a)corn
f(i)re
z(e)bra
m(u)sic
(e)vent
(o)cean

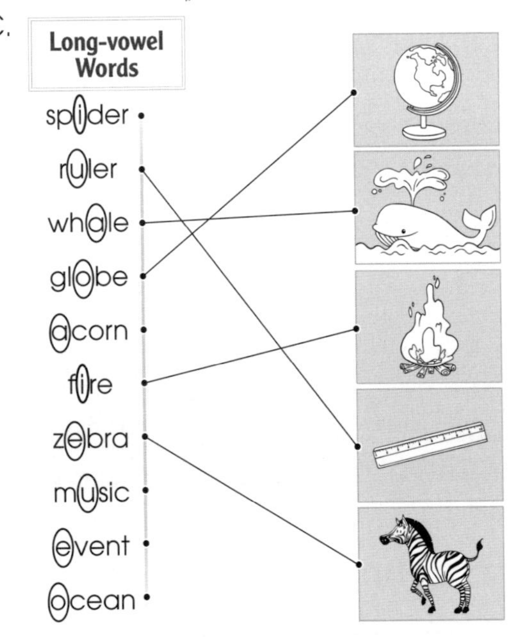

D. All about Plants

(blue) **Most** plants start as a seed. (green) **Usually**, (green) **you** plant the seed in the garden or the yard, in the (red) **shade** or the sun.

If (green) **you** (green) **use** a small (red) **spade**, (green) **you** can dig a (blue) **hole** to (blue) **poke** the seed down and cover it with soil. (green) **You** plant the seed and let the sun shine down on it. When it sprouts and the stem gets stronger, leaves begin to come out.

---

10 Y as a Vowel

A. 1. i   2. e
   3. e   4. e
   5. e   6. i
   7. i   8. i

B. 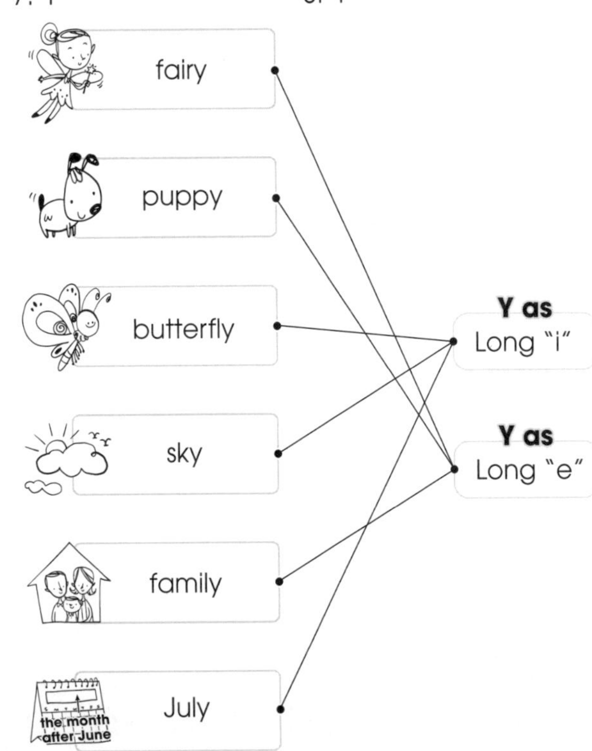

C. Y as Long "i" (in red): my ; try ; fly ; dry ; fry
    Y as Long "e" (in blue): funny ; buddy ; sunny ; pony ; Mary
    1. Mary   2. funny

3. Buddy   4. dry
5. try   6. sunny
7. fly   8. my
9. fry   10. pony

D. The Coin Collection

<u>Brittany</u> has a coin collection. She started it when she was six years old. She put the coins in a jar labelled "(My) Coins".

The first coins she got were from <u>Italy</u>, which her mom gave her after a trip there. Since then, <u>many</u> of her <u>family</u> members have given her coins for gifts. Her dad will (fly) to China in (July) and he will (try) to find some special coins for her. <u>Brittany's</u> favourite coin is one from Sri Lanka. It is large and <u>heavy</u>.

11   Vowel Digraphs

A.

B. 1. nail   2. snail
3. tray   4. jay
5. pay   6. say
7. paint   8. play
9. jail

C. 1. bee   2. jeans
3. tea   4. team
5. bean   6. meat
7. weed   8. week

9. see   10. seed

D. (Individual answers)

E. Adventure at the (Sea)

(Dear) (Jayden,)

We went to Sharaz on (Thursday). On our (way), we heard about a sunken ship in the (deep) (Sea). The story goes like this – a pirate ship got caught in the (rain) there a long time ago. It sank and a chest with precious gems and gold (beads) went down with it.

At first, we were (afraid) of the water, but then we decided to look for the ship. We boarded a small ship. Then we dived under the water. When we (reached) the ship, we swam inside and guess what? We found the chest!

I'll show you some photos when we're home.

Your friend,

(Dean)

12   Vowel Digraph: oo

A. 1. (in green)   2. (in blue)
3. (in green)   4. (in blue)
5. (in blue)   6. (in blue)
7. (in green)

B. Long oo: smoothie, roots, boot, noodles, zoo
Short oo: brook, hood, foot
(Individual examples)

C. 1. short ; long
2. cook ; book ; look ; cookbook
3. fool ; pool ; cool ; drool

D. <u>Noor's Smoothie</u> Recipe

<u>Noor</u> was a very (good) (cook). But she did not want to make the same <u>food</u> every day. So she (stood) in the kitchen and (looked) around. Finally, she decided to put some apples, strawberries, bananas, and three <u>scoops</u> of

chocolate ice cream into the blender. She pushed the red button and "<u>whoosh</u>" it went as it (shook) the small (wooden) table. She excitedly poured the mixture into her glass. <u>Noor</u> hummed in a (good) <u>mood</u> as she drank the delicious <u>smoothie</u>.

13 Diphthongs

A. 1. ou
   3. ou
   5. oy
   7. oi

2. oi
4. ow
6. oy
8. ow

B. 1. oy ; royal
   3. ow ; town

2. oi ; noise
4. ou ; mouth

C. ou: trout, found, shout, out
   ow: shower, towel, down
   oi: boil, coin, voice, avoid
   oy: voyage, loyal, employ, joy

D. R(oy) the T(oy) Robot

   R(oy) was very ann(oy)ed with his sister, J(oy). She was ar(ou)nd two years old and enj(oy)ed destr(oy)ing his things. She even sp(oi)led his favourite drawing of blue cl(ou)ds over a sea of tr(ou)t and the one with a cr(ow)d of silly cl(ow)ns. At first, R(oy) yelled at her in a l(ou)d v(oi)ce. Then he heard her cry on the c(ou)ch. So he decided to surprise her. He took a piece of f(oi)l, some br(ow)n paper, and a metal c(oi)l. After a lot of hard work, "R(oy) the T(oy) Robot" went to his sister and they both played till their mother was back home.

14 Rhyming Words

A. (Colour each rhyming pair with the same colour.)
   cap – map
   tea – tree
   knot – pot

tub – cub

B. 1. book ; <s>door</s>
   2. duck ; <s>quack</s>
   3. cake ; <s>cage</s>
   4. frog ; <s>wok</s>
   5. sun ; <s>mom</s>
   6. plane ; <s>man</s>

C.

D. (Circle each pair or group of rhyming words with the same colour.)
   Rhyming pairs/groups:
   deep – sheep – deep – sleep
   cat – rat
   bear – hare – pear
   dog – frog
   moose – goose

Review 1

A. 1. middle

2. 

3. knife

4. cl

5. 

6. S

7. wheel ; thumb ; chair

8. short vowel

9. long "a"

10. 

11. ai

12. hook

13. 

14. diphthong

15. bite ; sight

16. 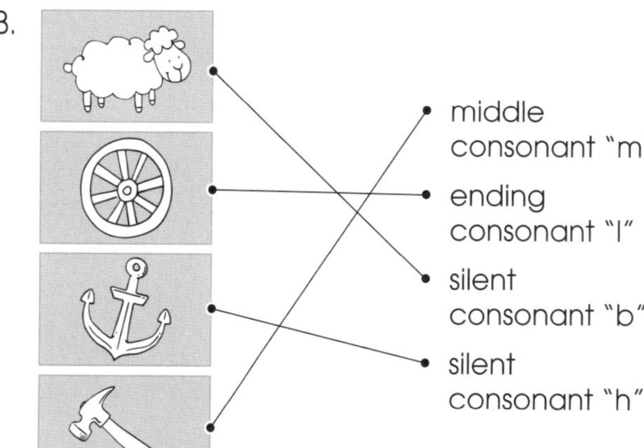

B.

- middle consonant "m"
- ending consonant "l"
- silent consonant "b"
- silent consonant "h"

C.
1. The gigantic giant, Gary, used magic to decorate the castle.
   (green, orange, red green, orange, green red, red, red)
2. There were cakes and candies in the garden on Carl's birthday.
   (red, red, orange, red)
3. The dancers celebrated as Andy played the guitar.
   (blue, blue, orange)

D. 1. cl   2. dr
3. st   4. fr
5. sk   6. fl

E. 1. 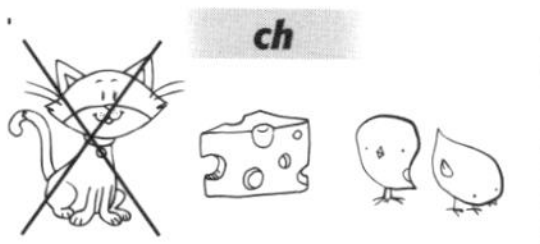

2. 

3. 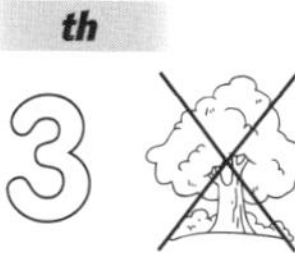

4. 

F. Short vowel: a ; u
Long vowel: i ; o
(Individual examples)

G.

	Short-vowel Word	Long-vowel Word
1.	Bill	grapes
2.	pink	slide
3.	mat	rose
4.	pet	bone
5.	rocks	night

H. 1. ee ; ee   2. ai ; ea
3. ai ; ay   4. oo ; oo

I. ou: clouds, outside
ow: crown, brown
oi: soil, noise
oy: boy, annoying

1 Nouns

A. Person: boy ; Timmy
Animal: dog ; Dalmatian
Place: city ; Toronto
Thing: game ; Frisbee

B. 1. parrot   2. fairy
3. foxes   4. dresses
5. brushes   6. chicks
7. bench   8. rat
9. kids

C.

carrot**s**   jam   popcorn

glass**es**   ball**s**   cheese

D. 1. water ; cups
2. bottles ; plastic
3. sand ; pots
4. faith ; heroes

E. Countable Noun: farm , market, cows , animals,
hens, eggs, sheep
Uncountable Noun: soil, dirt, air, water, wool, milk

2 Articles

A. a: house, uniform, violin
an: apricot, umbrella, idea, album
the: South Pole, CN Tower, RCMP,
St. Lawrence River
(Individual examples)

B. 1. the sun
2. an owl
3. an elephant
4. a rainbow ; a unicorn
5. a lamp
6. the Earth
7. the Olympic Games
8. an airplane

C. 1. the   2. an ; a
3. the ; the   4. The
5. the ; the ; a   6. the ; an
7. A   8. an
9. a ; the   10. the

D. (Individual writing)

3 Pronouns

A.

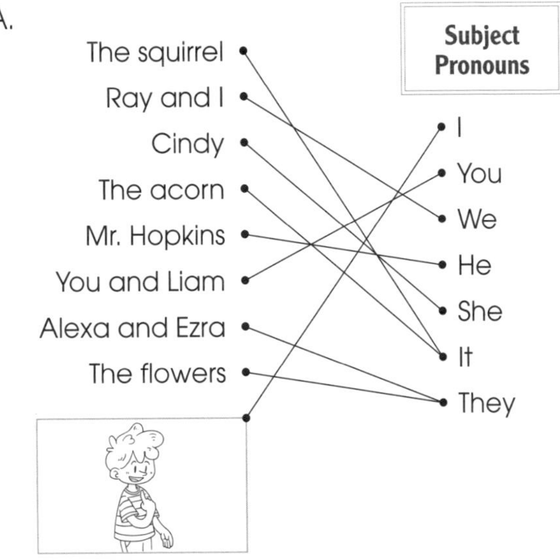

B. 1. We   2. They
3. She   4. It
5. I

C. They ; We ; He ; It

D. 1. you   2. it
3. them   4. him
5. us ; her

E. 1. her   2. them
3. us   4. you
5. him   6. us
7. it   8. him ; them

F. 1. us   2. it
3. them   4. him
5. us   6. her

4 Present Tense Verbs

A. 1. sing ; singing
2. laughs ; laughing
3. break ; breaking
4. leap ; leaps
5. snows ; snowing
6. find ; finding

B. 1. shines
2. walking
3. chat
4. live
5. waving
6. looking

C. 1. eat
2. gets
3. stay
4. blowing
5. plays
6. collecting

D. 1. are
2. are
3. is
4. is
5. is
6. are
7. are
8. are ; am

E. A. I am reading a letter.
B. The calves are playing happily.
C. Gavin is swinging in the tree.

5 Past Tense Verbs

A.

c	e	p	d	r	h	l	c	o	l	r	f	a
o		l	i	t	e	b	u	z	z	e	d	
b	a	d	s	g	e	r	a	s	l	a	e	t
r	s	h	l	r	t	u	r	o	i	c	b	e
c	l	o	s	e	d	s	e	r	f	h	u	r
o	j	u	c	a	m	h	a	i	t	e	z	a
l		c	o	l	l	e	c	t	e	d	s	s
e	p	b	r	u	s	d	d	b	d		c	e
c	o	r	e	a	d		k	m	c	e	o	d
d	q	t	d	i	s	l	i	k	e	d	s	g

B. Dodo **carryed** / (**carried**) a backpack to school yesterday. He **learnd** / (**learned**) some funny tricks at the dog school. He (**balanced**) / **balanceed** himself with one hand on a plank on a ball. After that, he **skiped** / (**skipped**) for an hour. Then he **hurryed** / (**hurried**) home for lunch. On his way home, he (**remembered**) / **rememberred** that there was no more dog food at home, so he **stoped** / (**stopped**) by a grocery store and **grabed** / (**grabbed**) some dog food. He also **tryed** / (**tried**) to look for a bone as a treat but he could not find one that he (**liked**) / **likeed**.

C. 1. stood
2. caught
3. burst
4. bought
5. wept
6. threw
7. taught
8. spread

D. 1. was
2. ✔
3. ✔
4. were

6 Adjectives

A.

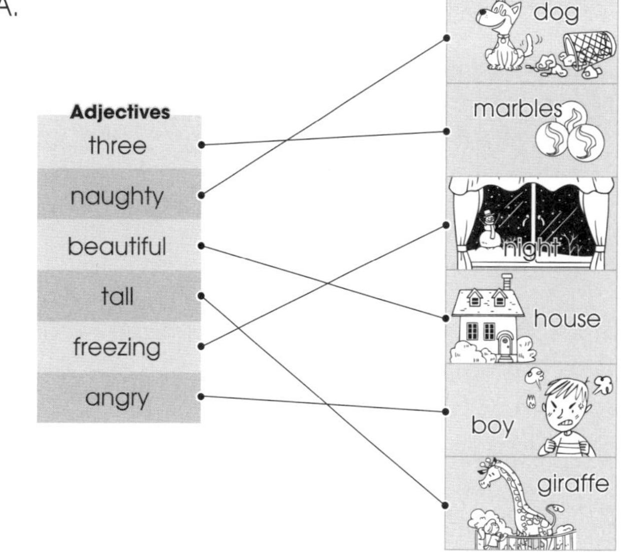

B. 1. apple
2. cat
3. diamond
4. sweater
5. candy
6. book
7. tree
8. girl
9. castle
10. ball

C. 1. Green
   2. juicy
   3. seven
   4. round
   5. spicy
   6. new ; yellow
   7. black ; white ; fresh
   8. puzzled
   9. lazy

D. 1. big
   2. pretty
   3. six
   4. scary
   5. red
   (Individual writing)

7 Prepositions

A. 1. in
   2. behind
   3. over
   4. on ; by
   5. between
   6. at ; in

B. Samuel is <u>under</u> ( ) [on] a cruise ship. He is sitting at (✔) a table <u>in</u> ( ) [on] the deck enjoying the cool breeze. There are some clouds <u>over</u> ( ) [in] the sky but the weather is still fine. There is a drink <u>under</u> ( ) [on] the table. Samuel does not know what is <u>in</u> (✔) the glass but he thinks it tastes amazing. A little bird is <u>in front of</u> ( ) [behind] Samuel. It seems to want to share the tranquil moment with him. The cruise ship is not too far <u>on</u> ( ) [from] the shore. Samuel can see people as tiny as ants <u>between</u> ( ) [on] the beach.

C. 1. on
   2. in
   3. at
   4. in
   5. on
   6. on
   7. at
   8. on

D. Marineland

Marineland is an adventure park (near) [blue] Niagara Falls, Ontario. There are many whales and dolphins (in) [blue] the park. If you put food (on) [blue] your hands, they will eat it right from your hands! Marineland is such a great place to visit. You can go there early (in) [red] the morning and spend a whole day there. Besides visiting the animals, you can go on the many rides (around) [blue] the park. You can also try different kinds of food (in) [blue] the restaurant and (at) [blue] the food kiosks. Why not go to Marineland (on) [red] a weekend (in) [red] the summer and enjoy all the fun?

8 Joining Words

A. 1. and
   2. but
   3. and
   4. or
   5. and ; or ; and
   6. but
   7. or
   8. but ; and
   9. but

B. 1. or
   2. and
   3. but
   4. but
   5. and ; or ; But ; and

C. 1. ✔
   2. Do you want to be a chef ~~or~~ [and] work in a restaurant?
   3. ✔
   4. I have to practise hard ~~but~~ [and] be better at dancing.
   5. My brother only has one day off in a week. It is Saturday ~~and~~ [or] Sunday.

D. 1. My sister brushed her hair and she put on her favourite dress.
   2. I wanted to show my picture to you but it got ruined in the rain.
   3. Rehearse more or you will not remember the lines.

E. Playing Soccer

Today I started soccer. My twin brother,

Michael, ∧(and) I went to a big field. There were lots

of children ∧(but) none were beginners like us. Some

of them were practising their skills ∧(and) others were

playing a game.

The coach told us to pick an orange

uniform ∧(or) a green one. I liked the green

uniform ∧(and/but) Michael liked the orange one.

Our coach was very nice ∧(and) friendly. She told us

that we would practise once a week, either

on Saturday ∧(or) Sunday. She said that the most

important thing was to have fun.

9 The Sentence: Subject and Predicate

A. (Check these boxes.)
1. Period
2. Capital Letter ; Period
3. Period
4. Capital Letter
5. Capital Letter ; Period
6. Capital Letter
7. Capital Letter
8. Capital Letter ; Period
9. Period

B. 1. Mrs. Maddison   2. Brad's father
3. The birthday cake   4. Nina
5. The children   6. Brad's parents
7. The children   8. They
9. Brad   10. Andy
11. The party

C. 1. E   2. F
3. B   4. C

5. A   6. G
7. D   8. H

D. (Individual answers)

10 Subjects and Objects

A. 1. The girl
2. The hungry lion
3. The hamburger on the plate
4. My mom and dad
5. The book on the shelf
6. She
7. Ted and his sister
8. The cute kitten
9. That boy over there
10. Kayla, Miles, and I
11. The busy beaver

B. 1. ice cream of any flavours
2. the vase by the window
3. ✗
4. an apple pie
5. a warm jacket
6. computer games
7. ✗
8. ✗
9. all the soup in the big bowl
10. Samuel and me

C. 1. Allen the Chipmunk ; S
2. The trees in the forest ; S
3. food and shelter ; O
4. nuts and seeds ; O
5. fresh fruit ; O
6. tall trees ; O
7. various fun games ; O
8. Their parents ; S
9. Allen and his friends ; O
10. one another ; O
11. different sounds ; O

D. (Individual writing)

11   Types of Sentences

A. A: .
   B: .
   C: ?
   D: .
   E: ?
   F: ?
   G: ?
   H: .
   Telling Sentence: A, B, D, H
   Asking Sentence: C, E, F, G

B. 1. The news is on at nine o'clock.
  2. It snows in the winter.
  3. This vase is made of glass.
  4. They are sitting at the table.

C. 1. When — is your birthday?
  2. Why — can't penguins fly?
  3. What — is under the chair?
  4. Did — you solve the puzzle?
  5. Who — has left the scarf here?
  6. How tall — is that building?

D. 1. Exclamatory Sentence
  2. Imperative Sentence
  3. Imperative Sentence
  4. Exclamatory Sentence
  5. Imperative Sentence
  6. Exclamatory Sentence
  7. Imperative Sentence
  8. Imperative Sentence
  9. Exclamatory Sentence
  10. Exclamatory Sentence

E. (Individual writing)

12   Punctuation and Capitalization

A. 1. !   2. .
  3. ?   4. .
  5. .   6. ?
  7. .   8. !
  9. !

B. 1. !   2. ?
  3. !   4. .
  5. ?   6. !
  7. ?   8. !
  9. .

C. 1. !
  2. ✔
  3. ?
  4. !
  5. ✔
  6. !

D.

E. 1. Last year's Halloween was a Friday.
  2. Was Mrs. Jevon at home on New Year's Day?
  3. Jennifer, Ray, and I loved our picnic lunch!
  4. The concert was held in Edmonton last August.
  5. "We Are the World" is such a great song!

13   Forming Negative Sentences

A. 1. ✔
  2. ✘
  3. ✔
  4. ✔
  5. ✔
  6. ✘

B. 1. Dad was ⌃not using the computer earlier.
  2. Zoey and Dennis were ⌃not at the party last night.
  3. They were ⌃not singing when the bell rang.
  4. Jacky was ⌃not waiting for the bus at two o'clock yesterday.
  5. We were ⌃not looking when the clown came out.
  6. Rachel and Percy were ⌃not classmates last year.
  7. The cherry pie we had this morning was ⌃not very delicious.
  8. Rhonda was ⌃not at home when Jane called.
  9. Sophia noticed that the machines were ⌃not functioning well.

C. 1. does not stop
  2. does not go
  3. do not grow
  4. does not sleep
  5. do not know
  6. do not want
  7. do not like

D. 1. Mom did not go to work last Saturday.
  2. I did not study in this school last year.
  3. Macy and Samuel did not play in the pool yesterday.
  4. Jason did not play video games last night.

14   Contractions

A. 1. he's   2. they're
  3. what's   4. I've
  5. there's   6. how's
  7. don't   8. they'll
  9. you've   10. doesn't
  11. didn't   12. shouldn't

B.
  1. I wasn't [was not] sure how I broke the toy.
  2. Where's [Where is] the box office?
  3. Isn't [Is not] this your lunch bag?
  4. ✔
  5. Katie can't [cannot] finish the whole pizza.
  6. ✔
  7. How's [How is] everyone doing?
  8. ✔
  9. There aren't [are not] any cookies left.
  10. I'm [I am] happy to have you as my friend.

C. (Circle these words.)
  couldn't ; here's ; she's ; we'd ; weren't ; hasn't ; they'll ; why's
  1. She's ; hasn't
  2. Here's
  3. weren't
  4. We'd
  5. They'll
  6. couldn't
  7. Why's

D. 1. It's chasing a rat.
  2. We'll have fun at the pool.
  3. That's the book I told you about.
  4. Let's take a rest under the tree.
  5. The children mustn't swim in the lake when no adults are around.

Review 2

A. 1. City   2. boxes
   3. The girls are eating honey.
   4. the sun   5. We
   6. The boy is playing.   7. round
   8. behind   9. in
  10. Are you staying or leaving today?
  11. Ada <u>loves animals</u>.
  12. We rock!   13. . or !
  14. I do not like singing.

B. Common Noun: kingdom ; king ; elf
   Proper Noun: Colourland ; King Edwin ; Coby

C. Then someone said, "Look what <u>we</u> have found! <u>It</u> is a note left for (us) by Coby."

To get all the colours back, Princess Lilian and Prince Ned have to search for one thing in each colour. When <u>they</u> have found (it) , <u>he</u> or <u>she</u> needs to touch (it) and say its colour! Then that colour will return to the kingdom. <u>I</u> will be hiding somewhere nearby to make sure <u>they</u> follow the rules.
Coby

D. King Edwin carefully **studyied** / (**studied**) Coby's note. Then he said, "My children (**are**) / **am** very brave. I **am allow** / (**am allowing**) them to begin the search today!"
The king asked Wilkin to accompany the children. Wilkin had an idea, "We (**are going**) / **is going** to look all over the woods just outside Colourland before we (**go**) / **went** any farther."

E. 1. between ; and
   2. under ; and
   3. on

F. 1. Lilian
   2. Ned
   3. (Individual answer)
   4. (Individual answer)

G. (The children) gathered <u>some fruits</u>. (They) ate <u>the oranges, peaches, and grapes</u>. (Lilian) said, "(I) love <u>fruits</u>! But (I) am worried. How are (we) going to find <u>yellow</u>?"
"Look!" said (Ned). (They) saw <u>some roses</u>. "Maybe (they) are yellow."
"But (roses) can be pink, red, or white," said (Wilkin).
"(That) reminds <u>me</u>! (We) have to find <u>red</u> as well!" (Lilian) said in a panic.

H. B
   A
   C
   D

I. ^AAfter they had found the colour red, the children retrieved the colour yellow with a sunflower and returned to ^CColourland (.)

"^LLet's celebrate (!) " cheered the people (.)

"^HHow have you been (?) " asked ^KKing ^EEdwin (.)

"^WWe are good (.) ^WWe had fun (!) " replied ^NNed (.)

"^LLook (,) " said ^LLilian as they saw ^CCoby disappear into thin air (.) ^HHe left behind a book titled ^MMagic ^SSpells (.)

1 Sense Words

A. 1. see ; eyes
   2. smell ; nose
   3. hear ; ears
   4. touch ; hands
   5. taste ; tongue

B.
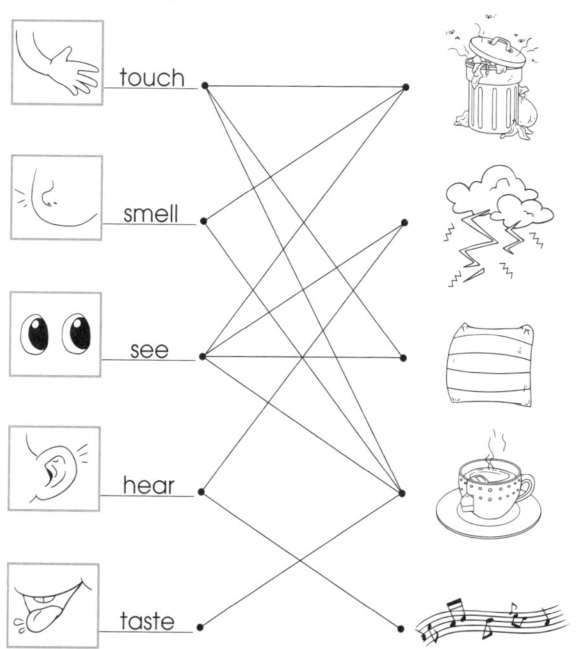

C. 1. hot   2. sharp
   3. fluffy   4. soft
   5. cold   6. hard
   7. rough   8. smooth
   9. sticky

D. (Individual drawings)
   1. sour   2. salty
   3. spicy   4. sweet
   5. bitter

2 Season Words

A. 1. spring   2. summer
   3. fall   4. winter

B. 1. warmer ; rainy
   2. cold ; snowy
   3. cool ; breezy
   4. hot ; sunny

C.

autumn	breezy
chilly	warm
windy	sunny
cozy	fall
scorching	cold
cloudless	hot

f	e	l	e	d	m	c	☀	i	s	y	e	a	j	g
b	☁	k	h	l	l		a	u	t	u	m	n	o
j		c	o	g	o	a	q	s	n	j	r	g	l	p
w	a	r	m	f	n	e	v	h	w	n	d	y	n	
i	u	h	p	a	q	s	c	o	z	y	m	t	u	☁
d	t	c	o	l	d	u	h	t	i	o	a	v	a	m	f
g	n	h	c	l	o	u	b	d	o	p	l	b	s	w	o
k	u	i	s	s	c	o	r	c	h	i	n	g	c	i	l
a	l	l	c	b	e	j	e	t	g		h	d	n	r
m	c	l	o	u	d	l	e	s	s		o	q	d	h
h	u	y	h	t	e	b	z	c	w	g	b	e	z	y	w
r	p	l	i	f	t	z	y	j	a	x	n	b	m	i	f

D. (Individual drawing and writing)

3 Camping Words

A. A: rope
   B: sleeping bag
   C: flashlight

B.
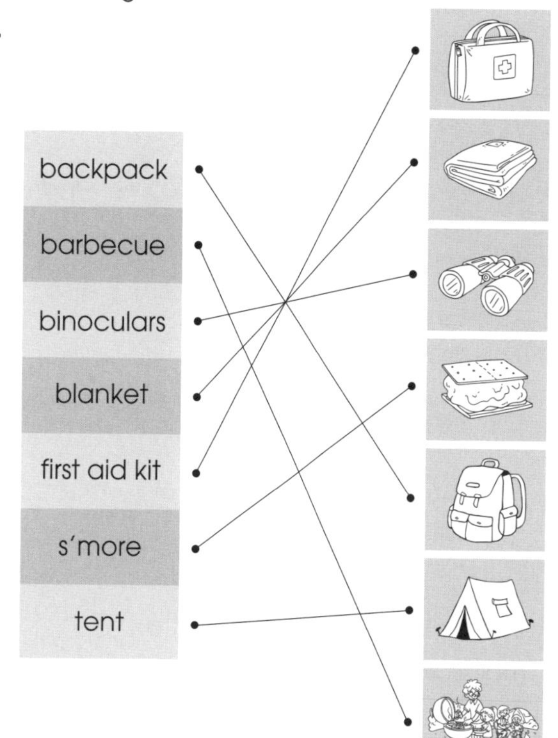

backpack	
barbecue	
binoculars	
blanket	
first aid kit	
s'more	
tent	

C. 1. marshmallow
   2. charcoal
   3. compass
   4. matches
   5. boots
   6. clothespin
   7. flask
   8. axe
   9. sunscreen
   10. lantern

D. 1. stargazing
   2. Wildlife watching
   3. hiking
   4. Canoeing

4 Community Words

A. 1. townhouse
   2. apartment building
   3. bungalow

B. A: library
   B: school
   C: swimming pool
   D: fire station
   E: park
   F: apartment building
   G: townhouse
   H: police station
   I: hospital
   J: supermarket
   K: bakery
   Q ; L ; O ; P ; M ; N

C.

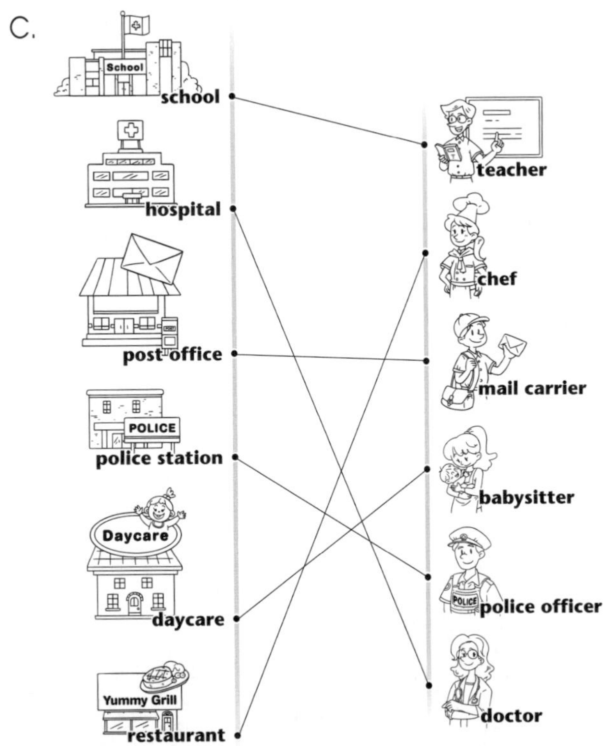

D. 1. chef
   2. doctor
   3. convenience store
   4. theatre
   5. mail carrier
   6. library

5 Polygon Words

A. 1. hexagon
   2. circle
   3. quadrilateral

B. 1. A   2. C
   3. C   4. A
   5. C   6. C ; A

C. (Individual tracing)
   1. 8 sides ; octagon
   2. 5 sides ; pentagon
   3. 3 sides ; triangle
   4. 4 sides ; quadrilateral
   5. 6 sides ; hexagon

D. (Suggested drawings)

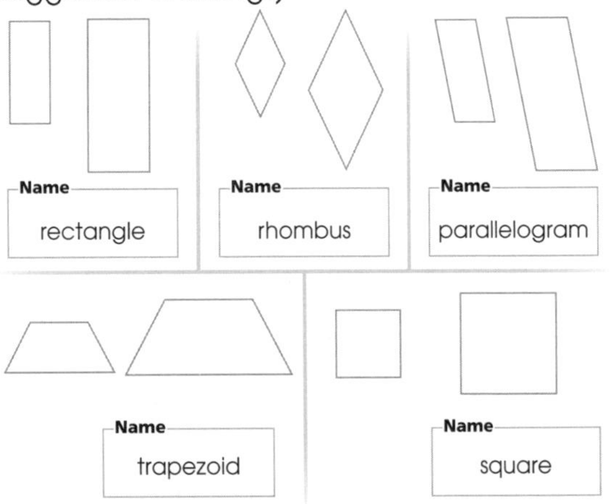

Name: rectangle

Name: rhombus

Name: parallelogram

Name: trapezoid

Name: square

6 Computer Words

A. 1. monitor
   2. screen
   3. modem

B.

C.

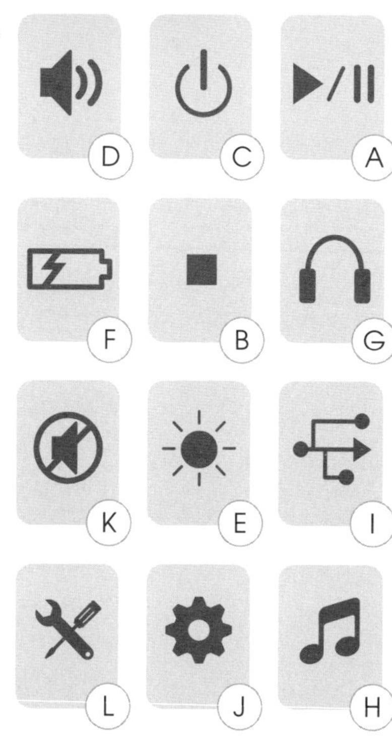

D. 1. music
   2. information
   3. buy
   4. communicate
   5. photos

7   Water Words

A. 1. sea
   2. pond
   3. brook
   4. stream
   5. lake
   6. creek
   7. river
   8. ocean

B. C ; A ; D ; B ; E
   1. Pacific Ocean
   2. Arctic Ocean
   3. Indian Ocean
   4. Southern Ocean
   5. Atlantic Ocean

C. 1. geyser
   2. delta
   3. glacier
   4. reservoir
   5. waterfall
   6. swamp
   7. fjord

D.

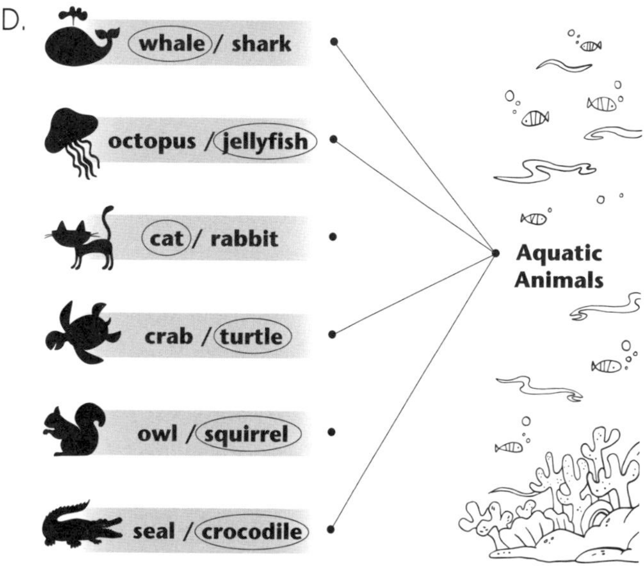

8   Synonyms

A. tasty: delicious ; yummy
   sad: unhappy
   pretty: beautiful
   big: large
   happy: glad
   Mom: mother
   picked: chose

B. 1. frightened
   2. shiny
   3. tiny
   4. drowsy
   5. hungry

C. 1. buddy ; pal
   2. leap ; hop
   3. furious ; mad
   4. smart ; intelligent
   5. courageous ; bold

D. 1. crying
   2. breezy
   3. tired
   4. little
   5. damp
   6. store
   7. hard
   8. fast
   9. dirty
   10. huge

E. 1. Little Ryan loves the fluffy bunny.
   2. Please shut the door behind you.
   3. Did you hear that weird noise?
   4. Hana's performance was awesome.
   5. Let's fill the pails with water.

9 Antonyms

A. (Colour these pairs of antonyms with different colours.)
hot – cold
thick – thin
wet – dry
day – night
short – long
less – more

B. (Cross out these words.)
1. messy
2. provide
3. afraid
4. open
5. large
6. plain

C. C ; A ; D ; E ; B

D. stay: go, depart, leave
wrong: correct, right, proper
sad: glad, happy, jolly
slow: fast, swift, speedy
easy: difficult, hard, challenging

E. (Circle these words.)
1. early – late
2. best – worst ; calm – windy
3. opened – closed ; went – came ; up – down
1. early ; late
2. best ; worst
   calm ; windy
3. opened ; closed
   went ; came
   up ; down

10 Homophones

A. 1. rode
   2. too
   3. blew
   4. sun
   5. tale
   6. sea
   7. knight
   8. deer

B. 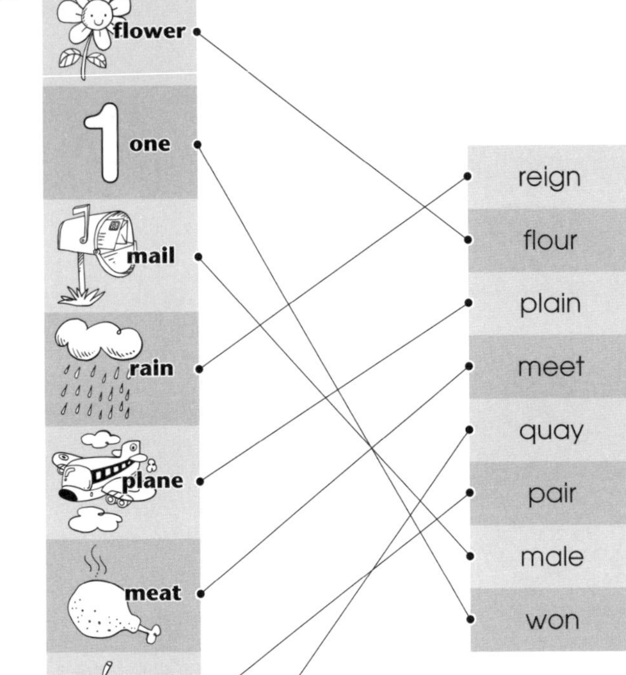

C. 1. bear
   2. ate
   3. by
   4. cents
   5. weight
   6. knew
   7. hear
   8. some
   9. flower
   10. sell
   11. bee
   12. write

D. 1. Kelly taught us how to tie a knot.
   2. I picked berries on my way to Grandma's house.
   3. Ricky played basketball for an hour.
   4. The hare hopped away when we got closer.

Review 3

A. 1. sight   2. winter
   3. compass   4. flask
   5. in a bakery   6. pentagon
   7. volume control   8. a computer word
   9. a glacier   10. a geyser
   11. drowsy   12. neighbour
   13. brave   14. leave
   15. our   16. wait

B.   Sense Word: see, hear, sweet, salty, smooth
   Season Word: fall, chilly, autumn, windy, cozy, cloudless
   Camping Word: camping, boots, tent, backpacks, canoeing, campsite, s'mores, barbecued, campfire, binoculars, stargazing

C. 1.

D. 1. rhombus
   2. octagon
   3. A: pentagon
     B: rectangle
     C: triangle

E. 1. monitor   2. CPU
   3. keyboard   4. mouse

F. 1. river   2. delta
   3. waterfall   4. pond
   5. turtle

G.

1   A Balloon Ride

A.

B. 1. excited

2.

3. her mom

4. trees

C. 1. The setting is the park in the morning.

2. The big adventure is a hot-air balloon ride.

3. The hot-air balloon is colourful.

D. 1. A Balloon Ride

2. Janet ; Janet's mom ; the man controlling the hot-air balloon

3.

4. morning

E. There is a burner in the hot-air balloon. The burner has to be lit. ~~You can light candles with matches.~~ It heats up the air in the balloon. ~~The children played a ball game.~~ The hot air makes the balloon rise into the sky.

F. (Cross out these sentences.)

B: She had a nightmare.

F: Some birds have wings but cannot fly.

Janet got up early. Then she got ready and went to the park. Before the man lit the burner, Janet jumped into the basket. After the balloon lifted off, Janet felt like a bird flying.

2   The Sun and the Ocean

A. 1. ✔

2. ✘

3. ✘

4. ✔

5. ✘

B. 1. Grandpa's grandma

2. friends

3. the Ocean

4. the Sun ; the Ocean

C. 1. Yes, it is a folk tale.

2. The rain falls to the earth.

3. He turns into rain when he misses his home.

D.

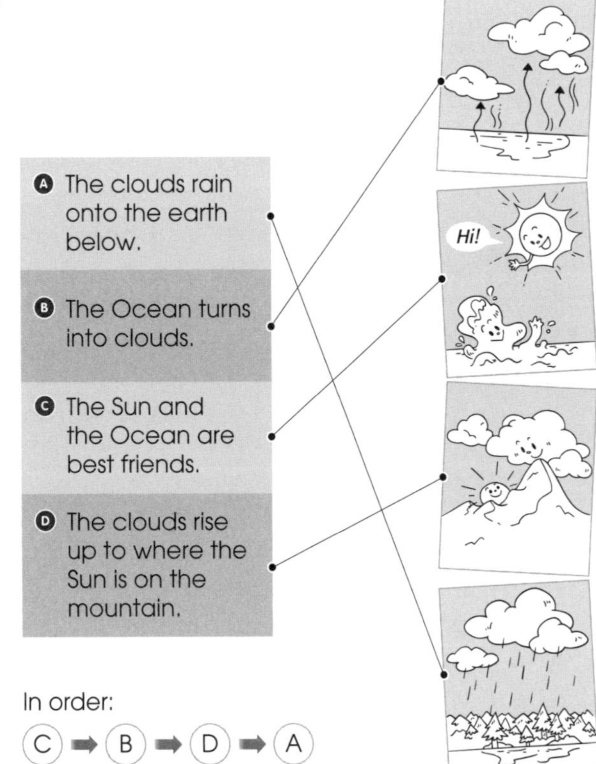

In order:

Ⓒ ➡ Ⓑ ➡ Ⓓ ➡ Ⓐ

E. The rain falls down to the earth. The Ocean becomes himself again. Then the Sun wants to visit the Ocean. He sets at dusk to meet his friend. The next morning, the Sun leaves his friend. He rises high up in the sky again.

(Individual drawing)

3 The Museum Trip

A. 1. Egyptian mummy
   2. the Bat Cave
   3. dinosaurs
B. 1. a museum
   2. his classmates
   3. to the ROM
   4.

C. 1. Sender: George
      Receivers: Grandpa and Grandma
   2. The full name of the ROM is the Royal Ontario
      Museum.
   3. He draws and writes about what he saw in the
      museum.
D. (Individual writing and drawing)
E. (Individual writing and drawing)

4 Alphabet Rhyme

A. 1. hive
   2. oar
   3. lamb
B. 1. eight
   2. 16
   3. kin
   4.

C. 1. It is a rhyme.
   2. There are four stanzas.
   3. bike – dike ; ear – gear ; five – hive ; inn – kin ;
      jam – lamb ; more – oar ; net – pet
D. (Individual drawings)
   Q
   road
   sail/sale
   T
E. (Individual writing)

5 Today Is My Birthday!

A. (Suggested drawing)

B. 1. today   2. seven years old
   3. the writer's friends   4. Mother
C. 1. It is his birthday.
   2. They will sing, eat, play, and run.
   3. hooray – birthday ; bake – cake ; sing – king ;
      run – fun
D. (Colour these boxes.)
   This poem has a title.
   This poem has rhyming words.
   This poem follows the AABB scheme.
   This poem describes feelings.
E. (Individual writing)

6 The Butterfly's Life Cycle

A. 4 ; 3 ; 1 ; 2
B. 1. a caterpillar
   2. a pupa
   3. a pupa
   4.

C. 1. The Butterfly's Life Cycle
   2. It is about the life cycle of a butterfly.
   3. There are four pictures. They show the four
      stages in the life cycle of a butterfly.

D. (Suggested diagram)

Title: _The Butterfly's Life Cycle_

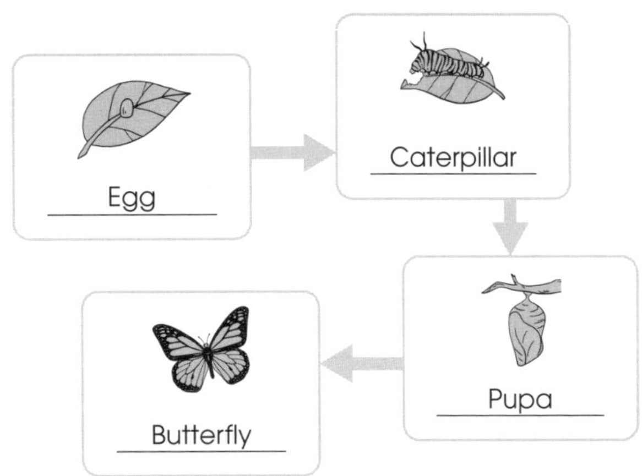

(Check these characteristics.)

arrows ; text ; title ; colour ; labels ; pictures

E. (Individual diagram)

---

7   Crispy Squares

A. 2 ; 3 ; 4 ; 1

B. 1. Step 1

   2. measuring cup

   3. a kitchen tool

   4.

C. 1. It provides instructions on how to make crispy squares.

   2. Rice crispies, marshmallows, and margarine are needed.

   3. It is used for stirring the marshmallows into the margarine.

D. Smoothie Recipe

Ingredients: 4 strawberries ; 2 ice cubes ; 1 peeled banana ; 1 cup of milk

Utensils: measuring cup ; glass ; blender

Directions:

   1. Put all the ingredients into the blender.

   2. Blend them for 1 minute.

   3. Pour the smoothie into a glass.

E. (Individual drawing and writing)

---

8   Jumbo the Gigantic Elephant

A. 1. jumbe – chief

   2. almost – nearly

   3. enormous – very big

   4. star – famous performer

B. 1. Victoria

   2. Swahili

   3. Jumbo

   4. 

C. 1. Jumbo was kept at the London Zoo in the early 1880s.

   2. He could carry up to 100 children.

   3. A zookeeper of the London Zoo gave Jumbo his name.

D. Date of the Accident: September 15, 1885

Place of the Accident: St. Thomas ; Ontario ; Canada

Whom Jumbo Wanted to Save: Tom Thumb

What Jumbo Was Struck by: a train

When Jumbo's Statue Was Erected: in 1985

Where Jumbo's Statue Was Erected: in St. Thomas

E. (Individual answer and drawing)

---

9   Bat Facts

A. 1. ✔

   2.

   3. ✔

   4. ✔

   5.

B. 1. not very hot or cold

   2. its hearing

   3. at night

   4.

C. 1. It contains facts.

   2. The subheadings are "Habitat", "Diet", and "Senses".

   3. They give birth to live young.

D. A bat flies at night without crashing. ~~This is because bats are magical animals.~~ It makes noise and listens for it to bounce back. This noise is called an echo. ~~An echo is created by an enchanted wand.~~ The echo tells a bat where an object is. Then the bat can avoid the object. ~~That is why no bats have crashed into the witch's castle.~~

A bat flies at night without crashing. It makes noise and listens for it to bounce back. This noise is called an echo. The echo tells a bat where an object is. Then the bat can avoid the object.

E. (Individual writing and drawing)

10 Big Red Rescuer

A. (Check these features.)
has light ; has a hose ; battery-operated ;
is red ; has sound ; has an extendable ladder

B. 1. water
2. a toy truck
3. save
4. 

C. 1. It is promoting a toy fire truck.
2. The audience is kids and parents.
3. Some words are in bold to catch the audience's attention.
D. 1. superwoman costume
2. parents ; young girls
3. to persuade
4. Be a Superwoman!
5. $15.99
6. B
7. B
E. (Individual answer and design)

Review 4

A. 1. characters
2. before, after, then
3. A folk tale
4. the sender's
5. addresses and a stamp
6. paragraphs
7. first ; second
8. a poem
9. graphic text
10. labels and pictures
11.
12. step-by-step instructions
13. contains fictional information
14. different subheadings
15. an ad
B. 1. ✔
2. ✘
3. ✘
4. ✔
5. ✔
C. 1. It is an informational text.
2. It helps spread pollen from one plant to another.
3. It makes honey by chewing the pollen and mixing it with its saliva.
4. (Individual answer)
D.

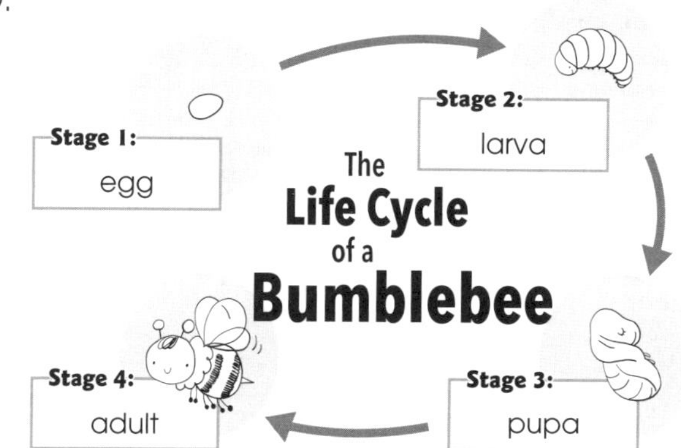

(Individual writing)
E. (Individual writing and design)

1.

3.

2.

4.

ide
at
am
cl
gl
ess
fl
bl

s e a g u l l b g s
h c l t e h c l a h
p n t s p a d e b e
a f m u i t o j u l
i b y n a x z v s l
l t o z s d r d e b
e u m b r e l l a
p i v c g k m a s f

coin
boat
loonie
jump
bat
dime
toonie
sea
quarter
nickel
ruler

b
a
g
c
t
d
r
a
i
e
v
n
p
e
m
q
k
w
r
Hi, Jimmy!

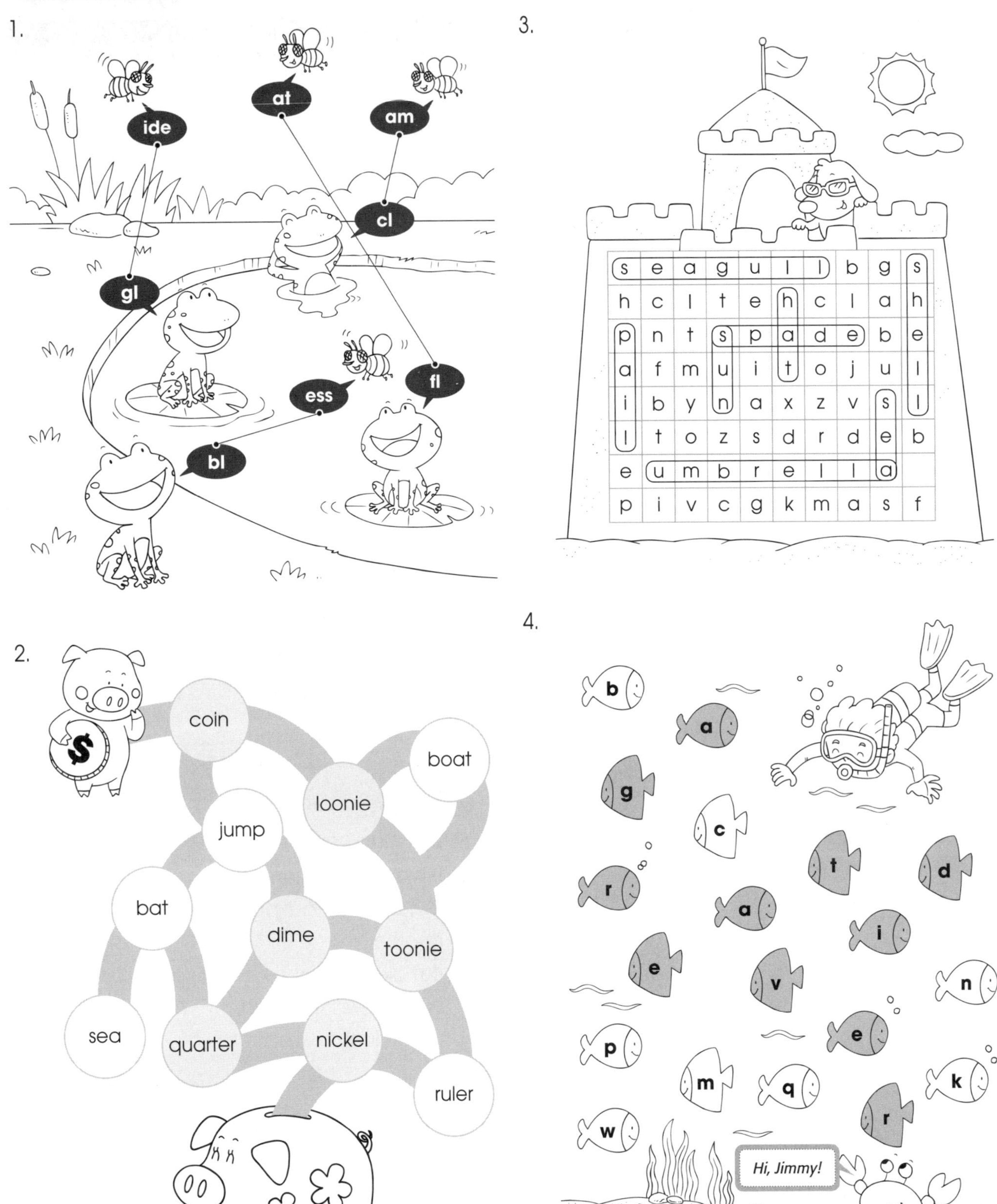

5.

	1			4			5		
A	M	O	U	S	E		F		
	I			G		B	B	I	R	D
	L	C		G			S		O
D	K	R	2 P	I	G		H		G
		A							
E	B	U	N	N	Y				
	B	O							
	I	S							
F	T	O	E	S					

6. 1. duckling
   2. puppy
   3. calf
   4. fawn
   5. piglet
   6. cub

7.

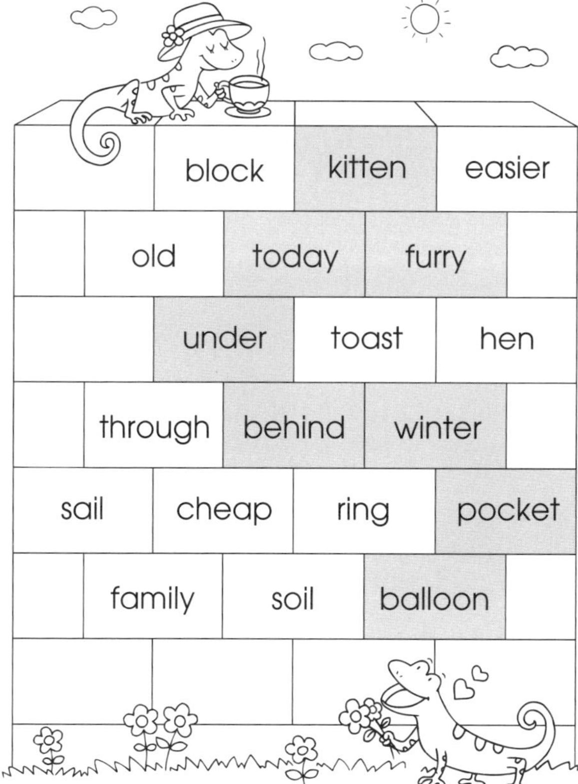

8. (Colour the rhyming pairs the same colour.)
   dim – swim
   dot – spot
   ink – pink
   bake – cake
   walk – talk

9.

10.

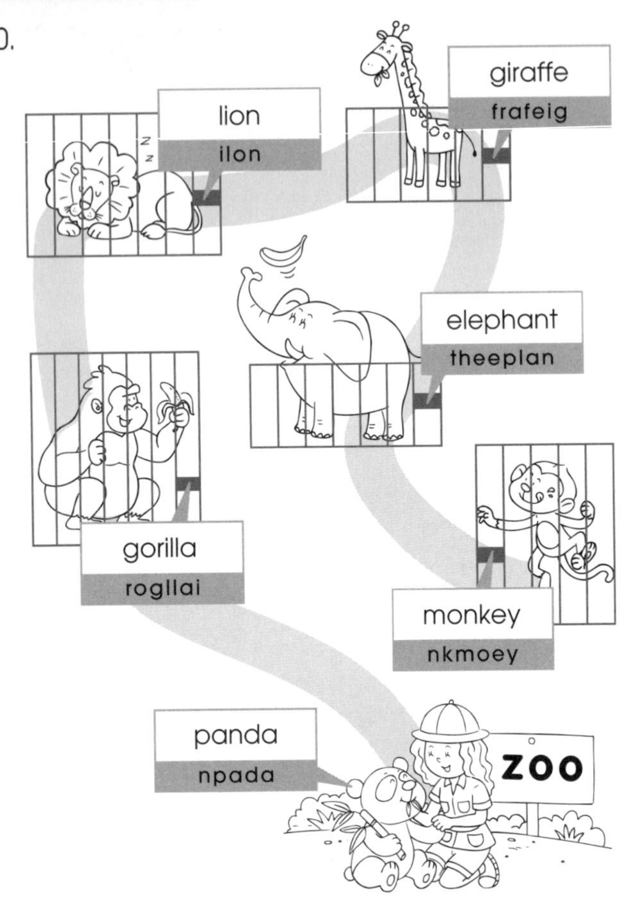

13. (Individual colouring)

11. (Colour the eggs with these words.)

den ; yen ; men ; pen ; Ben

12. (Individual drawing)

1. cat
2. rabbit
3. fish
4. octopus
5. snake

Language Games

Join each frog to a fly to form a word.

2 Help the piglet save his pocket money in a piggy bank. Colour the coins with "money" words to make a path to the piggy bank.

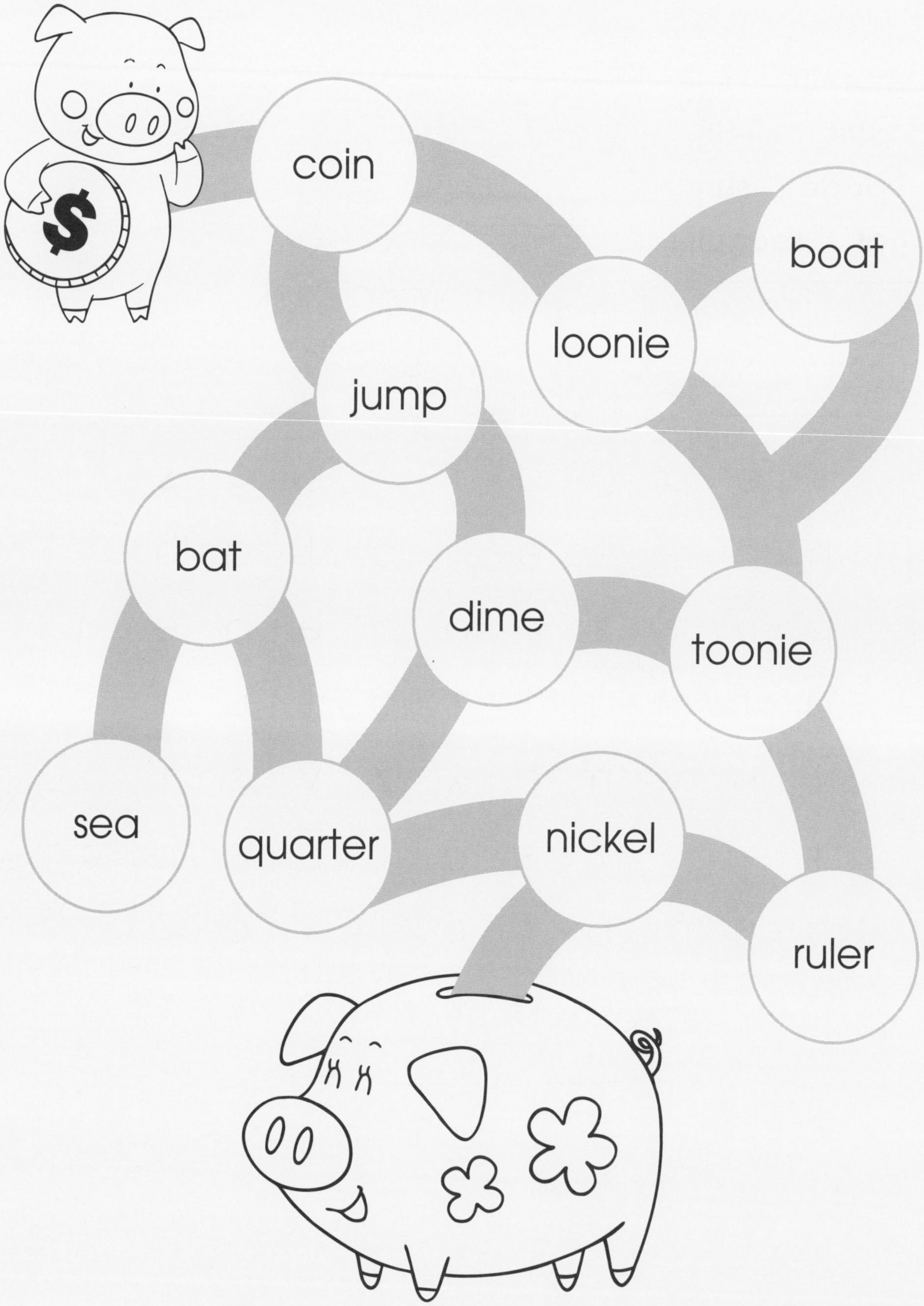

3

Circle the "beach" words in the word search.

umbrella   sea
pail   shell
spade   sun
hat   seagull

s	e	a	g	u	l	l	b	g	s
h	c	l	t	e	h	c	l	a	h
p	n	t	s	p	a	d	e	b	e
a	f	m	u	i	t	o	j	u	l
i	b	y	n	a	x	z	v	s	l
l	t	o	z	s	d	r	d	e	b
e	u	m	b	r	e	l	l	a	a
p	i	v	c	g	k	m	a	s	f

4 Colour the fish Jimmy has met by following the letters in the words "a great diver".

5 Read the clues and complete the crossword puzzle.

Across

A This pet likes to run on a turning wheel.

B A canary is one.

C This pet may be named Porky.

D If your pet rabbit was named King Rabbitoh, what would its initials be?

E another name for a rabbit

F A bird's claws are its _____ .

Down

1 what pet cats like to drink

2 Bugs Bunny is one.

3 Rabbits like to twitch their _____ .

4 A pet frog or a pet snake may lay these.

5 We keep these in a bowl or tank.

6 This pet has been called "Man's Best Friend".

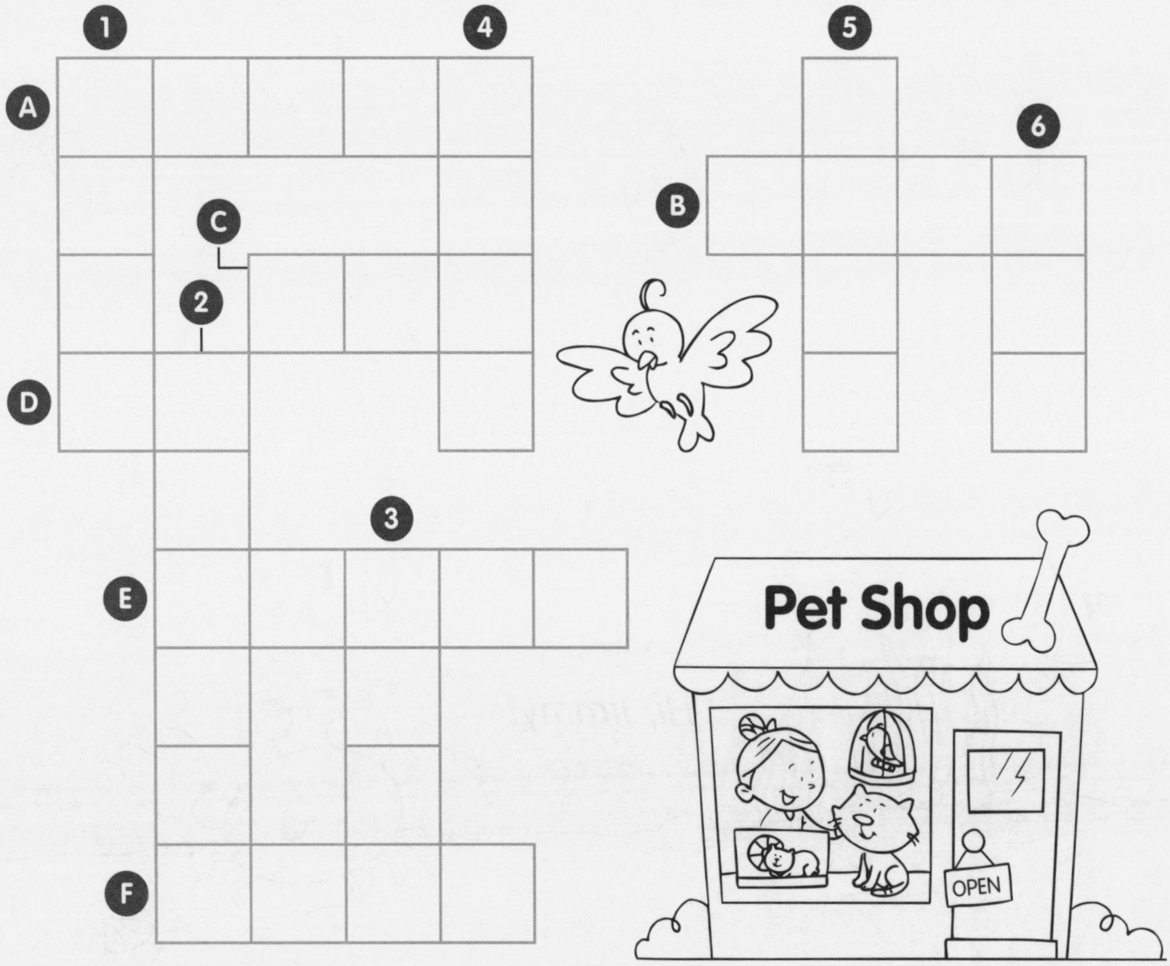

6

Look at the shadows of the baby animals. Write what they are.

1. 

2. 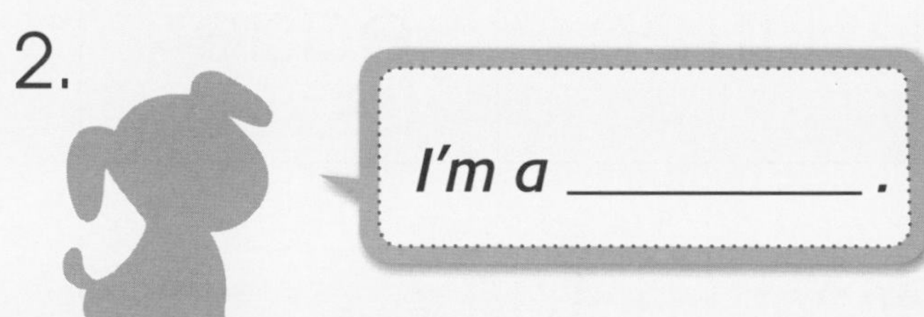

3. 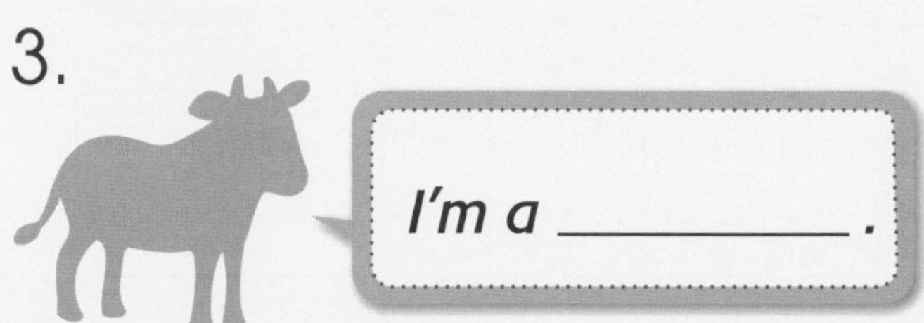

4.

5.

6. 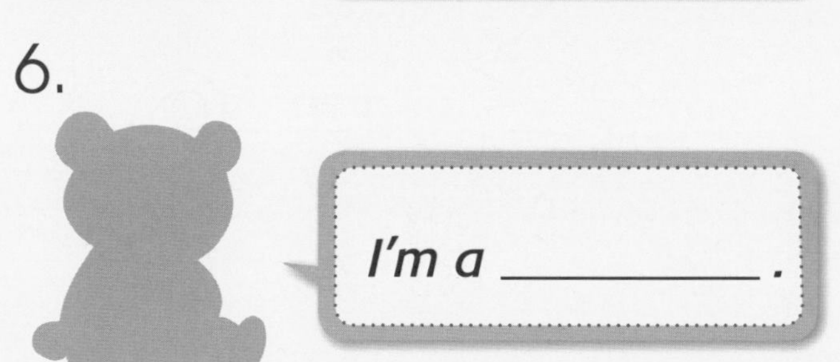

7 Help Leo the Lizard find his way up the wall by colouring the two-syllable words.

block	kitten	easier
old	today	furry
under	toast	hen
through	behind	winter
sail	cheap	ring	pocket
family	soil	balloon

8 Help the animals find their eggs by colouring each rhyming pair the same colour.

9 Circle the animal words in the word search.

duck	sheep	horse	goat	pig
	dog	goose	turkey	
rabbit	cow	chicken	pigeon	

```
            l
      s  y  a  n  p
   c  s  h  e  e  p  g  s  o
   g  e  t  o  x  h  l  w  b  c  e
p  i  a  c  b  p  s  k  j  r  v  p  l
c  d  g  l  j  g  d  g  o  a  t  i  n
h  o  r  s  e  z  w  o  i  b  n  g  d
r  g  d  h  x  t  q  o  u  b  k  e  i
k  n  j  m  d  u  y  s  p  i  g  o  b
b  o  a  v  u  r  h  e  z  t  y  n  h
l  c  h  i  c  k  e  n  v  s  o  r  c
e  j  f  e  k  e  q  r  t  a        a
z  u  x  v  i  y  m  c  o  w        x  r
a  c  v  e  r  w  f  n  i        s  d
```

10 Unscramble the letters to help the zookeeper write the names of the animals.

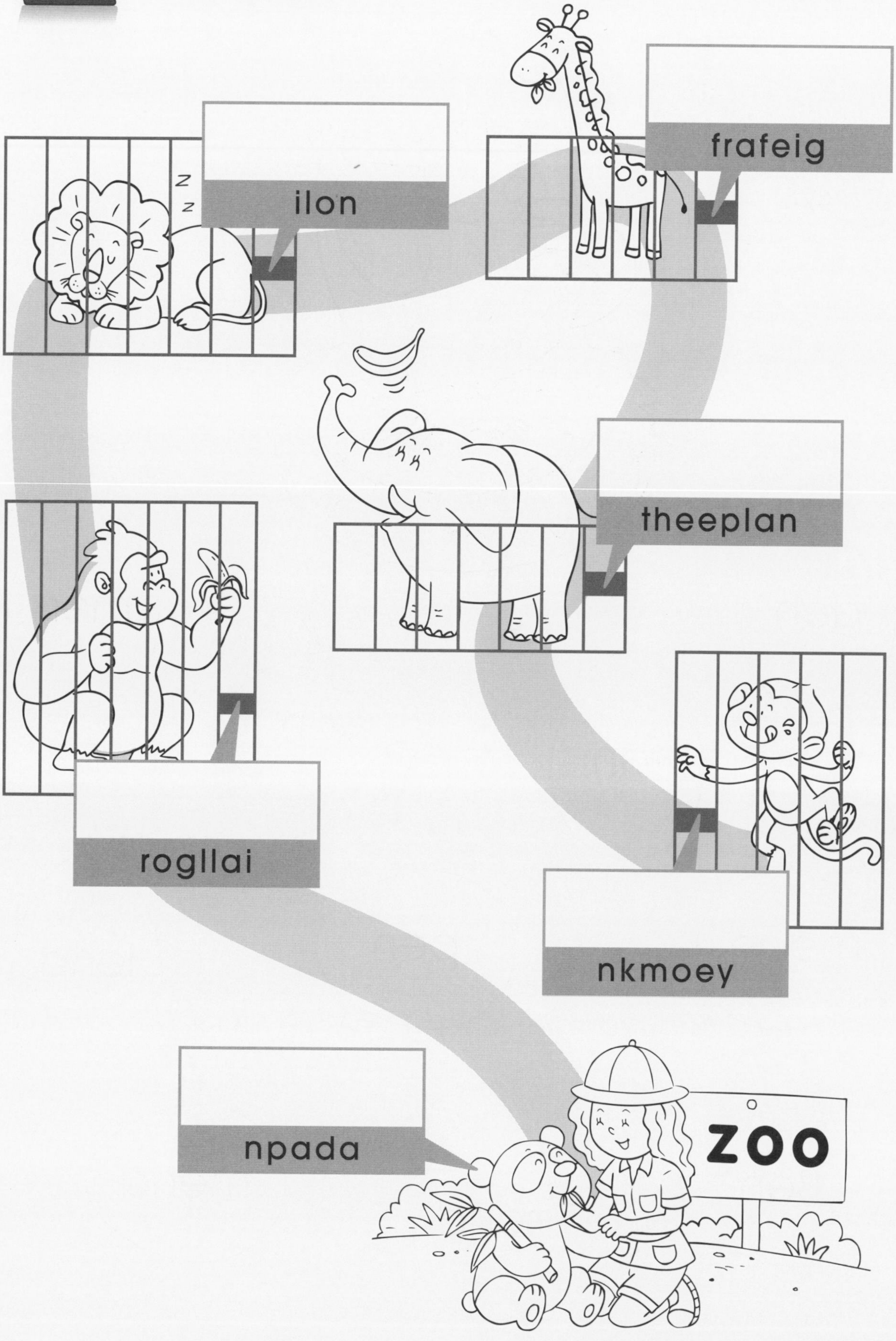

11 Help Mother Hen find her eggs by colouring the eggs that rhyme with "hen".

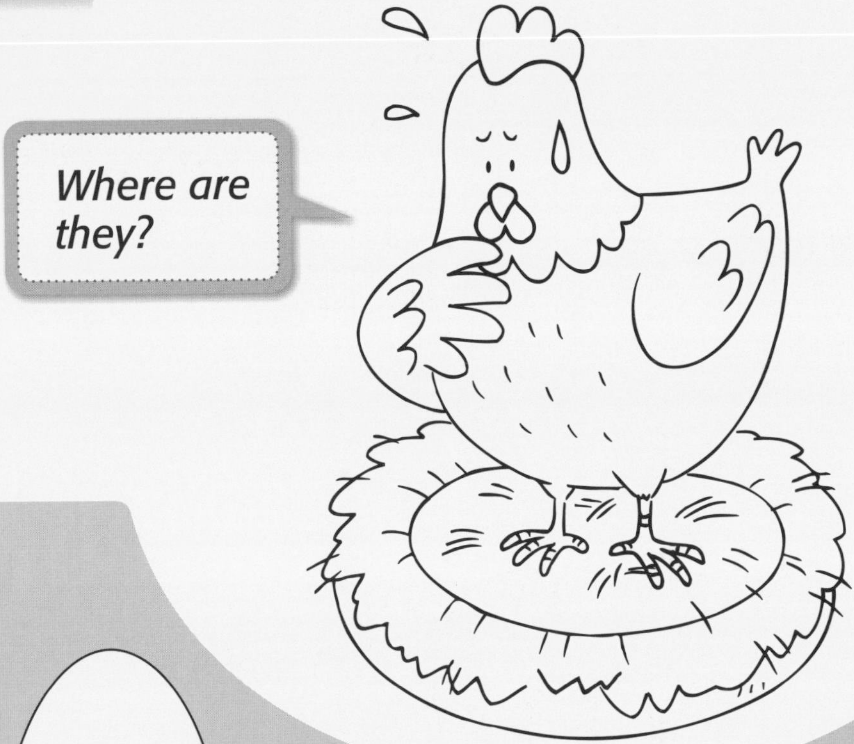

12   **Draw and write the names of the animals on Carol's sticker sheet.**

My Sticker Sheet

1.

2.

3.

4.

5.

13 Find and circle the colour words in the word search. Then colour them the correct colours.

b	p	e	j	p	u	r	p	l	e	b
c	i	p	g	r	e	e	n	i	d	r
f	n	s	l	c	y	s	o	a	f	o
j	k	o	a	t	e	m	e	y	t	w
b	o	r	v	h	l	b	l	u	e	n
l	r	a	b	z	l	w	d	i		
a	i	n	m	x	o	z	o	z		
c	d	g	e	p	w	q				
k	a	e	h	b	j	f	a			
g	r	e	d	w	h	i	t	e		

Language Game

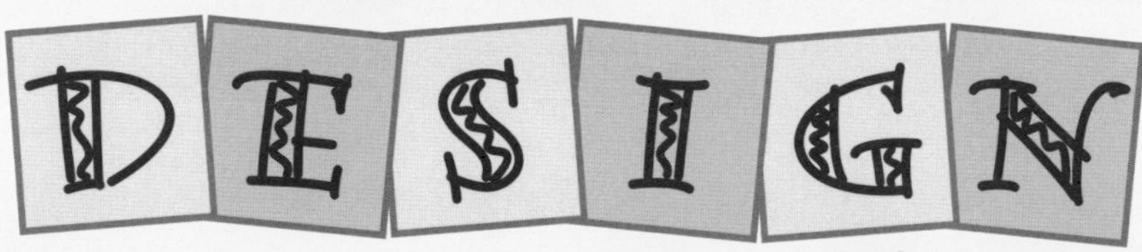

Challenge

We have an exciting Language Game Design Challenge! Submit your design to win a prize if your entry is selected and posted on our website!

Entry Rules:

- You have a passion for learning English.
- *Complete EnglishSmart* is your favourite learning tool.
- You are between 6 and 14 years old.

How to Enter:

1. Use the back of this page to create your own language game.
2. Give your language game a title.
3. Make sure the language game is fun!

My Contact Information

Name: _______________________________________ Age: ___________

School: ______________________________________ Grade: _________

E-mail: ______________________________________

Parent's Signature

Scan and e-mail this form and your language game to: *ca-info@popularworld.com* or mail it to: 15 Wertheim Court, Units 602-603, Richmond Hill, Ontario, Canada L4B 3H7.

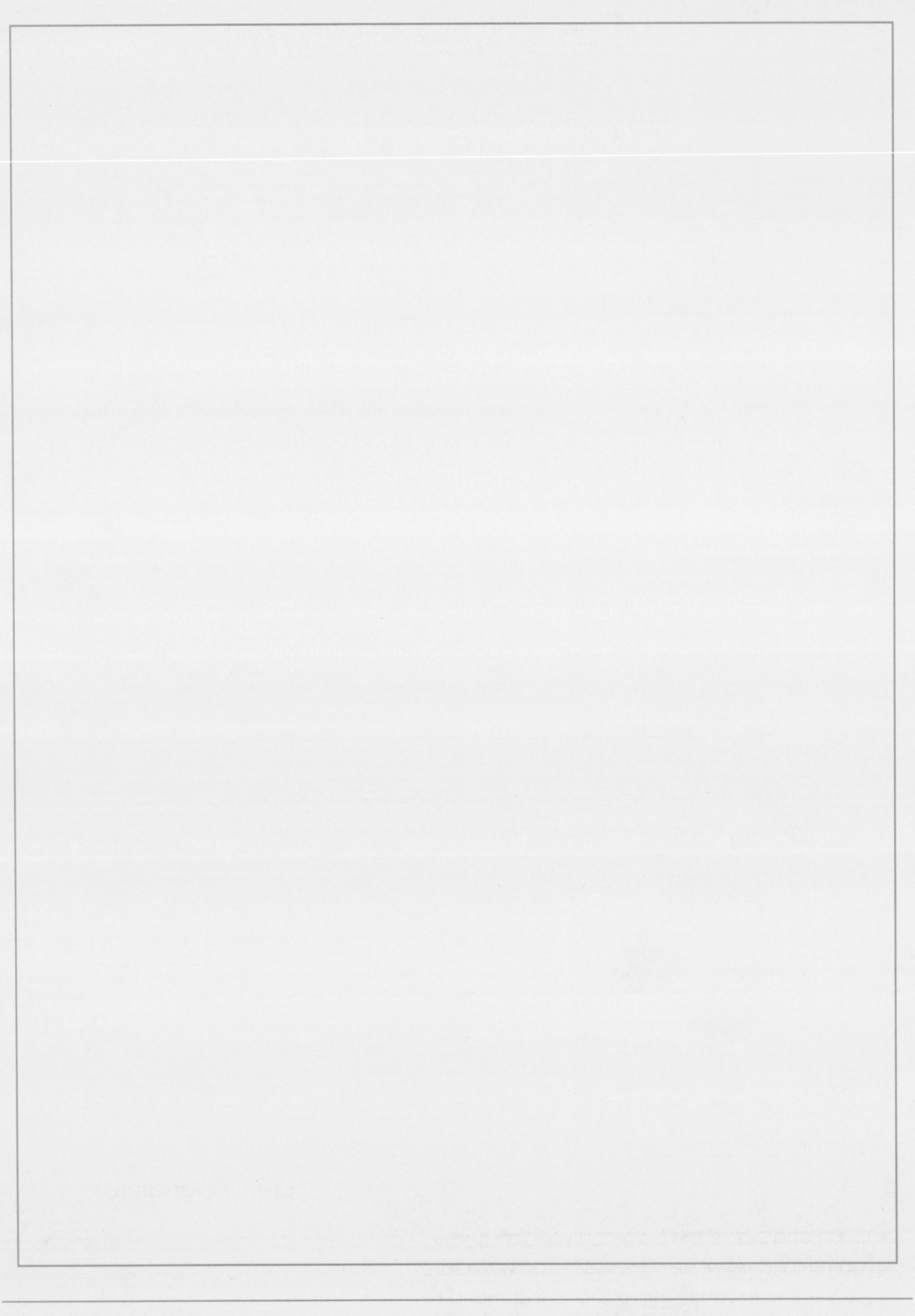

Popular Book Canada retains the right to use all the entries for promotional purposes. The chosen entries will be posted on our website and the winners will be contacted regarding the prize.

 Complete EnglishSmart (Grade 2)